Kids in the Middle

The Micropolitics of Special Education

Edited by
Marshall Strax, Carol Strax, and Bruce S. Cooper

ROWMAN & LITTLEFIELD EDUCATION

A division of
ROWMAN & LITTLEFIELD PUBLISHERS, INC.
Lanham • New York • Toronto • Plymouth, UK

KH

Published by Rowman & Littlefield Education
A division of Rowman & Littlefield Publishers, Inc.
A wholly owned subsidary of The Rowman & Littlefield Publishing Group, Inc.
4501 Forbes Boulevard, Suite 200, Lanham, Maryland 20706
www.rowman.com

Estover Road, Plymouth PL6 7PY, United Kingdom

British Library Cataloguing in Publication Information Available

Library of Congress Cataloging-in-Publication Data
  Kids in the middle : the micropolitics of special education / [edited by] Marshall
Strax, Carol Strax, and Bruce S. Cooper.
     p. cm.
  Summary: "Children with disabilities, their parents, teachers, administrators,
advocates, attorneys, and adult educators, all have a key role to play in the micropolitics of special education. The children—in the middle—are pivotal in the growing
special education saga. This book brings together people with disabilities and others
who advocate for their cause with expertise in special education law, administration,
severe and profound disabilities, ethics, foundations, finance, teaching, disability
rights, and culture. All these people work together to develop an awareness that beyond
the administrative aspects of special education and the Individuals with Disabilities
Education Act (IDEA) are micro-political issues that affect how children with disabilities
are educated."—Provided by publisher.
  ISBN 978-1-60709-846-1 (hardback) — ISBN 978-1-60709-847-8 (paper) —
ISBN 978-1-60709-848-5 (electronic)
  1. Special education—Political aspects—United States. 2. Special education—Law
and legislation—United States. 3. Children with disabilities—Education—United States.
I. Strax, Marshall. II. Strax, Carol. III. Cooper, Bruce S.
  LC3981.K47 2012
  371.90973—dc23

                                                              2011052507

Printed in the United States of America

11/26/12

Contents

Acknowledgments

My chapters in this book would not have been possible without the generosity of adolescents with disabilities, parents of children with disabilities, school administrators, advocates, adult educators, and attorneys. They all gave generously of their time to help inform me in my writing. I would especially like to thank the parents and adolescents who were so willing to share their stories—and their pain—so that others might benefit in the future. I am humbled by their fortitude and valor in navigating life and the field of special education. Working with them, learning their stories, and getting to know them were an honor and inspiration.—CS

I thank Sister Francis Raftery and Dr. James Dlugos from the College of Saint Elizabeth for allowing me the time and support to develop the concept of this book. Sister Teresa Bruno provided the creative and intellectual space to complete this project.—MS

Foreword

Kids in the Middle is an informative, accessible, and deeply moving account of the history and present status of special education in the United States. Having taught for a lifetime at every level from sixth grade through graduate school, I was surprised at how much I did not know about special education, and I'm grateful for what I've learned here. Like most well-educated people, I knew something of the early history of special education and our shameful and insensitive treatment of children with disabilities, but I was not fully aware of the difficulties faced today by both parents and children when the children are "classified." This is in part, perhaps, because one of my own children benefited from an exceptional program of special education in a public elementary school. He and his best friend (also in the program) persevered to complete their college degrees. Neither of these boys was a behavior problem, and they had no physical disabilities; both were "declassified" in high school. For both boys, temporary classification triggered the help they needed.

Understandably, parents and children experience some ambivalence about being "classified." On the one hand, many parents seek energetically to achieve classification so that their children will get the help they need. On the other hand, there is still a stigma attached to classification and, once classified, it is hard for students to escape that status. Further, special education is very expensive, and so there is constant pressure to reduce the number of newly classified students. There is something of an enigma here. Instead of obstructing initial classification to keep the numbers down, educators should identify problems early, provide needed help, and work toward "declassifying" their increasingly competent students. We cannot save money by ignoring early warning signs.

To address the twin problems of cost and stigma, many schools have adopted a program called Response to Intervention (RTI). The idea is to intervene with special help at the earliest signs of learning difficulties, thereby avoiding classification. The idea is certainly a good one, but its implementation takes a variety of forms, and we can't say with certainty how successful any one form will be. It seems, however, to be a step in the right direction.

I finished reading this book with concern about the concept of *inclusion*, and I hope other readers will be similarly prodded to think deeply about it. To include special education students in all the social activities of the school—if they wish to participate—seems exactly right. But in academic activities, what is meant by "full inclusion"? If a child is kept in a regular class all day, might he or she be deprived of special help desperately needed? Can that help be provided in a regular classroom? I think the answer to that question must be "sometimes." Cases differ, and within "cases" (or types of disability), individuals differ. We should avoid the temptation to settle everything with one sweeping generalization; few educational problems can be solved by recipe.

The tendency to universalize is a huge mistake made now in general education—to prepare *everyone* for college, even though many students would profit from a form of top-notch vocational education. Instead of pushing for "full inclusion," we might better think in terms of a full array of opportunities from which students may, with appropriate guidance, make their own choices. Not every student can profit from traditional academic preparation, and perhaps some special education students will not profit from being forced into "full inclusion."

I thank the authors of *Kids in the Middle* for giving us so much to think about.

Nel Noddings
Lee Jacks Professor of Education Emerita
Stanford University

Preface

Children with disabilities, their parents, teachers, administrators, advocates, attorneys, and adult educators all have a key role to play in the micropolitics of special education. The children—in the middle—are pivotal in the growing special education saga.

This book brings together people with disabilities and others who advocate for their cause with expertise in special education law, administration, severe and profound disabilities, ethics, foundations, finance, teaching, disability rights, and culture. All these people work together to develop an awareness that beyond the administrative aspects of special education and the Individuals with Disabilities Education Act (IDEA) are micropolitical issues that affect how children with disabilities are educated.

Political scientists look at the actions of the U.S. president, Congress, and the courts, but they often ignore politics on the familial and local levels, where parents and children come together with schools, school districts, and the system. What happens when children with disabilities meet school personnel and go into the classrooms? What are people feeling and doing at the personal and inter-personal levels—person to person, child and system, parent and advocate? Not understanding these key roles, actions, concerns, beliefs, and feelings probably means that education for children with disabilities will not evolve and improve as it should.

An important motive in writing this book is to promote a new model of special education to help with the goal of transforming special education as we know it— from an approach grounded in the concepts of promises, privilege, and power— into a system built on caring, compassion, and the common good. The special education system is arranged to the liking of those who profit most from it—those who wield the power to maintain intact arrangements that benefit them. "History shows no examples of the powerful voluntarily relinquishing their power to the powerless" (Smith and Max-Neef 2011, 13).

The reader will be taken on a fascinating journey through special education in the past, present, and future. On this journey, the micropolitics of special education will be seen through the eyes and experiences of children with disabilities, their parents and advocates, adult educators, and school administrators. Real stories come from real people!

Historically, children with disabilities were often excluded from education in American schools. When these children were finally allowed to attend school in the later part of the twentieth century, the norm was to segregate them. Their educational and psychosocial needs were usually not met. While children with other "diversities" such as race and gender often attended public schools that offered an education that was deemed "separate but equal" (*Plessy v. Ferguson* 1896) (*Plessy*), children with intellectual, developmental, behavioral, physical, and other disabilities were cloistered away in institutional settings or kept at home where they received little or no comprehensive, appropriate education (University of Oregon 1997).

In 1954 the U.S. Supreme Court in *Brown v. Board of Education* (*Brown*) overturned *Plessy*, ending separate but equal schooling in the United States. However, as recently as 1963, the year that the term *learning disability* was defined, only 23 percent of children with disabilities were served in American public schools. In 1975 when the Education for All Handicapped Children Act (EAHCA), now known as the IDEA, was passed, about one in eight children with disabilities was still totally excluded from public education and another three in eight children were receiving an *inappropriate* program in public schools.

Between the 1954 *Brown* ruling and 1977 when federal regulations were implemented for the EAHCA—and Section 504 of the Rehabilitation Act (Section 504)—the courts and U.S. Congress engaged in a legal drama that allowed children with disabilities and their advocates to transcend their terrible exclusion from American schools and arrive at the possible—a free appropriate public education for all.

Milestones in this legal drama included: (1) passage of the Civil Rights Act (1964) that eliminated major forms of racial and social discrimination; (2) the *Mills* decision (*Mills v. Board of Education of the District of Columbia* 1972), which extended educational rights to children with disabilities; and (3) Title IX of the Education Amendments of 1972 that prohibited discrimination on the basis of gender in federally funded programs.

Since the passage of the EAHCA in 1975, and Section 504 of the Rehabilitation Act in 1973, the United States has expanded its educational programs for children with disabilities—a line of policy development that is on par with efforts to desegregate education and provide gender equity. In fact, at this point, over 13 percent of American children are classified as children with disabilities and are entitled to special education services in their schools, districts, or outside programs at public expense.

Over the years, subsequent reauthorizations of the IDEA sought to further integrate all children with disabilities into the educational mainstream. For example, in 1990 the classifications of autism and traumatic brain injury were added, giving voice to the needs of these children. The requirement to educate all children together, referred to as *education in the least restrictive environment,* was reinforced in 1990, 1997, and 2004. Attention to the academic quality of special education was the focus of the 1997 and 2004 federal reauthorizations.

However, in a world of No Child Left Behind (2006), many children with disabilities are still left behind and are given labels identifying them as different. Their education may be equitable, but it is certainly not equal. Like children of other minority groups, their needs still are not always met in American schools. Even the concept of equity in education is problematic. As Kozol (1991) points out, equity is "something that resembles equity but never reaches it: something close enough to equity to silence criticism by approximating justice, but far enough from equity to guarantee the benefits enjoyed by privilege" (175).

Thirty-seven years after the passage of EAHCA (1975) and thirty-five years after its implementation, cultural and contextual borders still stand, dividing parents, children, and their school districts. Students of color are classified as children with disabilities in higher percentages than white children. Children from lower socioeconomic status (SES) families are more likely to be found in special education settings than children from higher SES families (U. S. Department of Education 2004). The percentage of litigation in education related to special education far exceeds the percentage of children evaluated or placed in special education.

In the past, leaders such as presidents Franklin D. Roosevelt and John F. Kennedy had to hide or manage their own disability status to succeed in American society. Thomas Eagleton, a person with a psychological disability, had to withdraw his nomination for U.S. vice president in 1972. At many school graduations the audience clapped louder for the students with visible disabilities.

Today, audiences often applaud louder for students with disabilities. Presidential and vice presidential candidates will discuss disabilities such as cancer or heart disease, but only when their illnesses are safely medically managed. Yet the faces and voices of people with disabilities are still not adequately heard or represented in political office, on television, or in the movies as primary characters in American life—faces and voices also missing from the ranks of teachers, principals, professors, and other education personnel.

Despite the progress of the last twenty-five years, barriers that include the following still interfere with meeting the needs of children with disabilities in American schools:

- Failure to federally fund the IDEA puts pressure on school districts.
- Competition for scarce resources leads to adversarial relationships between stakeholders.
- Parents cannot navigate the special education system without in-service education.
- Parents and children without financial means cannot take advantage of their due process rights.
- Correct diagnosis of disability is often too late to take advantage of early intervention.
- Labeling (classifying) children identifies them as different from the norm.
- Transition to adulthood planning is insufficient.
- The discipline, testing, classification, placement, and initiation of services provisions outlined in the IDEA have resulted in successful educational experiences for some students with disabilities, but in misery, boredom, and wasted lives for others.
- The special education system atomizes children instead of socializing them into the mainstream of school life.
- The administration of special education services has been highly technical and bureaucratic.
- Many administrators manage special education programs in their districts using the same classical bureaucratic top-down management style that they use with all other programs under their control.
- Administrators adhere rigidly to federal and state laws and regulations for special education, making no attempt to grasp the spirit of the law and the unique qualities of children in special education programs.

Our book, *Kids in the Middle: The Micropolitics of Special Education*, is divided into four sections. Part I, "Politics of the Past: From Segregation to Integration," explores the nature of the micropolitics of special education, and the politics of legislation and litigation leading to the passage of the Individuals with Disabilities Education Act.

Part II, "Politics of the Present: Law and Finance," and Part III, "Politics of the Present: Reality on the Ground," describe the politics resulting from issues of law and finance and the micropolitics involved in delivering services to children with disabilities in the present. Part IV, "Politics of the Future," discusses the perceptions of providers and consumers in the arena of special education of the micropolitics necessary to develop an ideal system of special education in the future.

The effects of policy development and program implementation at the federal, state, and local levels on children with disabilities and their educators, families, parents, communities, and taxpayers will be explored. We hope this book will encourage people in the general public and professionals in schooling to be moved to action and to refuse to accept mediocre solutions to the problems that exist in educating children with disabilities.

REFERENCES

Brown v. Board of Education, 347 U.S. 483 (1954).

Civil Rights Act of 1964, Title IV, 42 U.S.C. § 2000c et seq. (2006).

Individuals with Disabilities Education Improvement Act, P.L. 108-446, 118 Stat. 2647 (2004), now codified, as amended, at 20 U.S.C. § 1400–91 (2006).

Kozol, J. (1991). *Savage inequalities: Children in America's schools.* New York: Crown.

Mills v. Board of Education of the District of Columbia, 348 F. Supp. 866 (D.D.C. 1972).

No Child Left Behind Act, 20 U.S.C. §§ 6301-7941 (2006).

Plessy v. Ferguson, 163 U.S. 537 (1896).

Rehabilitation Act, Section 504, 29 U.S.C. § 794 (2006).

Smith, P. B., and M. Max-Neef. (2011). *Economics unmasked. From power and greed to compassion and the common good.* Devon, UK: Green Books.

Title IX of the Education Amendments of 1972, 20 U.S.C.A. 1681 (1972).

United States Department of Education. (2004). *Twenty-sixth annual report to Congress on the implementation of the Individuals with Disabilities Education Act.* Washington, DC: Author.

University of Oregon, producer. (1997). *Abandoned to their fate: A history of the social policy toward people with disabilities from the Middle Ages through the twentieth century.* Videotape. IRIS Media Inc.

I

POLITICS OF THE PAST: FROM SEGREGATION TO INTEGRATION

A new model of special education sets the stage for the rest of the book. After a thorough grounding in the politics of special education, the reader takes a short journey from a world where people with disabilities were segregated, through attempts by individuals to challenge the system, to the passage of legislation that guaranteed the integration of children with disabilities in schools. Part I introduces our concept of politics of special education, with a historical view of equity, politics in general education, and special education politics in particular.

Chapter 1, "Borderline: The Political Divide in Special Education," begins by defining politics in the context of special education in the United States as the competition for scarce resources. The roots of the cultural and contextual borders that separate the stakeholders involved in providing an education to children with disabilities are explored. Three ethical frames that create a multidimensional framework for evaluating issues that arise in special education are examined.

Next, two approaches to educating children with disabilities—special education and disability studies—will be considered. After presenting some examples of political issues inherent in both methodologies, key stakeholders in the education of children with disabilities will enter into a dialogue with the goal of reconciling all the ambiguities and inconsistencies of special education.

Chapter 2, "Schooling Tommy in the Past: A Personal Perspective," is an autobiographical case study that chronicles the education of a child with cerebral palsy from elementary school through college and medical school in the 1940s, 1950s, and 1960s. The case study exposes the cultural and contextual borders that existed and the micropolitical issues that arose in the education of Tommy. The politics and power struggles Tommy and his parents had to negotiate as critical *border crossings* will be discussed.

Chapter 3, "Free At Last? Legislation for Children with Disabilities," discusses the political and legal actions that led to the passing and implementation of the Education for All Handicapped Children Act in 1975 and Section 504 of the Rehabilitation Act of 1973, which ushered in the contemporary world of special education as we know it. After the Civil Rights Act was passed in 1964, 75 percent of children with disabilities still did not have their educational needs met in public schools. Many children were segregated in or excluded from schools. From the very late 1960s through the late 1970s, parents and advocates of children with disabilities sought to attain civil rights for the children in the arena of education.

1

Borderline

The Political Divide in Special Education

Marshall Strax

*B*onnie *drove down the hall, through the automatic door, and went outside. A cool breeze blew across her face as she looked up at the clouds
in the sky and sighed. Birds were flying south for the winter. It was October
and Bonnie smelled fall in the air. With severe cerebral palsy, she used a
wheelchair for mobility and a computerized communication board to speak.*

*Bright and creative, Bonnie was an artiste. Her specialty was the theater,
but the wheelchair and communication board she used were metaphoric
borders around her. She had attended a school for children with disabilities
and lived in a rehabilitation setting. Unable to interact with the world by
herself, she depended on adaptive equipment to be her passport to another
world. And so was the dance. . . .*

INTRODUCTION

All people have their story and it is important to hear this narrative told in their
own voice, a voice that comes from deep inside, reflecting who they are and the
experiences of their life. Parts will be happy, many will be generic facts, and others will be of oppression, pain, and suffering. One can empathize with another's
life chronicle but can never know what other persons experience, especially when
they are not of the same societally defined diverse group.

One cannot begin to know what it is like to live and go to school in the United
States as a person with a disability unless one is a person with a disability. Life
experiences and social interactions are unique. The ways in which one navigates
the cultural, contextual, physical, intellectual, psychological, and social terrains,
and surmounts the barriers to human interaction that appear along the journey, are
affected by how one is identified by the dominant culture.

Max-Neef (2010) suggests that when one is speaking and interacting with other people who have lived their lives in a different social, cultural, and contextual environment, one's own language is totally inadequate. An opportunity to invent a new language is created—communication that is coherent with the environment and the experiences of the other.

All the professional stakeholders involved in the education of children with disabilities may be knowledgeable professionals in their field and believe they know all about educating the children; however, knowledge in general and understanding in particular are two different issues. Knowledge may allow one to empathize with the plight of another, but only by living a life can an individual truly understand the needs of the other.

Over the years I have worked with hundreds of students with disabilities at the elementary, secondary, and postsecondary levels. Regardless of what psychological reports, evaluation statistics, and Individualized Education Programs (IEPs) have said, I have been struck by the creativity of the students—their ability to develop networks of cooperation and mutual aid and to find ways to survive and succeed educationally.

Under the direction of the Individuals with Disabilities Education Act (IDEA) (2004), educators know how to educate children with disabilities but often do not do so. Concerns abound over the cost of resources and interpretations of the laws putting stakeholders—children, parents, teachers, psychologists, administrators, and others—in competition with one another. However, the resources are there; it is just a matter of how society chooses to spend them.

Politics, according to the *Merriam-Webster's Dictionary* (2011), is the "competition between competing interest groups or individuals for power and leadership . . . in a particular area of experience especially as seen or dealt with from a political point of view" (www.merriam-webster.com/dictionary/politics). Interrelationships between the people, groups, or organizations in a particular area of life are especially critical insofar as they involve power and influence or conflict.

Smith and Max-Neef (2011) posit that "political power is subservient to economic power, simply because economic and financial power give political power to those who have it, and, inversely, those without economic power are bereft of the means to wield political power" (11). Therefore, politics, in the context of special education in the United States, grows out of the competition for scarce resources.

A NEW MODEL

Historically, children with disabilities were excluded, segregated, and underserved in American schools. In 1975, when federal legislation was passed creating special education as we know it today, 18 percent of children with disabilities were excluded from schools even though all fifty states had passed compulsory

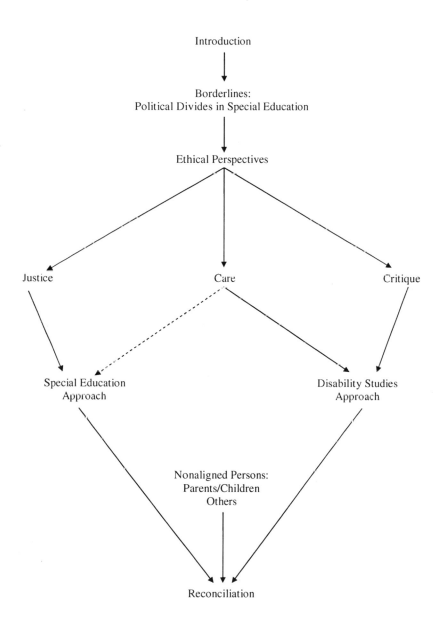

Introduction

Borderlines:
Political Divides in Special Education

Ethical Perspectives

Justice   Care   Critique

Special Education   Disability Studies
Approach   Approach

Nonaligned Persons:
Parents/Children
Others

Reconciliation

Figure 1.1. A New Model

school attendance laws. In addition, 55 percent of children with disabilities were not receiving any school services related to their unique learning needs.

As with earlier civil rights struggles, the purpose of the IDEA was to integrate children with disabilities into the mainstream of education to the greatest extent possible. Over the last thirty-five years, legislation and litigation have tweaked the IDEA. However, a dearth of activity has taken place to critique the basic structures of the laws and the problems that still exist in schooling children with disabilities.

A comprehensive approach to educate children with disabilities in the twenty-first century is overdue. Special education, as we know it today, essentially dictated by the mandates of the IDEA, needs to be rethought. Too many borderlines still divide stakeholders in the process of educating these children. The voices of the children, and their parents and advocates, have been muted. Moral dimensions of special education need to be explored. New perspectives on disability from social sciences other than education and law should be considered. The process is in need of a serious review and revision.

A new model, as shown in figure 1.1, begins with a description of seven qualities that keep people from constructively interacting and working with one another and goes on to examine three ethical frames that create a multidimensional framework for evaluating issues that arise in special education. Next, two approaches for educating children with disabilities—Special Education and Disability Studies—are considered. The ethical grounding of these approaches is discussed. After considering some examples of political issues inherent in both methodologies, key stakeholders will enter into a dialogue informed by all components of the model with the goal of reconciling all the ambiguities and inconsistencies therein, coming to a consensus, and implementing a better educational experience for children with disabilities.

BORDERLINES

The roots of the cultural and contextual borders are explored, those that separate the many stakeholders involved in providing an education to children with disabilities. These borders keep people from interacting and working constructively with one another in the same way that stone walls, fences, rivers, mountains, and arbitrary human territorial borders create physical barriers to everyday interaction. Following are descriptions of borderlines that must be crossed.

- Resources equal political power: "No just society ever existed but not all societies are equally unjust. There are great differences in the degree of justice. . . . The distribution of economic and financial power determines how just a society is. Politics and economics cannot be separated" (Smith and Max-Neef 2011, 10).

- The social sciences are not hard sciences: Special education is a social science concerned with the complete education of children with disabilities and all the complexities involved in describing the interaction of human beings in social settings. However, special education is administered and implemented through a *systems management approach* as described by Apple (2004), based on the work of Taylor (1911) and others. The approach assumes a superficial rationality championing objective thought, the sanctity of statistical analysis, competition between groups, hierarchy, heuristics, the categorization of people, and reductionism.

- Language is not politically neutral: "The ground rules regulating significant discourse become in effect the expression of power" (Bowers 1987, 13). When parents meet with education professionals schooled in the language of law, psychological assessment, and educational jargon, the unequal terrain creates a vertical wall parents cannot scale alone. The people who prevail control the language of discourse and the way terms are defined. Questions posed that appear neutral are not. It is important to understand who formulates questions, answers questions, and gets their voices heard without trepidation and hindrance.

- A label is more than a word: Children with disabilities are labeled with one of thirteen classifications mandated by the IDEA. Many educators believe that labeling is a perfectly reasonable way to classify children by ability for their educational benefit. Others believe labeling is representative of a stratified society that is concerned explicitly with the classification of people and implicitly with measuring their value differentials (Apple 2004).

- Identity politics leads to identity powerlessness: Stakeholders identify and advocate for whatever group they believe they are part of. When stakeholders self-divide into competing groups, the power of numbers in the political process at every level is lost. For example, if all the parents of all the children (greater than six million) with disabilities worked together in solidarity, this group would be a political force to be reckoned with. Inclusion of all people with disabilities into this constituency would totally change the political dynamics of disability in the United States.

- Prisoners have no political power: Plato (1892), in book 7 of *The Republic*, was one of the first to intellectualize the predicament of human beings as prisoners of their thoughts and actions. All people have thoughts, beliefs, and ideas, both rational and irrational, that they believe are important. "Whether through our upbringing, schooling, reading, or whatever, we all have relatively fixed valuations concerning the world about us, and whether we like it or not, we carry them with us into our work and social science" (Smith and Max-Neef 2011, 57). When people refuse to be open to new ideas and to critically challenge their inner beliefs because of the comfort level provided, they become prisoners of their own thoughts.

- Not only the British have colonized: The education of children with disabilities is dependent on the resources made available by politicians and on the politicians' benevolence. With little or no role in, knowledge about, or relationship to the children and their families, political leaders wield the power to influence and alter the lives and destinies of these constituents. This hegemonic behavior by political and educational elites leads to the oppression and exploitation of the students through systemic structures beyond their control. Essentially, the children and their families are colonized through the maldistribution of resources and implementation of federal legislation or lack thereof. These structures—including the IDEA, and funding—have the power to alter the children's destinies and lives.

FRAMES AND PERSPECTIVES

Starratt (1991) suggests that a more complete response to the ethical issues occurring in everyday school life can be guided by three complementary modes of ethical thought—the ethic of justice, the ethic of caring, and the ethic of critique. The three ethics work together to inform, strengthen, and compensate for the weaknesses of each other ethic (see figure 1.2). A brief description of each follows.

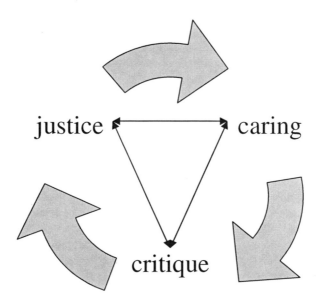

Figure 1.2. The Three Ethics

Justice

The American system of justice is based on the idea of a social basis for morality and that moral rules may be changed over time. The rules of government or society should be determined by the consent of the governed. People are self-interested and in constant competition and conflict with one another, thereby making it necessary for them to establish a government to make and enforce laws. Reasoning is a two-directional phased activity in which people use their general ideas to guide actions that direct their general ideas. The general rules are relative to particular judgments, which in turn are relative to rules (Fox and DeMarco 1990).

Rawls (1971) believed that citizens share an idea of a well-ordered society in which all people are free and equal: "Each person is to have an equal right to the most extensive system of equal liberties compatible with a similar system of liberty for all. . . . Social and economic inequalities are just only if they result in compensating benefits for everyone—the least advantaged in particular" (1971, 302).

Kohlberg's (1981) stages of moral development find many American adults with an orientation toward authority, a reliance on fixed rules, regulations, laws, and policies, and a belief in maintaining the social order—and the status quo—for its own sake. Moral principles are universal and applied to moral dilemmas through deductive, formal, and abstract thinking. Emphasis is placed on the legal point of view but only with the possibility of changing law in terms of the rational consideration of social unity.

In the context of special education, justice provides a legal framework that maintains the social order in the process of educating children with disabilities. Policy, law, and regulations intermingle in a symbiotic relationship carried out at the federal, state, and local levels. Law is constantly in flux and open to change as evidenced by over thirty years of litigation and reauthorization. The stated goal is to provide compensating benefits to children with disabilities—who have been disadvantaged in the past—while maintaining an ongoing system, providing an equitable and fair education to all.

Caring

Caring expands the idea of morality to include concern for interconnection, harmony, and nonviolence with an emphasis on attachments, self-sacrifice, selfishness, and a consideration of relationships as primary. Moral dilemmas are contextual and are resolved through inductive thinking (Gilligan 1977). For Noddings (1984), caring is characterized by a move away from self. *Caring* educators seek to meet their *cared-for* children and their parents in a reciprocal relationship where each learns from the other. The goal is to maximize human relationships and the potential of the children.

When *caring* persons can see the other's reality as a possibility for themselves, they must act to eliminate intolerable situations, reduce pain, fill needs, and help actualize others. For the *caring* person the essential part of caring is to apprehend the *cared-for* person's reality and try to feel what that person feels (Kierkegaard 1846/1941). Starratt (1990) suggests that in this ethic, children should not be used as a means to an end, but constitute an end in themselves.

In the context of special education, *caring* educators would strive to maximize the social, academic, and cognitive potential of children with disabilities. They would meet the children and their parents in a reciprocal relationship—where each person can try to feel and understand the other—and maximize all the dimensions of that relationship. The children's needs come first. When educators are making placement, programmatic, instructional, and other decisions concerning the education of children with disabilities, the children should always be the end of the decision-making process, not the means to someone else's end.

Critique

Starratt's (1990, 1991, 1994) concept of critique is the application of critical theory to education from an ethical perspective, as he explains: "Schools, as important institutions in the social fabric, disproportionately benefit some groups in society and fail others. As a bureaucratic organization, the school may exhibit structural properties which promote a misuse of power and authority among its members" (Starratt 1990, 18).

Critical theory finds its roots in the Frankfurt school of philosophers and others whose ideas are similar. When considering social relationships, social customs, and social institutions with various power relationships at work within them, critical theorists concern themselves with ongoing competitive struggles between societal groups for the power to define the status quo of the social order. Their focus includes the use of language, ground rules of discourse, and structural arrangements in society that allow some groups to exhibit an advantage over others in defining the status quo (Starratt 1990, 1991, 1994).

Society operates under a complex set of formal laws and informal rules that have been created by certain groups to benefit some citizens at the expense of others. In our industrial-commercial society, some groups create and perpetuate the labels—terms used to identify other subordinate groups. The dominant groups set up, run, and control our social system (Apple 2004). They use their hegemony over sources of power—such as the schools, universities, courts, election processes, boards of directors, sources of funding, media, discourse, and language—to control others.

Language gives the dominant groups the ability to determine the meaning of everyday words that allow the ordering of groups of people, organizations, and individuals—such as stakeholders—as dominant and subordinate. To understand how dominant groups use the power of language to control in this way, one must evaluate who benefits from the way things are, who defines the terms, who is in control, and who creates the myths behind the ways people relate to one another.

To think critically, one must be aware that political and social decisions are never neutral (Zinn 2002). They are a reflection of the power, interests, and influence of controlling groups, legitimized by laws, customs, and narrow, objective, reductionist descriptions of concepts of social science (Apple 2004; Giroux 1988, 1991, 2005).

In the context of special education, an ethic of critique would propel all stakeholders constantly to question the roots of the process of testing, classifying, and placing children with disabilities in, and the results of special education, raising these key questions:

- Whose rules, regulations, and laws define the process?
- Whose language defines the terms and labels?
- Who controls the discourse?
- Whose authority are we orientated to?
- Whose social, economic, and political order are we maintaining?
- Whose status quo are we maintaining?
- Who benefits from the way things are and who loses?

Most special and regular educators are not sensitive to issues that arise in the education of children with disabilities from a perspective of critique (Strax 1992). In my conversations with students, teachers, and other professionals in the special education arena over the last nineteen years, I have found that there continues to be an inability or lack of desire to critique the legal, social, and political structures involved in the education of children with disabilities. The first step to a comprehensive review of special education as we know it will need to begin with this critique.

Summary

Uniting the three ethical themes—justice, caring, and critique—creates a complete compassionate environment where the strengths of one substitute for the weaknesses of the other. As Starratt (1991) suggests:

> The ethic of critique assumes a point of view about social justice and human rights and about the way communities ought to govern themselves. The ethic of justice assumes an ability to perceive injustice in the social order as well as some minimal level of caring about relationships in that social order. The ethic of caring does not ignore the demands of community governance issues, but claims that caring is the ideal fulfillment of all social relationships . . . each ethic needs the very strong convictions embedded in the other. (198)

Starratt continues:

> The ethic of justice needs the profound commitment to the dignity of the individual
> person found in the ethic of caring. The ethic of caring needs the larger attention to
> social order and fairness of the ethic of justice if it is to avoid an entirely idiosyn-
> cratic involvement in social policy. The ethic of critique requires an ethic of caring
> if it is to avoid the cynical and depressing ravings of the habitual malcontent, and the
> ethic of justice requires the profound social analysis of the ethic of critique to move
> beyond the naïve fine-tuning of inequalities built into the very structures by which
> justice is supposed to be measured. (198)

People, such as children with disabilities, who did not succeed by the rules of
American society—which until recently was grounded in a liberal philosophy—
were targets of an attempted rescue by a constantly expanding central government
trying to keep its capitalistic economy afloat through a growing welfare state (Bowers 1987). In the current neoliberal climate, the future of this safety net is under
attack (Smith and Max-Neef 2011).

SPECIAL EDUCATION

The Special Education approach to educating children with disabilities, developed over many years and clearly defined and codified in the IDEA (2004), is the
dominant methodology taught in most schools of education in the United States
and articulated by most education professionals in the field. This approach has
its roots in the classical concepts of *scientific management* (Taylor 1911) and
bureaucracy (Weber 1925/1947). Frederick Taylor's principles of scientific management concentrate on technical issues such as time and motion, rigid discipline
on the job, and focus on the task to be performed. His principles of administration
as management are fixed on coordinating small tasks to accomplish the overall
job as efficiently as possible.

Max Weber believed that bureaucracy was a theory best suited to large, complex enterprises performing services for many clients. He saw organizations as
having characteristics such as a division of labor in specialization, a hierarchy
of authority, rules and regulations, and an impersonal orientation. Authority
relationships are an integral part of life in formal school organizations and are
the main factors underlying most student-teacher, teacher-principal, and student-
principal relationships. The exercise of authority in schools usually does not
involve coercion. Weber (1925/1947) defines authority as "the probability that
certain specific commands (or all commands) from a given source will be obeyed
by a given group of persons" (152).

Examples of bureaucracy include federal and state departments of education
and, of course, school districts and schools. New manifestations of older classical concepts such as management by objectives, competency-based programs,

and accountability programs are often referred to as "neoscientific" administrative concepts. Federal interventions in public schooling, such as the IDEA, are organized and administered utilizing classical and neoscientific concepts of bureaucracy.

Thus, special education, as we know it today, is a rational, heuristic, neoscientific, bureaucratic process relying on concepts such as objectivity, superficial rationality, task analysis, accountability, and the division of people into categories. Couched in the language of a justice ethic, special education practices follow the mandates of the IDEA—appearing to be caring, but on closer inspection only attempting to provide the just concepts of fairness and equity.

Special education is administered as a dual system. Some systemic functions are loosely joined and others are tightly fixed. The core technical activities of professionals are loosely coupled (Weick 1976). First, for example, teachers and psychologists have autonomy within broad school district and IDEA guidelines to carry out their professional tasks as they see fit. Everyday relationships are often caring. All other activities under the IDEA are more tightly coupled (Bidwell 1965). Second, provisions of the laws mandating organization, administration, and implementation must be carried out in a rigid fashion, leaving professional and familial stakeholders little latitude in doing their tasks.

In 1975, Congress passed the Education for All Handicapped Children Act (EAHCA), currently codified as the Individuals with Disabilities Education Act (IDEA), in answer to a situation in which children with disabilities had fallen through the safety net of American society. The IDEA, as an extension of the Civil Rights Act of 1964 and of Section 504 of the Rehabilitation Act of 1973, sought to equalize educational opportunities for all children, regardless of disability. In addition, this overdue legislation gave children with disabilities more of an equal chance to succeed educationally because of the increased per-student federal and state aid it prescribed.

The IDEA mandates a free appropriate education in the least restrictive environment for all children aged three to twenty-one and provides a comprehensive system of due process to settle disputes between stakeholders. All special education services—including evaluations, instruction, professional and supportive personnel, materials, and therapies—are provided to all children with disabilities from age three to twenty-one.

Children are identified as students with disabilities and provided special education through a process of assessment, classification, and placement guided by a clear set of hierarchical requirements. The assessment process is dominated by standardized individual psychoeducational evaluation instruments administered by psychologists, educators, therapists, and other health-care professionals. The criteria for classification, as a person with one of thirteen disabilities, are dominated by statistically derived scores and clinical medical diagnoses. Children are then given an *appropriate* special education placement based on this assessment and classification process.

The term *appropriate* is subjective. The first U.S. Supreme Court case to address any issue of the IDEA was concerned with precisely what this term meant. In *Board of Education v. Rowley* (1982), the Court ruled that school districts are obligated only to provide an appropriate floor of opportunity to students with disabilities and they do not have to maximize their educational potential. The Court mediated in this dispute to balance the demands of competing interest groups in trying to create a system in which everyone can be given an equal opportunity to compete for rewards in our society.

The IDEA requires school officials to give children with disabilities an appropriate education in the least restrictive environment. The term *least restrictive environment* mandates that children with disabilities must be educated to the maximum extent possible with children in regular education classrooms. The law allows for a variety of alternative teaching structures including team teaching, consultive special educators in the regular education classrooms, instructional support personnel, accommodations for learning and test taking, and assistive technology.

Children without disabilities may benefit from alternative teaching structures designed for children with disabilities in the regular classroom without violating the funding provisions of the law. In addition, the regular education teacher becomes a member of the child's IEP team, ensuring grade-appropriate content in the education goals listed within.

IEPs contain sequenced, developmental, cognitive, and behavioral prescriptions designed to document school districts' compliance with the IDEA. These plans are an attempt to equalize educational opportunities for students with disabilities through a regimented system of rules and regulations specifying a program that, if followed and documented, should develop a successful student.

The IDEA provides a comprehensive system of due process to settle disputes between stakeholders in the entire process of educating children with disabilities. Parents and students of legal age must give their consent at various stages of the assessment, classification, placement, IEP development, and instructional delivery process. School officials often have competing concerns. The system of due process provides extensive details and timelines that must be followed. Stakeholders have opportunities to resolve differences at every level from local meetings to the U.S. Supreme Court.

Additional tenets of the IDEA follow (for a full review of the IDEA, see chapter 4).

- Students attending nonpublic and charter schools are now eligible for a certain level of special education services at public expense.
- Parents are allowed full review of all records.
- Children with disabilities who carry weapons and/or drugs and those who may be a danger to themselves or others can be removed from school and

placed in alternative placements ensuring the continuation of their education for up to forty-five days.
* The IEP team must provide a behavior plan based on a behavioral assessment.

The delivery of special education services now appears to protect the rights of students with disabilities while bringing more stakeholders into the educational process in a spirit of cooperation and community.

DISABILITY STUDIES

Even though the current Special Education approach to educating students with disabilities—developed through legislation such as the IDEA and Section 504 of the Rehabilitation Act of 1973—has been refined through reauthorized legislation and litigation, many people believe this approach failed to fully meet the needs of the children. Since the 1990s, the Disability Studies approach has gained currency with many people with disabilities, their advocates, and scholars and practitioners. Disability studies continues to emerge as a major methodology taught in many schools of education in the United States and articulated by a growing number of education professionals in the field.

This method, which continues to gain momentum, approaches through a social model the education of, and service provision to, students with disabilities. The voices of people with disabilities that describe stigmatizing, oppressive experiences in the dominant social culture are a driving force in developing new strategies to educate children with disabilities. Ideally, disability studies will engage with studies in other forms of oppression such as racism, sexism, and homophobia in setting a new standard for collaboration across oppressions in the dominant culture of the United States and provide an example to put an end to identity politics.

Disability studies, an interdisciplinary field, concerns itself with the culture, history, experiences, and contributions of people with disabilities (Wikipedia 2008). This approach is based on the premise that people with disabilities are at a disadvantage in a society that defines and responds to them as different (Johnstone 2001). Davis (1997) suggests that students of disability studies should engage subject matter from other disciplines—such as the social sciences, humanities, history, and literature from political, cultural, social, economic, and other perspectives—to understand that different attitudes toward disability are relevant in different time periods and in different places.

This area of study should include postsecondary students, with and without disabilities, attending professional programs that prepare them to be service providers and advocates for people with disabilities. Disability studies replaces the idea of disability as an individual deficit or defect needing to be remedied through medical intervention or rehabilitation, believing in the exploration of new destigmatizing approaches through collective social science responses to issues that arise in the education and development of people with disabilities.

Unlike the Special Education approach, Disability Studies seeks to understand the history, origin, and development of conceptual ideas about disability, and to develop strategies to improve the lives of all people. When children do not reach their full educational, social, and economic potential, it is a loss to all society. One dollar spent on a child's development saves society one thousand dollars during the child's lifetime (Committee for Economic Development 1989).

Thus, the ethic of caring and critique provides a moral path to reaching the goals of disability studies. Caring asks educators of children with disabilities to maximize student potential, create reciprocal relationships between stakeholders, and respect the voices of the children and their advocates when making decisions with the end being the child. As Davis (1997) suggests, stakeholders approaching the education of children with disabilities from a disability studies perspective will question the current Special Education approach—who benefits from the way things are and why.

NONALIGNED PERSONS

Many stakeholders involved in the process of educating children with disabilities do not identify with either the Special Education or Disability Studies approaches. To develop an identity one must be cognizant of what these approaches are. Even though special education has a major effect on their lives, destinies, and in some cases income and working conditions, many stakeholders have very little knowledge and/or understanding about either approach.

Unknowledgeable stakeholders include most parents and children, adult people with disabilities and their supporters, and some teachers. Limited knowledge and understanding place stakeholders in a subordinate position whenever they are involved in any interaction or activity, including giving consent. They become atomized, as individuals left on their own to confront or be confronted by the enormous special education bureaucracy.

RECONCILIATION

A comprehensive approach to educate children with disabilities in the twenty-first century should begin with a reconciliation of the many ideas, perspectives, and differences in thinking of the stakeholders in educating children with disabilities. This process must begin with dialogue, starting with a debate between stakeholders who believe in the Special Education approach and those who support the Disability Studies approach. "It's not a matter of where the train is going, it's deciding whether to get on" (Starkey, Zemeckis, Goetzman, and Teitler 2004).

Supporters of the Special Education approach would draw attention to the legislative mandates that provide funding. Without the billions of dollars provided by federal, state, and local education agencies, there would be no comprehensive services provided to the children. The clock would be rolled back to the pre-IDEA era. Disability Studies supporters would retort that the federal government's failure to adequately fund the IDEA has led to increased financial burdens on state and local education agencies. This places stakeholders in other areas of education in a political competition to grab the decreased number of dollars that remain. The threat of losing all federal funding if IDEA mandates are not carried out keeps special education funding flowing from state and local sources.

Disability Studies advocates would point to the IDEA as an attempt to solve a social science problem using hard science. The IDEA's reliance on objective reasoning—based on statistical data to create a prescription (IEP) to cure a disability—is considered an unduly simplistic way to approach all the complexities of a human being interacting within a multifaceted social system, such as a school. Supporters of the Special Education approach would identify the IEP and its supporting data as a framework for teachers, therapists, and other professionals to follow to educate the children and provide for accountability of results.

The IDEA mandates the labeling of children with one or more of thirteen classifications of disability. To proponents of the Special Education approach, labeling is an excellent way to identify children by category, allowing for the provision of improved services. Critically thinking Disability Studies professionals believe labels divide people into categories with value differentials; the children are thus considered different, deviant, or not as good.

These professionals would go on to mention how parents of children with disabilities and other interested parties organize themselves into advocacy groups by disability categories. These groups raise money for research, provide parent outreach, community education, and political advocacy—organized around one particular disability. This effort leads to an identity politics where different disability groups compete with one another in the political process at every level rather than joining together into a supportive interpolitical block titled People with Disabilities.

Supporters of the Special Education approach would indicate that the concept of disability as diversity would lead to its own identity politics just as other diverse groups are plagued by identity politics. Disability supporters, for example, could easily divide themselves into identity groups such as veterans, children, seniors, Asians, African Americans, women, men, and so on.

Over the years, incremental changes have been made to special education, as we know it, through the political and legal process. People who champion the Special Education approach perceive the procedural due process as the ideal way to afford stakeholders an equal chance to have their grievances heard. Disability Studies devotees would draw attention to the unequal ability of stakeholders to access advocates and attorneys to take advantage of their due process rights.

One might wonder where the dialogue toward reconciliation and unity should begin. The debate among advocates of both the Special Education and Disability Studies approaches to educating children with disabilities should also include education professionals, scholars, and practitioners. A conversation beginning with this debate is a dialogue that begins in the middle. In the past, the top-down dialogue creating special education as we know it flowed down from the U.S. Congress and the courts to the schools and communities.

Freire (1968/1970) believed that people oppressed and exploited through systemic structures beyond their control need to create a dialogue to critically understand their situation, explore possibilities for liberation, and carry out a plan to achieve it. The education of children with disabilities would start with a conversation among parents, older children, and their closest advocates. This bottom-up discourse would begin with the voices never heard—everyday people talking with one another on the local level with the goal of understanding and solving the common issues that arise in the education of all children with disabilities.

Upon reaching consensus, this discourse would continue across larger geographic areas, eventually involving other stakeholders higher on the hierarchy such as local educators, attorneys, and politicians, and later state and federal educators and politicians. Agreement would have to occur at each level of dialogue before moving to a higher level. Implementation of new ideas resulting from these accords could be piloted at every level.

A word of caution: neoliberal economic policies have created an economic and political environment in the United States where funding for all social programs, including education, is under attack. With money flowing out of social programs and school district budgets, and Republican governors dismantling social programs, the future of special education—IDEA and Section 504—as we know it is brought into question.

The U.S. Supreme Court has usually upheld Congress's intent under Section 504 and IDEA, and Congress has generally supported disability legislation in a bipartisan manner. School districts are already under increased pressure to compete against other government agencies for shrinking federal dollars. Stakeholders must decide for themselves whether now is the appropriate time to implement a comprehensive plan to educate children with disabilities in the twenty-first century. The future of special education as we know it is unclear.

In the future will districts be required to fund disability services in private and charter schools? Could this lead to the resegregation of children with disabilities? Might children with disabilities through standardized testing and Adequate Yearly Progress (AYP) become a *political football* in the drive to break up public education by increasing the number of failing schools?

In writing this chapter, I hope to heighten readers' awareness of the possible effects that the IDEA could have on children and encourage everyone to carefully examine the law's provisions. Readers may then draw their own conclusions on the current state of disability legislation and any need for further change. New legislation will reflect the political climate of the legislature creating it. Educators and stakeholders will have to plan carefully the timing of any further attempts to revise or totally rewrite disability legislation.

QUESTIONS FOR DISCUSSION

1. How would the concept of the IDEA be different from several left- and right-wing perspectives in the United States?
2. What borderlines appear in the process of educating children with disabilities? What borderlines have you crossed during your education?
3. Which aspects of the Special Education approach do you support? Why? Which aspects of the Disability Studies approach do you support? Why?
4. What is your ideal comprehensive belief about the education of children with disabilities in the twenty-first century?

REFERENCES

Apple, M. W. (2004). *Ideology and curriculum*. 3rd ed. New York: Routledge.

Bidwell, C. E. (1965). The school as a formal organization. In *Handbook of organization*, ed. J. G. Marsh, 972–1022. Chicago: Rand McNally.

Board of Education of Hendrick Hudson Central School District v. Rowley, 458 U.S. 176 (1982).

Bowers, C. A. (1987). *Elements of a post-liberal theory of education*. New York: Teachers College Press.

Civil Rights Act of 1964, Title IV, 42 U.S.C. § 2000c et seq. (2006).

Committee for Economic Development (1989). *Children in need: Investment strategy for the educationally disadvantaged*. New York: Author.

Davis, L. (1997). *The disability studies reader*. New York: Routledge.

Education for All Handicapped Children Act, P.L. 94-142, 89 Stat. 773 (1975), now codified, as amended, at 20 U.S.C. §§ 1400–82 (2006).

Fox, R. M., and J. P. DeMarco. (1990). *Moral reasoning: A philosophic approach to applied ethics*. Chicago: Holt, Rinehart and Winston.

Freire, P. (1970). *Pedagogy of the oppressed*. Trans. M. B. Ramos. New York: Herder and Herder. (Orig. pub. 1968.)

Gilligan, C. (1977). In a different voice: Women's conception of self and of morality. *Harvard Educational Review* 49 (4): 481–517.

Giroux, H. A. (1988). *Schooling and the struggle for public life*. Minneapolis: University of Minnesota Press.

———. (1991). *Postmodernism, feminism, and cultural politics*. Albany: State University of New York Press.

———. (2005). *Border crossings: Cultural workers and the politics of education*. New York: Routledge.

Individuals with Disabilities Education Improvement Act, P.L. 108–446, 118 Stat. 2647 (2004), now codified, as amended, at 20 U.S.C. § 1400–91 (2006).

Johnstone, D. (2001). *An introduction to disability studies*. Hastings, East Sussex, UK: David Fulton Publishers.

Kierkegaard, S. (1941). *Concluding unscientific postscript*. Trans. D. F. Swerson and W. Lowrie. Princeton, NJ: Princeton University Press. (Orig. pub. 1846.)

Kohlberg, L. (1981). *The philosophy of moral development*. San Francisco: Harper & Row.

Max-Neef, M. (2010). Chilean economist Manfred Max-Neef on barefoot economics, poverty and why the U.S. is becoming an "underdeveloping nation." November 26. Audio transcript. Retrieved from www.democracynow.org.

Merriam-Webster. (2011). S.v. "Politics." June 13. Retrieved from www.merriamwebster .com/dictionary/politics.

Noddings, N. (1984). *Caring: A feminine approach to ethics and moral education.* Berkeley: University of California Press.

Plato. (1892). *The republic*. Trans. B. Jowett. New York: Oxford University Press.

Rawls, J. (1971). *A theory of justice*. Cambridge, MA: Harvard University Press.

Rehabilitation Act, Section 504, 29 U.S.C. § 794 (2006).

Smith, P. B., and M. Max-Neef. (2011). *Economics unmasked: From power and greed to compassion and the common good*. Devon, UK: Green Books.

Starkey, S., R. Zemeckis, G. Goetzman, and W. Teitler, producers (2004). *Polar express*. DVD. Warner Home Video.

Starratt, R. J. (1990). Supervision and ethical consciousness. Unpublished manuscript.

———. (1991). Building an ethical school: A theory for practice in educational leadership. *Educational Administration Quarterly* 27 (2): 185–202.

———. (1994). *Building an ethical school*. New York: Falmer Press.

Strax, M. (1992). Principal's sensitivities to ethical issues that arise in the education of disabled students. Unpublished diss., Fordham University, New York.

Taylor, F. W. (1911). *Principles of scientific management*. New York: Harper & Row.

Weber, M. (1947). *The theory of social and economic organization*. Ed. T. Parsons, trans. A. M. Henderson and T. Parsons. New York: Free Press. (Orig. pub. 1925.)

Weick, K. E. (1976). Educational organizations as loosely coupled systems. *Administrative Science Quarterly* 21:1–19.

Wikipedia. (2008). S.v. "Disability Studies." Retrieved from en.wikipedia.org/wiki/disability_studies, October 4.

Zinn, H. (2002). *You can't be neutral on a moving train: A personal history of our times.* Boston: Beacon Press.

2

Schooling Tommy in the Past

A Personal Perspective

Thomas E. Strax, Lisa Luciano, and Anna Dunn

New York, March 5, 1942. It was a typical cold, dreary, winter day. The United States was at war. Four people played out their roles at Beth Israel Hospital awaiting the birth of a baby. A grandmother sat patiently in the visitors' area waiting for the doctor's announcement. The mother, laboring for three days with a baby that was breach, was now giving birth. Her husband, a physician, was allowed to be in attendance while the obstetrician delivered the baby. The child, a boy, born after an extremely long and painful labor, was blue, not breathing, and had obvious weakness of his right arm and leg. When a spinal tap was performed, blood was found in his cerebral spinal fluid. He was a mess and in obvious trouble.

The obstetrician stood there, looked at the child, and did nothing. The infant's father wanted everything done to keep the baby alive. Finally, as the baby stabilized, the obstetrician left the room and walked down to the visitors' area to speak to the grandmother. The emotions of the grandmother were those of joy and excitement; however, they immediately turned to dismay, horror, and anger as the physician said, "The parents are young and healthy; the baby is better off dead." This was the first day of my life, a life that would encompass a multidecade odyssey and battle for the civil rights of individuals with disabilities.

Twenty-four years later, as an adult, the boy was in a lecture hall as a third-year medical student at the New York University School of Medicine listening to the same obstetrician giving a lecture in obstetrics to his third-year class. The student just sat there and smiled because he was now a successful medical student. Another forty-three years passed and this boy, now a grandfather, presided over a Thanksgiving table, thinking about being blessed with a son and daughter who stand up against injustice; their spouses; his four grandchildren;

and the beautiful woman whom he adores. But I am getting ahead of myself; let me start at the beginning.

GETTING INTO SCHOOL

Five years after the fateful March evening, the little boy was ready to attend school. However, New York City law stated that "no handicapped child" was permitted to attend public school, as society at the time was very different from how it is now. The prevailing attitude was that children and adults with disabilities should be protected in institutions or kept at home, instead of participating as active members of society. These individuals should be guided, raised, and protected by their parents.

My parents, who had been among the founders of United Cerebral Palsy (UCP), which advocates for the humane protection of children and young adults, had a radical idea. They wanted me to grow up being able to live independently. To accomplish this goal I would need education and social experiences with other children. In the event that I didn't flourish academically, my parents and grandparents began saving money to buy a store or grocery that would provide me with a stable income.

My parents' first attempt to get me accepted into public school was unsuccessful. They immediately filed a suit against the City of New York on the premise that I deserved an education. Their second action was to obtain assistance from my great-uncle, who was very powerful in the political system in New York City, and who worked behind the scenes finessing the court. With these two plans under way, I was examined by the chief of orthopedics for the Board of Education. His job was to identify children who were handicapped, and therefore, under the law, would be denied access to public school.

The chief of orthopedics was a friend of my father's who had served with him in the navy during World War II. This physician may have been the first individual to ever use the semantic difference between the words *handicapped* and *disabled.* After examining me he said that I had a number of physical disabilities; however, I was not handicapped! This difference opened the door for my admission to school. The courts also ruled in my favor.

After I started school, my parents received a letter from the superintendent of the Board of Education telling them that they had made a great mistake, should remove me from school, and should institutionalize me with my tested IQ of 40. Years later when I graduated from high school and went to college, my father sent this former superintendent a copy of my high school grades.

On the first day of school, my mother brought me to the bus stop. When the bus driver arrived, he opened the door, took one look at me, and said that he was not taking a *cripple* on his bus. He closed the door and drove off. Under the union contract the bus driver was like a captain of a ship, able to deny any child access to the bus. My father's friends suggested that he try approaching the bus driver by using his union contacts. Having served in the Pacific during World War II with the current tugboat union president, Dad approached him about our school bus dilemma.

I remember the bus driver as being extremely kind and friendly, and taking good care of me. Fifty years would pass before I was told what actually happened—that night, three longshoremen visited the bus driver and told him that if I wasn't on the bus the next day, he would be at the bottom of the East River. At midnight the bus driver called my father and pleaded with him to let me ride the bus.

THE ELEMENTARY AND HIGH SCHOOL YEARS

The first seven years of public school are a total blur to me. My first four report cards listed my grades as *present*. In the sixth grade, I was a year and a half behind. In the eighth grade, I was reading at a sixth-grade level and receiving Ds for behavior. My teacher wrote in my yearbook that if she ever had another two students like me and my friend JS, she would quit teaching.

The summer of 1954 was a magical one. I was sent to sleepaway camp with able-bodied children, and I played ball, ran, and did the fun things that all young adolescent boys do. Acceptance by a peer group and acceptance of my disability, movement, and coordination made me more confident physiologically and socially. Increased interaction with peers and others increased my linguistic skills and coordination. Physiological improvement led to improved concentration on academics

Perhaps it was the magic of the Catskill Mountains, because when I started the ninth grade, for some reason, everything managed to fall into place. My second report card had all As. With a new group of friends, who were among the leaders of my high school class, and driven by my desire to go to college and become a physician, I never looked back.

The psychosexual and psychosocial development of an adult occurs in a succession of stages. Each stage incorporates the preceding stage and builds on it. Arrest of this maturational process can occur at any point from a variety of causes. Physical disability has a high potential to alter the developmental trajectory.

Adolescence is a very difficult time for all children. Having a disability just adds to the stress. The adolescent has five developmental tasks (Strax 1991):

- Find an identity.
- Be accepted into a peer group.
- Separate from parents.
- Find a loving relationship outside the family.
- Find a vocation.

The path to personal independence takes many experiences to gain an identity. One needs accepting family and friends. However, an education, social skills, financial stability, spirit, drive, and the occasional reality check to shake things up a bit are also needed. My parents, sisters, and friends gave me chances to succeed, fail, and learn from both experiences.

COLLEGE AND MEDICAL SCHOOL

In high school I did well enough to be asked to participate in a special program that the State of New York initiated in the early 1950s to find high school students with disabilities who had the intellectual ability to warrant a college education. The state decided that it would pay for four years of higher education for children with disabilities. At the time, this program was not based on financial need or eligibility.

Upon receiving an invitation to participate, I accepted. When the guidance counselor was informed that my college major was to be premed, I was told that the program coordinator did not feel that medicine was a viable vocation for me. The state refused to pay for my college education unless I was willing to become an engineer. I did not want to be an engineer. When this information was given to my parents, my mother said, "What if he gets into medical school?" At that point, the representative of the program said, "Well, if he gets into medical school, we will pay for four years of medical education." This was said with a snicker. The program administrators were quite surprised, however, when I came back four years later and asked them to pay for my education at the New York University (NYU) School of Medicine.

All my high school teachers were extremely supportive and kind, allowing me a few extra accommodations, which at that time were acts of personal kindness rather than things that they were obligated to provide. These included oral examinations and copies of some lectures that were given to the class. Two teachers who had a great influence on my decision to become a mentor/teacher were my high school history and biology teachers.

They took interest in me as a person and were kind, yet they demanded I tow the mark. The history teacher, who lived near me, brought over notes. I loved history. The biology teacher died before my senior year of high school. The whole class loved him. Both teachers were very accommodating and gave me oral exams, teaching me a skill that was very valuable in college, medical school, and my professional life.

College was very different. I lived in the school dorms, learned to drive, and slowly came to realize that I was, at first, the only person on campus with a physical disability. Most of the professors were extremely helpful and gave me an opportunity to prove myself. Unfortunately, a small group of individuals seemed to go out of their way to stop something they considered to be unacceptable. Most notably, a professor actually said that he had given me a lower grade because I needed some help to set up my lab equipment in organic chemistry. A second teacher gave me a grade that was based purely on what he felt like giving me and not on my performance on the final examination.

DISABILITY, HANDICAP, AND SOCIETAL ATTITUDES

The United States in the 1940s, 1950s, and 1960s was growing very rapidly. However, attitudes did not change. Children with disabilities were kept at home, where they were protected, sheltered, and not integrated into society. It was common to sterilize women with developmental disabilities. Fifty to a hundred thousand young women and adolescent girls with disabilities were sterilized. Many children were institutionalized on the recommendation of their physicians, and in many cases families were discouraged from visiting their *deformed* children. No one knows how many hundreds of thousands of children with disabilities were locked away forever.

At that time all the agencies that raised money for children and young adults with disabilities had the same message in their advertisements: give to the poor, defenseless, and crippled. That attitude and that message continued until the early 1970s. I can still hear the voices singing, "Look and see they are walking, look and see they are talking" when I watched the UCP telethon as a child. Nowadays, our society still contains people who believe that infants with physical and mental disabilities do not have the right to live (Marquis 2002). These individuals believe that parents and physicians have a responsibility to put such children to death. This way, they will not suffer or be a burden to our society, thereby leaving room for children who are normal (Vehmas 2002).

Personal Perspective

Our society has slowly changed. More and more people, even if they are at first skeptical, are willing to give others a chance. The conceptual difference between a disability, which is something that causes us to have trouble doing an activity we are not required to do, and a handicap, which is something that we need to be able to do but that our disability prevents us from doing, is an important one. Many people assume that my disability is a recent development and are shocked to find out that I have had cerebral palsy since birth, that I have children and grandchildren, and am still practicing medicine, driving a car, and participating in other life activities of able-bodied people.

Many children do not have parents who have the knowledge, finances, contacts, and strength to do what my parents did. One of every ten families knows the tragedy of having a child born less than perfect (Kaiser Permanente 2004). About 20 percent of the U.S. population has a disability. People with disabilities represent the single largest minority group in the United States—larger than African Americans, Latinos, and Asians combined (Centers for Disease Control and Prevention 2001a, 2001b). Almost one-third of Caucasian widows in America, who are over 65 years old and have a physical disability, do not have enough money to buy food. This number rises to 49.5 percent if she is a woman of color, a point of national shame (Klesges et al. 2001).

I was fortunate enough to have parents who had the vision, direction, knowledge, and emotional strength to resist the prevailing treatment and attitude toward children with disabilities. My parents paid a price for defending my right to attend school, send me to a sleepaway camp with able-bodied children, and to live independently. They were ostracized and thrown out of United Cerebral Palsy. Aunts and uncles were horrified by my parents' desire to let me go my way and achieve what I could. When the Cub Scouts would not accept me into a local den, my mother petitioned the Scouts to allow her to initiate her own den for boys in the neighborhood. The same thing happened with the Boy Scouts.

When dealing with children with developmental disabilities, parents and guardians must have a plan and a goal similar to one for able-bodied children. Children with disabilities, who are expected to live in society, should be allowed to grow up healthy, happy, and able to take care of themselves in a competitive environment. The plan should include alternative options, such as putting away money to purchase a store or to provide placement in a residential facility.

Important, too, is that parents should remember that they may not have the answers to all the questions about their child's capabilities for a number of years. The critical issue is that if children are able to succeed in society, they need to be mainstreamed early and have experiences with the able-bodied population. Children must learn how to live with their disability and other individuals' reactions, a reality that can be extremely difficult for parents who are afraid that their children are going to be hurt. Everybody gets hurt at some point and children with disabilities—and their parents—need to persevere.

Parents should also try not to waste their time placing blame on each other for this or that situation. All children (with and without disabilities) should be treated the same. Children with disabilities need consistent feedback to avoid making excuses and blaming their disability when they fail. No one else will make excuses for them. People have to take responsibility for their actions. Parents must also remember that they will probably not be around for their children's entire lives; therefore, they must give them the opportunity to grow, become emotionally stable, and achieve independence.

Many parents and young adults with disabilities who see me professionally have asked me how I handle a variety of situations. The way I cope may not be appropriate for another individual. It is critical to remember that the more we keep our eye on the goal and allow independence, the greater the chance for success in life. This strategy applies to all children, with or without physical disabilities. Children who are overprotected and whose parents make excuses for them will grow up weak and unable to handle the rigors of the society that they will have to live in.

One last suggestion: do not forget the emotional needs of our abled-bodied children or give them the responsibility of caring for and protecting their sibling with disabilities. My parents forced my middle sister to make a number of sacrifices. Even though I appreciate those sacrifices, I realize how unfair they were to her.

Attitude and bias by educators should not have a place in the education of a child with a disability; however, they do. If children have a developmental disability, it helps to be visually appealing (Nosek et al. 2004). In 1970, a fire occurred in an experimental school for preschool children with developmental disabilities. The Archdioceses of New York offered the school an opportunity to integrate these children with able-bodied children in the preschool programs of the Archdiocese at the Riverside Church. At the time I was chief resident in physical medicine and rehabilitation at NYU's medical school and had been doing some work at the experimental school. I was asked to work with the archdioceses to facilitate this integration.

During that process I met with a number of teachers and administrators of this program. Three basic issues were apparent. First, the teachers were afraid that the able-bodied children would taunt and torture the children with physical disabilities. I assured them that bigotry is a learned behavior and suggested that they explain to the class that Johnny or Amy had been very sick when they were born, and because of that, they walk or talk a little bit differently.

Second, teachers were concerned that time spent instructing children would be consumed by continuously assisting the children with disabilities. Understanding children's zest for helping their teacher, I suggested the teachers assign some of the more accelerated able-bodied students to assist Johnny or Amy in setting up the day's activities. This strategy allows children to feel rewarded, and assists the teacher in maintaining flow in the lessons. During this process the children would understand that Johnny and Amy were children like them, not to be feared, and to be treated as friends and classmates.

The third problem was the most pervasive one, one that I've heard from many individuals who must interface with people with disabilities in their employment: physical appearance. People fear having to work with an individual who has a grotesque appearance and who displays difficulty in walking or handling objects. Flight attendants do not want to serve people with mental and physical disabilities who are unattractive, dysarthric, and/or drooling. This problem requires an extremely strong response from the administrative leadership: this is part of your job and if you don't want to do it, find a new job. Fortunately, that approach was chosen and surprisingly, things worked out well.

CONCLUSION

Societal attitudes, education, and quality of life for children and adults with developmental disabilities have changed a great deal since the 1940s, 1950s, and 1960s. I have enjoyed my life in the civil rights battle to assist some of the *weakest* members of our society. Standing up for others has given me joy and sense of purpose. Parents need to be willing to communicate their desires and fears to one another and develop a mutually agreed-on educational and instructional plan for all their children (Weiss 2000). They should seek out help and advice from knowledgeable professionals. The goal of this plan should be to allow the child as much independence as possible.

Parents should give their children needed constructive feedback and the opportunity to make mistakes and to learn from them, and to take responsibility for their actions. This is facilitated by both parents and a supportive peer group. Through their inner drive, opportunity, strength, weakness, supportive parents, peers, and luck, children will accomplish a great deal. I did!

QUESTIONS FOR DISCUSSION

1. The more things change, the more they stay the same. Do you think Tommy's testing, evaluation, placement, and K–12 education would be the same today as it was in the 1940s and 1950s? Why? Give examples.
2. Would you be comfortable being examined and treated by a doctor with cerebral palsy? Why or why not?
3. If Tommy were born to and raised by parents who were uneducated and without resources, what would the outcome of this case study have been?
4. Flight attendants do not want to serve people with mental and physical disabilities who are unattractive, dysarthric, and/or drooling. Do you? Why? Why not?

REFERENCES

Centers for Disease Control and Prevention. (2001a). Prevalence of disabilities and associated health conditions among adults—U.S. 1999. *MMWR Morb Mort Wkly Rep* 50 (7): 120–25. (Pub. erratum in MMWR *Morb Mortal Wkly Rep 2001* 50 (8): 149.)

Centers for Disease Control and Prevention. (2001b). Disability and secondary conditions. Chap. 6 of *Healthy people*. Washington, DC: U.S. Government Printing Office.

Kaiser Permanente National Diversity Council and Kaiser Permanente National Diversity Department. (2004). *A provider's handbook on culturally competent care: Individuals with disabilities.* Oakland, CA: Kaiser Permanente.

Klesges, L., M. Pahor, R. Shorr, J. Wan, J. Williamson, and J. Guralnik. (2001). Financial difficulty in acquiring food among elderly disabled women: Results from the Women's Health and Aging Study. *American Journal of Public Health* 9: 68–75.

Marquis, D. (2002). Culture of death. Letter. *Hastings Center Report* 32 (5): 5–6.

Nosek, M. A., D. H. Rintala, and M. E. Young, et al. Center for Research on Women with Disabilities. National study of women with physical disabilities: Special summary. www.bcm.tme.edu/crowd/national study/SPECIALS.htm. Accessed June 2004.

Strax, T. E. (1991). Psychological issues faced by adolescents and young adults with disabilities. *Pediatric Annals* 20 (9): 507–11.

Vehmas, S. (2002). Is it wrong to deliberately conceive or give birth to a child with mental retardation? *Journal of Medical Philosophy* 27: 47–63.

Weiss, S. C. (2000). Parental decisions and physician responsibilities. *Journal of the American Medical Association* 248: 1142–45.

3

❖ ❖

Free at Last?

Legislation for Children with Disabilities

Allan G. Osborne Jr. and Charles J. Russo

INTRODUCTION

Although all fifty states now have laws requiring school systems to provide special education services to qualified students with disabilities, prior to 1975 most states did not have any comprehensive special education legislation. The federal government offered financial incentives for states to make some level of services available but did not require states, and consequently local school districts, to offer special education services to students with disabilities until the passage in 1975 of the Education for All Handicapped Children Act (EAHCA) (currently known as the Individuals with Disabilities Education Act [IDEA]) (2006). Before enactment of the EAHCA, the states that had statutes mandating special education services were in the minority.

Prior to the EAHCA's requirement that states receiving federal funds pass their own laws safeguarding the educational rights of students with disabilities, most public schools routinely excluded children who were difficult to educate. Federal and state courts generally upheld these exclusionary practices until the early 1970s. The federal government intervened as a result of the long-term efforts of advocates of individuals with disabilities. Initially, the battle for the educational rights of students with disabilities was fought in the courts, much of it an outgrowth of the civil rights movement.

The purpose of this chapter is to present an overview of the events and forces that led to the enactment of federal legislation protecting the rights of students with disabilities. A historical review of the social conditions, political actions, and legal proceedings sets the stage for the passage of the EAHCA. The exclusionary practices of the schools before the enactment of the EAHCA and the struggle to gain equal educational opportunity rights for all students, including those with disabilities, are highlighted. This chapter serves as an introduction to chapter 4, which analyzes various sections of the federal statutes and regulations along with litigation over the implementation of the various statutes.

A word about the language used in this chapter is appropriate at this juncture. Over the years the terms used to identify and describe various disabilities have changed. While we certainly recognize the need to use current terminology, the court decisions reviewed in this chapter often used expressions that are now outdated and considered to be politically incorrect. To keep the flavor of these decisions intact, and to avoid mistranslation of the terms, in some instances we have used the original language of the courts. The reader should understand that the terminology used herein is that of the courts—and not ours.

EXCLUSIONARY PRACTICES UPHELD

Prior to the 1970s, public schools more often than not excluded students with disabilities from the educational process. As a rule these exclusionary practices were not only endorsed, but actually encouraged, by courts. A decision handed down during the closing years of the nineteenth century, *Watson v. City of Cambridge* (1893), provides an example of the judicial thinking prevalent during the period. In this case, the Supreme Judicial Court of Massachusetts approved the exclusion of a student who was mentally retarded because he was too "weak minded" to profit from instruction.

Observing that school records showed that the child was "troublesome" and unable to care for himself physically, and noting that by law the school committee (as school boards in Massachusetts are known) had general charge of the schools, the court refused to interfere with school officials' judgment to exclude him. The court added that if acts of disorder interfered with the operation of the schools, whether committed voluntarily or because of "imbecility," the school committee should have the authority to exclude the offender without being overruled by a jury that lacked expertise in educational matters.

The situation was no better a quarter of a century later, as evidenced by a Supreme Court of Wisconsin ruling that permitted the exclusion of a student who had a form of paralysis (*State ex rel. Beattie v. Board of Education of Antigo* 1919). The student had normal intelligence, but his paralysis caused him to drool and make facial contortions. He was enrolled in a public school through fifth grade but was excluded after that when school authorities alleged that his physical appearance nauseated teachers and other students, his disability required an undue amount of his teacher's time, and he had a negative effect on the discipline and progress of the school.

Although school personnel recommended that he attend a day school for students with hearing impairments and defective speech, the student refused and was supported by his parents. The court affirmed the school board's decision not to reinstate the student, insisting that his right to attend the public schools was not absolute when his presence there was harmful to the best interests of others. The court even went so far as to suggest that since the child's attendance was not in the best interests of the school, the board had a duty to exclude him.

A state appeals court in Ohio recognized the predicament created by exclusionary practices that conflicted with compulsory education statutes, even as it acknowledged the state's authority to exclude certain students (*Board of Education of Cleveland Heights v. State ex rel. Goldman* 1934). The controversy revolved around the state's compulsory attendance law, which required children between the ages of six and eighteen to attend school. However, the court determined that the Ohio Department of Education had the right to consider whether certain children were not capable of benefiting from instruction.

The dispute arose when a school board in one community promulgated a regulation to exclude any child with an IQ score below 50, and pursuant to that regulation removed a student with IQ test scores that ranged from 45 to 61. The court conceded that the Ohio Department of Education could prohibit the attendance of some students, but ordered the child's reinstatement because he had been excluded by a local board rather than the state. In its written opinion, the court observed that education was so essential that it was compulsory between certain ages.

EFFECT OF THE CIVIL RIGHTS MOVEMENT ON SPECIAL EDUCATION

The greatest advancements in the field of special education came during the latter half of the twentieth century. These improvements occurred through a combination of greater professional knowledge, scientifically based research, social initiatives, and legal mandates resulting from challenges brought by concerned parents, educators, and citizens. The advancements in legal rights for individuals with disabilities can be directly traced to the civil rights movement in the United States, particularly as a result of hard-won milestone court cases and civil rights legislation.

Brown v. Board of Education

In the landmark school desegregation case *Brown v. Board of Education* (*Brown* 1954), the U.S. Supreme Court, albeit unknowingly, established the legal precedent for decisions in future right-to-education cases litigated on behalf of students with disabilities. Writing for a unanimous court, Chief Justice Earl Warren portrayed education as the most important function of government. Warren, acknowledging that education was necessary for citizens to exercise their most basic civic responsibilities, stated:

In these days, it is doubtful that any child may reasonably be expected to succeed in life if he is denied the opportunity of an education. Such an opportunity, where the State has undertaken to provide it, is a right that must be made available to all on equal terms. (*Brown* 1954, 493)

As will be discussed below, many subsequent federal and state courts cited Warren's comments to justify granting equal educational opportunity rights to students with disabilities. Consequently, students with disabilities became known as the *other minority* as they, and their parents and advocacy groups, sought the same rights to equal educational opportunities that had been given to racial and ethnic minorities (Osborne 1988).

The Civil Rights Act of 1964

The Civil Rights Act of 1964 was enacted to eliminate major forms of discrimination and end racial segregation in the United States. Once implemented, the Civil Rights Act, particularly Titles IV and VI, had an immense effect on public schools, particularly those in the South. In essence the Civil Rights Act made it unlawful to segregate the races in public schools, housing, or employment. Title IV required public school boards to desegregate their districts while prohibiting officials from making student assignments based on a student's race, color, religion, or national origin. Congress enacted Title IV both to provide an enforcement mechanism for *Brown* and to authorize the withdrawal of federal funds from programs that practiced discrimination.

Title VI prohibited recipients of federal funds, including public school systems, from discriminating against individuals on the basis of race, color, or national origin. Recipients of federal funds that violate Title VI are subject to termination of those funds or other actions by the U.S. Department of Justice.

EQUAL EDUCATIONAL OPPORTUNITIES FOR ALL STUDENTS

The movement to gain equal educational opportunity rights for students with disabilities gained energy in the late 1960s and early 1970s when parents and other activists brought lawsuits seeking educational equality for the poor, language minorities, and racial minorities. Not all these cases were successful, but, as with *Brown*, much of the language in many court opinions had direct implications for the cause of students with disabilities.

Discriminatory Tracking Outlawed

Only a few years after the passage of the Civil Rights Act, the federal trial court in Washington, D.C., as part of much larger litigation dealing with educational equity, established that the tracking system used by the city's public schools was discriminatory (*Hobson v. Hansen* 1969). Under the D.C. district's tracking system, children were placed in curriculum levels as early as elementary school based on an ability assessment that relied heavily on nationally normed standardized aptitude tests. Once so placed, students found it difficult to ever advance out of their assigned tracks.

After hearing evidence that the tests may have produced inaccurate and misleading results when used with populations other than white middle-class students, the court ordered school authorities to abolish the tracking system. The court was convinced that using such tests with poor minority students often resulted in their being placed according to environmental and psychological factors rather than innate ability. The court further observed that the school board lacked the ability to obtain test results that accurately reflected the innate learning abilities of a majority of its students, and therefore found that the students' placements in lower tracks were not justified.

The court consequently ruled that tracking denied the class of students who were in the lower tracks equal educational opportunities because they received a limited curriculum. Additionally, the court surmised that school officials denied students in the lower tracks equal educational opportunities by failing to provide them with compensatory educational services to help bring them back into the mainstream of public education.

Culturally Biased Testing Practices Prohibited

In two important decisions, courts prohibited school districts from placing students in segregated programs on the basis of culturally biased assessments. In the first case, which was decided by a federal trial court in California, the issue concerned the placement of a Spanish-speaking student in a class for children with mental retardation on the basis of an IQ test administered in English (*Diana v. State Board of Education* 1970, 1973). The issue was similar in the second case, except that the student was African American (*Larry P. v. Riles* 1972, 1974, 1979, 1984).

In the latter lawsuit, the Ninth Circuit decided that standardized IQ tests were inappropriate insofar as they had not been validated for the class of students on whom they were being used. The court found that the use of such tests resulted in the students' being placed disproportionately in special education classes. In both cases, the respective courts ordered the school boards to develop nondiscriminatory procedures for placing students in special education classes. Conversely, during the same time period, a federal trial court in Illinois wrote that standardized IQ tests commonly used in schools were neither culturally nor racially biased (*Parents in Action on Special Education v. Hannon* 1980).

Remedial Instruction for Language Minorities

In another landmark decision, *Lau v. Nichols* (1974), the U.S. Supreme Court
ruled that failing to provide remedial English language instruction to non-
English-speaking students violated Title VI of the Civil Rights Act. In a class
action lawsuit brought on behalf of Chinese students in the San Francisco school
system—who did not speak English and who had not been provided with English
language instruction—the Court held that denying the students the chance to receive remedial instruction deprived them of meaningful opportunities to participate in public education. The Court insisted that the school board, as a recipient
of federal funds, was bound by Title VI—as well as a regulation promulgated by
the then U.S. Department of Health, Education, and Welfare—to take affirmative
steps to rectify language deficiencies.

Funding Equality

Plaintiffs in several lawsuits alleged that students from low-income families were
discriminated against when the quality of education they received was based
on school district wealth. In a majority of these cases, schools were financed
largely by local property taxes; this resulted in greater disparities in educational
expenditures among a state's school districts. The unequal expenditure levels, the
plaintiffs alleged, had a direct impact on the quality of education that the students
received.

Nevertheless, in its only federal case to date directly addressing school finance
at the state level, in *San Antonio v. Rodriguez* (*Rodriguez*) (1973), the U.S.
Supreme Court rejected the contention that such disparities violated the federal
Constitution. Finding that low-income students were not a suspect class and that
education was not a fundamental right, the Court wrote that the U.S. Constitution
did not require absolute equality, at least where wealth was concerned.

The U.S. Supreme Court in *Rodriguez* outlined the criteria for what constitutes a suspect class: a group "saddled with such disabilities or subjected to
such a history of purposeful unequal treatment, or relegated to such a position
of political powerlessness as to command extraordinary protection from the
majoritarian political process" (28). Determining whether a particular group
qualifies as a suspect class under equal protection examination requires the
courts to use what is known as the *strict scrutiny test*, a criterion that entails
a higher standard for governmental units, including public schools, to justify
unequal treatment.

On the other hand, when assessing a claim under the *rational relations test*—
one based on the "due process" clause that is not necessarily mentioned in the
Constitution dealing with issues of the general welfare—courts require only
governmental units to meet a lower standard of duty. Thus, identification as a
suspect class makes it easier for plaintiffs to show that disparate treatment was

discriminatory. In its written opinion, the U.S. Supreme Court explained that "education, of course, is not among the rights afforded explicit protection under our Federal Constitution. Nor do we find any basis for saying it is implicitly so protected" (35).

The Supreme Court of California, in an important decision on school finance, applied the strict scrutiny test to rule that the state's school finance system violated the equal protection clause of the California Constitution inasmuch as the system's inadequacies failed to serve a compelling state interest (*Serrano v. Priest* 1971). Similar litigation has occurred in many other states over the past forty years, with the courts evenly divided over whether challenged financing systems meet state constitutional requirements.

NEW EDUCATION RIGHTS FOR STUDENTS WITH DISABILITIES

Although the court decisions discussed above, which resulted in gains in equal educational opportunities for the poor, language minorities, and racial minorities, did not apply to students with disabilities as a group, the rulings served as persuasive precedent in later disputes over access to public school programs for these children. Students with disabilities succeeded in gaining full access to public school systems when their parents and advocates used the earlier decisions granting equal educational opportunities to other groups.

Although the initial gains made by students with disabilities occurred exclusively in lower courts, they still are considered to be landmark decisions. In spite of their limited precedential value, these lower-court decisions provided the impetus for Congress to enact sweeping legislation mandating a free appropriate public education for students with disabilities, regardless of the severity or nature of their disabilities. These cases are significant because they helped establish the basic substantive legal requirements and due process rights that are now contained in the IDEA.

Right to an Education

In one of the first cases that established the educational rights of students with disabilities, *Wolf v. State of Utah* (1969), a state court declared, in language that was remarkably similar to portions of *Brown*, that children with mental retardation were entitled to a free appropriate public education under the state constitution. The dispute began when a lawsuit was filed on behalf of two children with mental retardation who were denied admission to public schools. Consequently, the children's parents were forced to enroll them in a private day-care center at their own expense.

In court, the parents pointed out that Utah's state constitution stated that the public school system should be open to all children, a provision that the state's Supreme Court had interpreted broadly in the past. Further, the parents claimed that other state statutes mandated that all children between the ages of six and twenty-one who had not completed high school were entitled to public education at taxpayers' expense. In light of these provisions, the court ordered the Utah Board of Education to ensure that the students received a free public education. In its opinion, the court stressed that segregating the children could be interpreted as denoting their inferiority, which would affect their motivation to learn.

The Supreme Court of North Dakota in 1974 also ascertained that a student with disabilities had a right to an education under the state's constitution. The dispute began when a child's parents moved to another state, leaving the child behind at the residential school in which she was enrolled. The school board that had been responsible for the child's tuition and the state's welfare department disagreed over which party should pay for the child's educational expenses.

The court placed the obligation on the school board, while acknowledging that the child had the right to have her tuition paid since students with disabilities were entitled to no less than other pupils under the state's constitution. In its opinion, the court observed, without deciding, that students with disabilities might constitute a suspect class because their disabilities were characteristics that were established solely by the accident of birth. The court noted that the deprivation of equal educational opportunities to students with disabilities was a similar denial of equal protection as had been held to be unconstitutional in racial discrimination cases.

In another groundbreaking lower-court case, *Panitch v. State of Wisconsin* (1977), a federal trial court insisted that not providing an appropriate education at public expense to students with mental retardation violated the equal protection clause of the Fourteenth Amendment of the U.S. Constitution. Wisconsin enacted legislation in 1973 that should have provided the relief the plaintiffs in this action sought. But by the time the court decided the case four years later, education officials had not yet carried out the law's dictates. The court, surmising that the delay was a sufficient indication of intentional discrimination in violation of the equal protection clause, ordered the state to provide an appropriate education at public expense to the students in question.

Free Appropriate Public Education and Due Process

Two now well-known class action lawsuits brought in federal courts, when taken together, have had a profound impact on the education of students with disabilities and established the basic principles of due process that are now part of the IDEA. The first, *Pennsylvania Association for Retarded Children v. Commonwealth of Pennsylvania (PARC)* (1971, 1972), was filed on behalf of a class identified as all individuals with mental retardation between the ages of six and twenty-one who were excluded from public schools.

Pennsylvania education officials justified the exclusions by pointing to four state statutes that they claimed relieved them of any obligation to educate children who, in the terminology used at that time,

- were certified as uneducable and untrainable by a school psychologist;
- had not attained a mental age of five years;
- were found unable to profit from education;
- were not functioning cognitively at ages eight to seventeen (the compulsary school ages).

The plaintiff class requested a declaration that the statutes were unconstitutional but also sought preliminary and permanent injunctions against their enforcement. After negotiations between the parties, *PARC* was settled by a stipulation and consent agreement that a federal trial court approved. Using language that foreshadowed the IDEA, the stipulations clearly stated that no children with mental retardation—or child thought to be mentally retarded—could be assigned to a special education program or be excluded from the public schools without due process. The consent agreement declared that school systems in the state had an obligation to provide all children with mental retardation with a free appropriate public education and training programs appropriate to their capacities.

Although *PARC* was a consent decree, which limited its precedential value, it had a considerable positive influence in terms of protecting the educational rights of students. Further, in establishing that students with mental retardation were entitled to receive a free appropriate public education, *PARC* paved the way for gaining educational rights for other students with disabilities. In giving the consent decree its imprimatur, the court stated that it would offer the students new hope in their quest for a life of dignity and self-sufficiency.

The second case, *Mills v. Board of Education of the District of Columbia* (*Mills*) (1972), extended educational rights to other categories of children with disabilities. In addition, *Mills* established the principle that a lack of funds was not a sufficient reason to deny services to students with disabilities. Most significantly, the court's written opinion in *Mills* provided much of the due process language that Congress later incorporated into the EAHCA (which later became the IDEA) and other federal statutes.

Mills was also a class action lawsuit but was brought on behalf of children in the District of Columbia who were excluded from the public schools after they had been classified as being behavior problems, mentally retarded, emotionally disturbed, and hyperactive. In court papers, the plaintiffs' attorneys estimated that approximately eighteen thousand out of twenty-two thousand students with disabilities in the District of Columbia were not receiving special education services at the time the lawsuit was filed. The plaintiff class sought a declaration of rights along with an order directing the school board to provide a publicly supported education to all students with disabilities either within the public schools or in alternative programs at public expense.

School officials acknowledged that the school board had the responsibility to provide a publicly supported education to meet the needs of all children within its boundaries and that it had failed to do so. Rather, they insisted that it was impossible to give the plaintiff class the relief it sought due to a lack of funds. Furthermore, school personnel admitted that they had not provided the excluded students with any due process procedures.

The federal trial court, quoting *Brown*, ordered the District of Columbia to expend available funds equitably so that no student would be denied an appropriate education. In issuing the order, the court pointed out that the U.S. Constitution, the District of Columbia Code, and the school board's own regulations all required the school board to provide a publicly supported education to all children, including those with disabilities.

The court emphasized that if sufficient funds were not available, existing dollars had to be distributed in such a manner that no child was entirely excluded, and that inadequacies could not be allowed to bear more heavily on one class of students. Moreover, the court directed school authorities to implement due process safeguards before any children were excluded from the public schools, reassigned, or had their special education services terminated. Concurrent with its order, the court spelled out elaborate due process procedures that it expected the school board to follow. These procedures are the basis for the due process safeguards that are now part of the IDEA.

A year after the EAHCA was passed, but before its implementation date, a federal trial court in West Virginia established that basic due process safeguards needed to be put in place before a student could be excluded from general education classes. The court, in *Hairston v. Drosick* (1976), ruled that a local school board had violated Section 504 of the Rehabilitation Act (which protects qualified persons with special needs from discrimination and extends equal opportunity) and the federal Constitution when officials refused to admit a minimally disabled child into its public schools without a legitimate educational reason.

The student, who had spina bifida, for example, was excluded from general classes even though she had the cognitive ability to attend public schools. In excluding the student, school officials did not give her parents any prior written notice or other due process safeguards. The court concluded that the actions of school officials, in excluding the student from general education and placing her in special education without a legitimate reason, violated Section 504; and their failure to provide prior written notice, the opportunity to be heard, and other basic procedural safeguards violated the due process clause of the Fourteenth Amendment.

One year before the EAHCA took effect, a federal court in Ohio determined that the due process procedures promulgated by the state were deficient. In *Cuyahoga County Association for Retarded Children and Adults v. Essex* (1976), plaintiffs challenged the state's system for educating children with mental retardation; they claimed, among other things, that such students were denied due process in the classification procedures provided for determining the education they received.

Although the court did find that the classification system used by the state was permissible, it ordered the Department of Education to propose supplemental regulations. The court found that the due process procedures were deficient on four grounds: (1) no school officials were obligated to provide notice, (2) no opportunity for review of evidence was afforded, (3) no right to introduce additional evidence was granted, and (4) there was no guarantee that the decision makers would receive all pertinent information before classifying students.

Free of All Costs

A year after the final pronouncements in *PARC* and *Mills* were issued, a family court in New York City, in *In re Downey* (1973), asserted that special education programs had to be free of all costs to parents. This court action was brought by the parents of a student with disabilities who attended an out-of-state school because the local school district did not have an adequate public facility that could meet his educational needs. Consequently, his parents challenged their having to pay the difference between the actual tuition costs and the state aid that they received.

The court was convinced that requiring the parents to contribute to the costs of their child's education violated the equal protection clauses of both the federal and state constitutions. The court ordered the school board to reimburse the parents for their out-of-pocket expenses. The court reasoned that since children, not their parents, had the right to receive an education, the opportunity should not be limited by the parents' inability to pay for it.

Adequate Education Defined

In another case from Pennsylvania, *Fialkowski v. Shapp* (*Fialkowski*) (1975), a federal trial court defined an adequate program for students with disabilities. The parents of two students with severe disabilities claimed that the children, who were classified as mentally retarded and thus came under the *PARC* decree, were not receiving an appropriate education because they were being taught academic subjects rather than self-help skills. School personnel, referring to the Supreme Court's decision in *Rodriguez*, responded that the claim should be dismissed because the students did not have a fundamental right to an education.

The court first ruled that *Rodriguez* was not controlling and then found that the students' education was not adequate insofar as their programs did not give students the tools they would need in life. In its ruling, the court agreed with the parents that the children could have constituted a suspect class. But the court did not find it necessary to consider this question because it was satisfied that the parents had presented a claim that warranted greater judicial scrutiny than was required by claims of unequal financial expenditures among school systems, such as had been brought in *Rodriguez*. One year later, the same court heard a class action suit filed on behalf of students with specific learning disabilities who alleged they were deprived of an education appropriate to their specialized needs. The plaintiffs in *Frederick L. v. Thomas* (1976, 1977) contended that students with specific learning disabilities who were not receiving instruction suited to their needs were being discriminated against. Thus, while children with no disabilities were receiving a free public education appropriate to their needs, mentally retarded children were being provided with a free public education suited to their needs, and some children with specific learning disabilities were receiving special instruction. For that reason, the plaintiffs alleged that students with specific learning disabilities who were not receiving an education designed to overcome their disabilities were denied equal educational opportunities.

The court refused to dismiss the lawsuit, convinced that denying these students appropriate educational services violated state special education statutes and regulations in addition to Section 504. The Third Circuit agreed that the trial court's remedial order requiring the local school board to submit a plan identifying all students with learning disabilities was neither an error nor an abuse of its discretion.

FEDERAL LEGISLATION

Education is not mentioned in the U.S. Constitution and is generally considered to be a function of state governments. Since the Tenth Amendment of the U.S. Constitution reserves powers not delegated to the federal government to the states, as long as those powers are not prohibited by the Constitution, education is recognized as being in the domain of the states. The U.S. Supreme Court has even stated that education is not a fundamental right under the U.S. Constitution (*San Antonio Independent School District v. Rodriguez* 1973). Thus, even though education is primarily a state responsibility, during the past century the federal government has become progressively more involved in public education. The federal government asserts its role by passing legislation and conditioning the receipt of funding to the states on their acceptance and implementation of the federal statutes.

Legislation mandating a free appropriate public education for students with disabilities provides one of the best examples of federal involvement in education. In the wake of several successful court judgments granting equal educational opportunity rights to students with disabilities, and with several other lawsuits on the horizon, Congress and the legislatures in several states passed new laws giving students with disabilities the right to a free appropriate public education. These statutes incorporated many of the legal principles that emerged from cases such as *PARC* and *Mills.* In passing the federal legislation, Congress pinned receipt of federal funds to states' acceptance and implementation of these laws. Thus, Congress can enforce the statutes by threatening states with the loss of federal dollars if the provisions of the laws are not met.

Three comprehensive federal statutes, as well as corresponding laws in all fifty states, currently govern the delivery of educational services to students with disabilities in the United States. First, the IDEA, with its mandate that states provide a free appropriate public education to all students with disabilities and extensive due process provisions, is the most comprehensive. Second, Section 504, which was passed before the IDEA, essentially prohibits recipients of federal funds from discriminating against all individuals with disabilities. Third, the Americans with Disabilities Act (ADA) extends Section 504's antidiscrimination provisions to the private sector. Each of these statutes is discussed in greater detail in the next chapter.

CONCLUSION

Individuals with disabilities, including students, were often treated as second-class citizens throughout much of the history of the United States. Students who required accommodations or special instruction generally were excluded completely from the educational process. Beginning in the nineteenth century, special schools and classes emerged for the education of children with disabilities. Even so, most of these facilities were run either by private or charitable organizations and were not publicly funded. The result was that children with disabilities still did not receive the same educational rights as their peers.

Midway through the twentieth century, racial, ethnic, and language minorities began successfully to assert their rights in the federal courts, leading to the congressional enactment of civil rights legislation to protect the rights of these individuals. These actions also set the stage for parents, and other advocates, to seek similar rights for students with disabilities. After several federal and state courts ruled in favor of granting equal educational opportunity rights to students with disabilities, Congress and state legislatures saw the writing on the wall and passed landmark legislation mandating a free appropriate public education for all students with disabilities. As will be discussed thoroughly in the next chapter, these laws have continued to be refined via amendments and court decisions.

QUESTIONS FOR DISCUSSION

1. What were the legal precedents for courts granting equal educational opportunity rights to children with disabilities?
2. How did the *PARC* and *Mills* court decisions lead to the passage of the IDEA?
3. What steps can advocates for children with disabilities take to ensure that the hard-won gains of the twentieth century are not lost?
4. If education is a function of state governments, why was it necessary for Congress to pass federal legislation mandating a free appropriate public education for students with disabilities?
5. What future legislation might be necessary in protecting and educating all children, including those with a range of needs and disabilities?

REFERENCES

Board of Education of Cleveland Heights v. State ex rel. Goldman, 47 Ohio App. 417 (Ohio Ct. App. 1934).

Brown v. Board of Education, 347 U.S. 483 (1954).

Civil Rights Act of 1964, Title IV, 42 U.S.C. § 2000c et seq. (2006).

Civil Rights Act of 1964, Title VI, 42 U.S.C. §§ 2000d et seq. (2006).

Cuyahoga County Association for Retarded Children and Adults v. Essex, 411 F. Supp. 46 (N.D. Ohio 1976).

Diana v. State Board of Education, Civ. No. C-70–37 RFP (N.D. Cal. 1970 and 1973).

Downey, In re, 72 Misc.2d 772 (N.Y. Fam. Ct. 1973).

Education for All Handicapped Children Act, P.L. 94-142, 89 Stat. 773 (1975), now codified, as amended, at 20 U.S.C. §§ 1400–82 (2006).

Fialkowski v. Shapp, 405 F. Supp. 946 (E.D. Pa. 1975).

Frederick L. v. Thomas, 408 F. Supp. 832, 419 F. Supp. 960 (E.D. Pa. 1976), affirmed, 557 F.2d 373 (3d Cir. 1977), appeal after remand, 578 F.3d 513 (3d Cir. 1978).

G.H., In re, 218 N.W.2d 441 (N.D. 1974).

Hairston v. Drosick, 423 F. Supp. 180 (S.D.W.V. 1976).

Hobson v. Hansen, 269 F. Supp. 401 (D.D.C. 1967), affirmed sub nom. *Smuck v. Hanson*, 408 F.2d 175 (D.C. Cir. 1969).

Individuals with Disabilities Education Act, P.L. 101-476, 104 Stat.1103(1990), now codified, as amended, at 20 U.S.C. § 1400–91 (2006).

Larry P. v. Riles, 343 F. Supp. 1306 (N.D. Cal. 1972), affirmed, 502 F.2d 963 (9th Cir. 1974), further action 495 F. Supp. 926 (N.D. Cal. 1979), affirmed, 793 F.2d 969 (9th Cir. 1984).

Lau v. Nichols, 414 U.S. 563 (1974).

Mills v. Board of Education of the District of Columbia, 348 F. Supp. 866 (D.D.C. 1972).

Osborne, A. G. (1988). *Complete legal guide to special education services*. West Nyack, NJ: Parker Publishing.

Panitch v. State of Wisconsin, 444 F. Supp. 320 (E.D. Wis. 1977).

Parents in Action on Special Education v. Hannon, 506 F. Supp. 831 (N.D. Ill. 1980).

Pennsylvania Association for Retarded Children v. Commonwealth of Pennsylvania, 334 F. Supp. 1257 (E.D. Pa. 1971), 343 F. Supp. 279 (E.D. Pa. 1972).

Rehabilitation Act, Section 504, 29 U.S.C. § 794 (2006).

San Antonio v. Rodriguez, 411 U.S. 1 (1973).

Serrano v. Priest, 5 Cal.3d 584, 487 P.2d 1241 (Cal. 1971).

State ex rel. Beattie v. Board of Education of Antigo, 169 Wis. 231 (Wis. 1919).

U.S. Constitution, Amendment X.

U.S. Constitution, Amendment XIV.

Watson v. City of Cambridge, 157 Mass. 561 (Mass. 1893).

Wolf v. State of Utah, Civ. No. 182646 (Utah Dist. Ct. 1969).

II

POLITICS OF THE PRESENT: LAW AND FINANCE

The Special Education approach to educating children with disabilities is clearly defined and codified in the IDEA. After a thorough grounding in legislation and litigation in special education, including Supreme Court cases, which defined special education in the current context, this section will explore school district policy, finance, and program development. A case study of an impartial hearing illustrates misunderstandings and controversies inherent in an adversarial system of due process. Part II ends with a discussion of the cultural and contextual borders—such as race, ethnicity, and socioeconomic class—that create adversarial forces that divide stakeholders involved in the education of children with disabilities.

Chapter 4, "The Limits of Freedom: Legislation and Litigation in Special Education," discusses legislation and litigation in special education. Martin Luther King Jr. pointed out that civil rights were not achieved by legislation alone. After the implementation of the Individuals with Disabilities Education Act, stakeholder groups opposed to one or more provisions of the Act attempted—through legal challenges—to give narrow interpretations to congressional intent and inadequate funding to programs, and to exclude certain children from civil and educational rights provided under IDEA.

The politics evident in the attempts to clarify key terms such as *free education*, *appropriate education*, *least restrictive environment*, *all children*, and *judicial due process* through legislation and case law will be discussed. Two civil rights statutes, Section 504 of the Rehabilitation Act and the Americans with Disabilities Act are also discussed.

Chapter 5, "The Costs and Benefits of Special Education," discusses issues of finance, school board policy, and program development in special education.

Federal and state legislation and litigation have sought to give school districts direction in the implementation of law and the development of programs to educate children with disabilities. However, different districts implement special education regulations and develop programs for children in different ways. The strategies school boards use to fund special education, control the services delivered to children with disabilities, cap the number of students served under the IDEA, and to manage, manipulate, and control all other aspects of educating children with disabilities will be discussed. This will include the funding disparities between school districts.

Chapter 6, "Kid in the Middle: A Case Study of an Impartial Hearing," explores the cultural and contextual borders, such as race, ethnicity, and socioeconomic class, and the social contexts of psychological evaluations. These borders stand as adversarial forces in dividing the energies, resources, and sense of community between stakeholders involved in the process of testing, classifying, placing, and developing an Individualized Educational Program (IEP) for children with disabilities.

A case study approach was used to help understand the source of these borders, how they constrain discussions and amicable solutions to problems, and how borders cause miscommunication and uncooperative behavior between school districts and people with disabilities. Suggestions to bridge cultural and contextual border crossings highlight the need for and indicate the content of preservice education, sensitivity training, and school district policy changes.

4

❖ ❖

The Limits of Freedom

Legislation and Litigation in Special Education

Charles J. Russo and Allan G. Osborne Jr.

INTRODUCTION

Congress reacted to the landmark federal court decisions in *Pennsylvania Association for Retarded Children v. Commonwealth of Pennsylvania* (1971, 1972) and *Mills v. Board of Education of the District of Columbia* (1972), discussed in the previous chapter, by passing major federal legislation to protect the rights of students with disabilities. The federal statutes, combined with similar state laws, entitle students with disabilities to a *free appropriate public education* (FAPE). Further, these statutes forbid discrimination against children with disabilities in any programs receiving federal funds, also including enforcement mechanisms and vehicles to resolve any disputes over their provisions.

This chapter begins where chapter 3 ended, reviewing the Individuals with Disabilities Education Act (IDEA) and its amendments, regulations, and major provisions. Included is an analysis of the most significant court decisions that have shaped our interpretation of the statutes and its regulations. Next, the chapter covers the two civil rights statutes: Section 504 of the Rehabilitation Act (Section 504) and the Americans with Disabilities Act (ADA). Although the civil rights statutes apply to all individuals with disabilities, they are presented here because of their implications for schools.

Note also that we refer to the federal special education law as the IDEA. Since the passage of the last amendments to this statute in 2004, the Individuals with Disabilities Education Improvement Act, many commentators have referred to the law itself by the name of the amendment. This practice is incorrect as the U.S. Code clearly states, "This chapter may be cited as the 'Individuals with Disabilities Education Act'" (20 U.S.C. § 1400(a)). We have chosen to refer to and cite the law by its official title.

INDIVIDUALS WITH DISABILITIES EDUCATION ACT

In 1975 Congress passed, and President Gerald Ford signed, Public Law 94–142, the Education for All Handicapped Children Act (EAHCA). The EAHCA was not an independent act, but rather was an amendment to previous legislation that provided funds to the states, encouraging, but not mandating, them to provide educational services to students with disabilities.

Importantly, the EAHCA, now known as the Individuals with Disabilities Education Act (IDEA), is permanent legislation, while previous laws expired unless they were reauthorized. Even though it is permanent legislation, the statute has been amended many times over the past thirty-five years. One of the most significant amendments, passed in 1990, gave the law its current title. The IDEA is basically a funding statute that applies only to states receiving federal funds. However, all states currently accept federal funds and are thus subject to the terms of the statute.

The IDEA requires states, and subsequently school districts, to provide a FAPE in the least restrictive environment to all students with disabilities between the ages of three and twenty-one, based on the contents of their Individualized Education Programs (IEPs). Teams made up of school personnel, in conferences with students' parents, must develop IEPs for all children who require special education and related services. The IDEA spells out the procedures to be followed to develop IEPs, and it mandates that certain information is to be included in the written documents. Significantly, the IDEA contains elaborate due process safeguards to protect the rights of students and their parents and to make sure that its provisions are carried out (Russo and Osborne 2008).

As stated above, the IDEA has been amended, or reauthorized, periodically since its inception in 1975. The first of those amendments, the Handicapped Children's Protection Act of 1986, added provisions for parents who prevail in litigation against school boards to recover their legal expenses. Another important amendment, passed later the same year—the Education of the Handicapped Amendments of 1986—offered grants to states to provide services to children with disabilities from birth to age two. The 1990 amendments, in addition to changing the statute's name, abrogated the states' Eleventh Amendment immunity to litigation, thus making it clear that parents could sue states and municipalities for failing to meet their statutory obligations.

Arguably, the most significant and far-reaching amendments were enacted in 1997 and 2004. The Individuals with Disabilities Education Act Amendments of 1997, which were passed after a great deal of controversy and debate, added disciplinary provisions to the statute and strengthened academic expectations and accountability for students with disabilities. The disciplinary provisions codified much of the case law that existed at the time.

The final provisions represent a compromise between the desires of advocates for students who did not want to see their rights weakened and school authorities, who were concerned about their ability to maintain discipline. The most recent amendments, the Individuals with Disabilities Education Improvement Act of 2004, now codified as the IDEA, modified the 1997 disciplinary provisions and brought the IDEA in line with other federal legislation, most significantly the No Child Left Behind Act (NCLB) (2006).

The key provisions of the IDEA, as it has been periodically amended and interpreted by the courts and refined through its implementing regulations (Assistance to the States for the Education of Children with Disabilities 2006) (IDEA Regulations), are outlined briefly below.

Entitlement, Eligibility, and Classification

The IDEA compels school boards to give students with disabilities a FAPE, consisting of any needed special education and related services (IDEA, 20 U.S.C. §§ 1401(9), 1412(a)(1)(A)). At the same time, the statute does not specify any substantive standards by which the adequacy of those services can be measured. The IDEA states that students are to be given specially designed instruction (IDEA, 20 U.S.C. § 1401(29)) in conformance with their IEPs (IDEA, 20 U.S.C. §§ 1401(14), 1414(d)). The Supreme Court has determined that students with disabilities are entitled to personalized instruction with support services sufficient to permit them to benefit from the education provided (*Board of Education of Hendrick Hudson Central School District v. Rowley* 1982) (*Rowley*). IEP teams first must determine whether students are even eligible for special education under the IDEA.

Students who have disabilities are not automatically covered by the IDEA. The statute defines students with disabilities as those who have at least one of any number of identified disabilities and who need special education and related services because of those impairments (IDEA, 20 U.S.C. § 1401(3)). Thus, students who have disabilities, but whose disabilities do not require special education, are not covered by the IDEA. The identified disabilities are further defined in the IDEA's implementing regulations (IDEA Regulations, 34 C.F.R. § 300.8).

Students with disabilities who have been enrolled in private schools by their parents do not have an individual entitlement to special education services. As a group, private school students are entitled to some benefits of the IDEA, but individual students do not have a right to receive services. Under the IDEA, school boards are required to spend only a proportionate share of their federal special education dollars to provide services to parentally placed private school students (IDEA, 20 U.S.C. § 1412(a)(10)(A)). Also important is that school boards are required to spend only a proportionate share of their federal special education dollars on private school students, but they are not required to spend any share of state or local funds on these students. Since the federal funds make up a very small portion of a school district's total budget, these dollars will not stretch far.

In an important change, the 2004 IDEA amendments modified the evaluation methods for students suspected of having learning disabilities. The new regulations no longer require IEP teams to consider whether children have severe discrepancies between achievement and intellectual ability in oral expression, listening comprehension, written expression, basic reading skill, reading comprehension, mathematical calculation, or mathematical reasoning (IDEA, 20 U.S.C. §§ 1402, 1407(b), 1414(b)(6)). Instead, school personnel now may use processes, known as *Response to Intervention* (RTI), which determine whether children respond to scientific research-based intervention as part of their evaluation procedures.

Procedural Safeguards

Congress recognized that IDEA's mandates would be hollow without an enforcement mechanism. For that reason, Congress included an elaborate system of due process safeguards in the legislation to make sure that school boards properly identify, evaluate, and place students with disabilities according to the law's mandates (IDEA, 20 U.S.C. § 1415). The statute mandates that school boards give the parents or guardians of children with disabilities the opportunity to participate in the development of the IEPs for and placement of their children (IDEA, 20 U.S.C. §§ 1414(d)(1)(B)(i), 1414(f)).

The law further requires school boards to provide written notice and obtain parental consent prior to evaluating any children (IDEA, 20 U.S.C. § 1414(a)(1) (D)) or making any initial placements (IDEA, 20 U.S.C. § 1415(b)(3)). Once students have been placed in special education, school boards must provide parents with proper notice before initiating any changes in placement (IDEA, 20 U.S.C. § 1415(b)(3)(A)). Still, while administrative or judicial actions are pending, school boards may not change students' placements without parental consent (IDEA, 20 U.S.C. § 1415(j)), hearing officers' orders (IDEA, 20 U.S.C. § 1415(k)(3)(B)(ii)), or court decrees (*Honig v. Doe* 1988).

IDEA places an affirmative duty on school boards to identify, locate, and evaluate all children with disabilities who reside within the school district (IDEA, 20 U.S.C. § 1412(a)(3)), including children who have been placed in private schools by their parents (IDEA, 20 U.S.C. § 1412(a)(10)(A)(ii)(I)). For private school students, the IDEA's regulations place obligations on the school boards in the districts where the private schools are located, not the districts in which students reside (IDEA Regulations, 34 C.F.R. § 300.131).

The law calls for school personnel to conduct initial evaluations before placing students in special education programs (IDEA, 20 U.S.C. § 1414(a)(1)(A)). These evaluations must be completed within sixty days of the date when school officials received parental consent to conduct them (IDEA, 20 U.S.C. § 1414(a) (1)(C)(i)(I)). All evaluations have to be multidisciplinary, meaning that they must consist of a variety of assessment tools and strategies to obtain relevant information in the suspected areas of disability (IDEA, 20 U.S.C. § 1414(b) (2), (3)). Students with disabilities may be entitled to independent evaluations at public expense if their parents disagree with a school board's evaluation (IDEA, 20 U.S.C. § 1415(b)(1)). Nevertheless, school boards can challenge requests for independent evaluations via administrative hearings, and parents are not entitled to obtain independent evaluations at public expense if the school board's evaluations are deemed to be appropriate (IDEA Regulations, 34 C.F.R. § 300.502(b)).

The dimensions of an IEP are also spelled out in the IDEA, which stipulates that all IEPs should contain the following six elements: (1) statements of students' current levels of educational performance, (2) annual goals and short-term objectives, (3) specific educational services to be provided, (4) the extent to which each child can participate in general education, (5) the dates of initiation and duration of services, and (6) evaluation criteria to determine if the objectives are being met (IDEA, 20 U.S.C. § 1414(d)(1)(A)).

In addition, IEP teams need to include statements concerning how students' disabilities affect their abilities to be involved in and progress in the general educational curriculum along with statements regarding any modifications that may be needed to allow the children to participate in the general curriculum. School personnel are required to review all IEPs at least annually, and students who have IEPs need to be reevaluated at least every three years (IDEA, 20 U.S.C. §§ 1414(d)(4)(A), (a)(2)(A)).When Congress amended the IDEA in 2004, some significant changes were made in the statute's procedural safeguards. In an important modification, the amendments added a clause establishing that states and local education agencies can neither be held liable for violating the IDEA's requirement of providing students with a FAPE nor be required to develop IEPs for children whose parents either refuse to consent to the receipt of special education services or fail to respond to requests to provide consent (IDEA, 20 U.S.C. § 1414(a)(1)(D)(ii)(II)(III)). This change significantly addressed a concern often expressed by school officials, that is, that they should not be held accountable when parents fail to cooperate. Even so, school personnel must take reasonable steps to secure parental cooperation.

Another change brought about by the amendments eliminated benchmarks and short-term objectives for children with disabilities, other than those children who take alternate assessments aligned to meet differing achievement standards. This provision also adds that the statement of the special education and related services and supplementary aids and services are to "be based on peer-reviewed research to the extent practicable" (IDEA, 20 U.S.C. §§ 1414(d), (f)).

These provisions bring the IDEA in line with NCLB and require school personnel to use best practices, as determined by federal law. Another important addition directs states to develop policies and procedures for preventing the overidentification or disproportionate representation by race and ethnicity of children with disabilities, to record the number of students from minority groups in special education classes, and to provide early intervening services for

children in groups deemed to be overrepresented (IDEA, 20 U.S.C. §§ 1412(a)
(24), 1418(d)(1)(A)(B)).

Dispute Resolution

A key, unique part of the IDEA is a comprehensive system to help to resolve disputes between parents and school boards. This process often involves meetings
between parents and school officials, including (a) mediation, (b) administrative
due process hearings, and, as a final resort, (c) appeals to the courts. In the 1997
IDEA amendments, Congress inserted language into the statute to provide for
the resolution of disputes through a mediation process as an alternative to an adversarial proceeding (IDEA, 20 U.S.C. § 1415(e)). Although mediation is volun-
tary—and may not be used to deny or delay the parents' right to an administrative
hearing—it provides an alternative to litigation. The 2004 IDEA amendments
also added a clause requiring school board officials to schedule a resolution session with the parents within fifteen days of the receipt of a complaint as another
means of settling disagreements without resort to litigation (IDEA, 20 U.S.C. §
1415(f)(1)(B)).

Parents may request impartial due process hearings if they disagree with any
school board decisions on proposed IEPs or any aspect of the provision of a
FAPE (20 U.S.C. §§ 1415(f) and 1415(g)). Any party not satisfied with the final
outcome of the administrative proceedings may appeal to state or federal courts
(IDEA, 20 U.S.C. § 1415(i)(2)(A)); however, all administrative remedies must
be exhausted prior to resorting to the courts unless it is not effective to do so.

The IDEA now includes a statute of limitations that requires parties to request
hearings within two years of the dates they knew or should have known about the
actions on which the complaints are based (IDEA, 20 U.S.C. § 1415(f)(3)(C)).
Even so, parents can be excused from meeting limitations periods if they can
show that school officials misrepresented that the problems complained of had
been resolved or that the officials withheld required information from the parents
(IDEA, 20 U.S.C. § 1415(f)(3)(D)).

The U.S. Supreme Court, in *Schaffer ex rel. Schaffer v. Weast* (2005), placed
the burden of proof in administrative proceedings on the parties challenging the
IEPs. This ruling effectively means that the burden of proving their claims is on
parents in due process hearings since they are the ones who typically challenge
IEPs. The IDEA empowers the courts to review the record of the administrative
proceedings, to hear additional evidence, and to "grant such relief as the court determines is appropriate" based on the preponderance of evidence standard (IDEA,
20 U.S.C. § 1415(i)(2)(C)(iii)). Even so, the U.S. Supreme Court has cautioned
judges not to substitute their views of proper educational methodology for that of
competent school authorities (*Rowley* 1982). The IDEA's statute of limitations
gives parties appealing final administrative decisions ninety days to do so unless
state law provides otherwise (IDEA, 20 U.S.C. § 1415(i)(2)(B)).

As mentioned earlier, the 1990 IDEA amendments specifically abrogated the states' Eleventh Amendment immunity to lawsuits in the federal courts for any actions that occurred after October 30, 1990 (IDEA, 20 U.S.C. § 1403). This amendment was passed in response to a 1989 Supreme Court ruling that the IDEA did not specifically abrogate the states' sovereign immunity (*Dellmuth v. Muth* 1989).

Placement

The IDEA's regulations require school boards to provide a "continuum of alternative placements" to meet the needs of students with disabilities for special education and related services (34 C.F.R. § 300.115). The continuum should range from placements in general public education on one end to private residential facilities on the other, but should also include homebound services. Even so, an important requirement for all IEP teams is to select placements in the least restrictive environment that are appropriate for each child and to remove students from general education settings only to the extent necessary to provide special education and related services (IDEA, 20 U.S.C. § 1412(a)(5)).

School boards must make all placements at public expense and need to ensure that they meet state educational standards (20 U.S.C. § 1401(9)). To be sure that placements continue to meet the changing needs of students, IEP teams should review them at least annually and revise them when necessary (20 U.S.C. § 1414(d)(4)).

The U.S. Supreme Court has stated that an appropriate education is one developed in compliance with the IDEA's procedures and is reasonably calculated to enable the child to receive educational benefits (*Rowley* 1982). Although states must adopt policies and procedures that are consistent with the IDEA, individual states may, and several do, provide greater benefits than those required by the federal law. When states do establish higher standards, courts will consider those standards when judging the appropriateness of challenged IEPs (Osborne and Russo 2007).

Related Services, Assistive Technology, Transition Services

The IDEA requires school boards to provide related, or supportive, services to students with disabilities if such services are needed to assist children in benefiting from their special education programs. The statute specifically enumerates transportation and such developmental, supportive, and corrective services as speech pathology, audiology, psychological services, physical therapy, occupational therapy, recreation (including therapeutic recreation), social work services, counseling services (including rehabilitation counseling), orientation and mobility services, medical services (for diagnostic or evaluative purposes only), and early identification and assessment as related services (20 U.S.C. § 1401(26)).

The Supreme Court has clarified that related services need be provided only to students receiving special education, and only those services that are necessary for the children to benefit from special education must be incorporated into their IEPs (*Irving Independent School District v. Tatro* 1984). The IDEA, however, does place some limitations on what might be considered related services. Medical services other than those that are specifically for diagnostic or evaluative purposes and medical devices that are surgically implanted or the replacement of such devices are specifically exempted in the statute (20 U.S.C. § 1401(26)).

The IDEA also requires school boards to provide students with disabilities with assistive technology devices and services when these are needed for students to receive a FAPE. The statute defines an *assistive technology device* as any item, piece of equipment, or product system that is used to increase, maintain, or improve the functional capabilities of individuals with disabilities. Such devices may include commercially available, modified, or customized equipment (20 U.S.C. § 1401(1)). An assistive technology service, under the IDEA, is designed to help an individual in the selection, acquisition, or use of an assistive technology device. Assistance includes evaluations of children's needs, provision of assistive technology devices, training in their use, coordination of other services with assistive technology, and maintenance and repair of devices (IDEA, 20 U.S.C. § 1401(2)).

Interestingly, assistive technology is not specifically included in either the definition of special education or related services; but it does fit within the definition of special education, as specially designed instruction, and within the definition of related services, as a developmental, corrective, or supportive service. Rather than include assistive technology within either of these two definitions, Congress chose to create assistive technology as a category separate from both special education and related services. Thus, assistive technology can be a special education service, a related service, or simply a supplementary aid or service (Regulations, 34 C.F.R. § 300.105).

To help students with disabilities to move from school to postschool activities such as postsecondary education, employment, vocational training, or independent living, the IDEA requires IEP teams to develop transition services, including related services, instruction, community experiences, and the acquisition of daily living skills (20 U.S.C. § 1401(34)). IEP teams need to include statements of needed transition services in students' IEPs beginning with the last IEP developed before they turn sixteen years of age (20 U.S.C. § 1414(d)(1)(A)(i)(VIII)).

Discipline

Congress amended the IDEA in 1997, adding specific provisions outlining disciplinary requirements for students with disabilities. Those procedures were further refined in the 2004 IDEA amendments (20 U.S.C. § 1415(k)). Prior to these amendments, courts frequently applied the IDEA's change in placement and status quo provisions to the disciplinary process. In fact, the current disciplinary procedures spelled out in the IDEA are largely a codification of the case law that developed prior to the 1997 amendments (Osborne and Russo 2009c).

In one such preamendment decision later incorporated into the statute, the Supreme Court emphasized that students with disabilities could not be expelled for disciplinary reasons where their infractions were manifestations of, or caused by, their disabilities (*Honig* 1988). When students are properly expelled, after a manifestation determination, the statue makes it clear that educational services must continue during expulsion periods (20 U.S.C. § 1415(k)(1)(D)). Another noteworthy provision requires school personnel to conduct functional behavioral assessments and to develop behavior intervention plans under specified circumstances (20 U.S.C. § 1415(k)(1)(D), (E)).

Even so, school authorities are not without recourse when students with disabilities misbehave. Administrators may suspend students with disabilities temporarily, and can subject them to other normal disciplinary sanctions that do not result in changes in their placements. If necessary, school authorities may seek a hearing officer or court intervention, pending completion of administrative due process hearings in situations where it can be shown that students are dangerous and school officials cannot reach an agreement with their parents concerning proper placements. Further, the current IDEA language allows school administrators to transfer students to interim alternative settings for up to forty-five days for violations involving possession of weapons or drugs or infliction of serious bodily injury (20 U.S.C. § 1415(k)(1)(G)).

Remedies

Unfortunately, school boards do not always live up to their responsibilities under the law. When courts find that boards fail to provide appropriate placements for students with disabilities, the IDEA empowers those courts to grant such relief as they determine to be appropriate (20 U.S.C. § 1415(i)(2)(C)(iii)). In most situations, the relief granted involves reimbursement of costs borne by parents in unilaterally obtaining appropriate services for their children. In an early case the Supreme Court ruled that courts can order school boards to reimburse parents for costs incurred in providing their children with special education and related services if the parents succeed in having their chosen placements declared to be appropriate (*Burlington School Committee v. Department of Education, Commonwealth of Massachusetts* 1985) (*Burlington*).

Prior to this decision, the IDEA did not specifically provide for reimbursement but only stated that courts could fashion appropriate relief. In later amendments to the IDEA, Congress corrected this omission by not only incorporating aspects of the *Burlington* ruling into the statute, but also adding clauses indicating that reimbursement awards may be limited when parents do not provide school boards with prior notice of their dissatisfaction with their children's placements and their intent to enroll them in private schools (20 U.S.C. § 1412(a)(10)(C)(iii)).

Reimbursement is allowed even when parents' chosen facilities are not state approved as long as the schools in question offer otherwise appropriate programs (*Florence County School District Four v. Carter* 1993) (*Carter*) and even if the students had not previously received services from the public schools (*Forest Grove School District v. T.A.* 2009) (*Forest Grove*). Even though Congress has amended the IDEA twice since *Carter,* it has not altered this judgment.

The *Forest Grove* decision settled a controversy that existed among federal circuits over congressional intent. Regarding a section of the 1997 IDEA amendments, some circuits interpreted the policy as prohibiting reimbursement in situations where parents enrolled children in private schools before they had ever received special education from a public agency (Osborne and Russo 2009b).

Awards of compensatory education services may be given in situations where the parents did not have the financial means to obtain private services while the litigation was pending. Compensatory education awards are designed to make up for the loss by providing the type and intensity of services to put the students in the position that they would have been in if the school board had provided the needed services in the first place.

In 1986, Congress amended the federal special education statute with the Handicapped Children's Protection Act. This amendment, which Congress passed specifically in response to a Supreme Court ruling that the law did not allow for recovery of attorneys' fees (*Smith v. Robinson* 1984), allows parents who prevail in a lawsuit pursuant to the IDEA to recover their legal expenses.

Another Supreme Court decision in a noneducation case, *Buckhannon Board and Care Home, Inc. v. West Virginia Department of Health and Human Resources* (2001) (*Buckhannon*), generated a new line of attorneys' fees litigation under the IDEA. In *Buckhannon* the Court struck down the so-called catalyst theory as a means for recovering attorneys' fees by deciding that a plaintiff must either receive an enforceable judgment on the merits or a court-ordered consent decree to be reimbursed for legal expenses. This decision has limited parents' abilities to recover legal costs when they obtain a settlement prior to a hearing, even when the threat of an impending hearing brought about, or was the catalyst for, the settlement. Although Congress has had the opportunity to amend the IDEA to abrogate this decision, it has chosen not to do so.

The high Court later determined, in *Arlington Central School District Board of Education v. Murphy* (2006), that parents could not be reimbursed for expert witness fees under the IDEA's attorney fees provision. This decision further limited parents' ability to recoup all expenses related to a hearing. Although Congress has had the opportunity to abrogate this decision by amending the IDEA to allow the recovery of expert witness fees by prevailing parents, it has not done so.

The IDEA is not the exclusive avenue through which parents may enforce the rights of children with disabilities. The statute specifically stipulates that none of its provisions can be interpreted to restrict or limit the rights, procedures, and remedies available under the Constitution, Section 504, or other federal statutes protecting the rights of students with disabilities (IDEA, 20 U.S.C. § 1415(l)). Litigations are frequently filed under Section 504, the ADA, and Section 1983 of the Civil Rights Act of 1871 in addition to the IDEA.

SECTION 504 OF THE REHABILITATION ACT

Section 504, the first civil rights legislation that specifically guaranteed the rights of individuals with disabilities, states:

> No otherwise qualified individual with a disability in the United States . . . shall, solely by reason of her or his disability, be excluded from the participation in, be denied the benefits of, or be subjected to discrimination under any program or activity receiving Federal financial assistance or under any program or activity conducted by any Executive agency or by the United States Postal Service.

Section 504's discrimination provisions are similar to those in Titles VI and VII of the Civil Rights Act of 1964, which forbid employment discrimination in programs that receive federal financial assistance on the basis of race, color, religion, sex, or national origin. Section 504 effectively prohibits discrimination by any recipient of federal funds in the provision of services or employment. Thus, Section 504 applies to school employees as well as students.

Individual with a Disability

Section 504 defines an individual with a disability as one "who (i) has a physical or mental impairment which substantially limits one or more of such person's major life activities, (ii) has a record of such an impairment, or (iii) is regarded as having such an impairment" (Rehabilitation Act, 29 U.S.C. § 706(7)(B)). The regulations implementing Section 504 define physical or mental impairments as including:

(A) Any physiological disorder or condition, cosmetic disfigurement, or anatomical loss affecting one or more of the following body systems: neurological; musculoskeletal; special sense organs; respiratory, including speech organs; cardiovascular; reproductive, digestive, genito-urinary; hemic and lymphatic; skin; and endocrine; or

(B) Any mental or psychological disorder, such as mental retardation, organic brain syndrome, emotional or mental illness, and specific learning disorders (Nondiscrimination on the Basis of Handicap in Programs or Activities Receiving Federal Financial Assistance 2006, 34 C.F.R. § 104.3(j)(2)(i)).

An explanatory comment accompanying the Section 504 regulations indicates that this definition merely provides examples of the types of impairments that are covered and is not meant to be exhaustive.

An individual must have a history of, or have been identified as having, mental or physical impairments that substantially limit one or more major life activities to qualify as having a record of an impairment. As defined by the Section 504 regulations, individuals who are regarded as having impairments are those who have the following:

(A) A physical or mental impairment that does not substantially limit major life activities but that is treated by a recipient as constituting such a limitation;

(B) A physical or mental impairment that substantially limits major life activities only as a result of the attitudes of others toward such impairment; or

(C) None of the impairments . . . but is treated by a recipient as having such an impairment (34 C.F.R. § 104.3(j)(2)(iv)).

"Major life activities means functions such as caring for one's self, performing manual tasks, walking, seeing, hearing, speaking, breathing, learning, and working" (34 C.F.R. § 104.3(j)(2)(i)).

Otherwise Qualified Individuals

In addition to having an impairment, an individual must be *otherwise qualified* to receive the protections of Section 504. In the school context a student is "otherwise qualified" when the child is

(i) of an age during which nonhandicapped persons are provided such services,

(ii) of any age during which it is mandatory under state law to provide such services to handicapped persons, or

(iii) [a student] to whom a state is required to provide a free appropriate public education [under the IDEA] (34 C.F.R. § 104.3(k)(2)).

Individuals who are otherwise qualified must be allowed to take part in any activities as long as they can do so with the provision of reasonable accommodations (34 C.F.R. § 104.39).

Once identified, otherwise qualified students are entitled to receive an appropriate public education, regardless of the nature or severity of their disabilities. Section 504's regulations include due process provisions to settle disputes regarding evaluation and placement. Those provisions are similar to, but not nearly as comprehensive as, those under the IDEA (Section 504 Regulations, 34 C.F.R. § 104.36).

Reasonable Accommodations

Under Section 504's requirement to provide reasonable accommodations for students with disabilities, school officials must give aid, benefits, and/or services that are comparable to those available to children who do not have disabilities. Thus, otherwise qualified students must have comparable facilities, materials, teacher quality, length of school term, and daily hours of instruction.

Further, programs for students with disabilities cannot be separate from those available to other students unless segregation is necessary for these students to receive an appropriate education. School districts are not forbidden to provide separate programs for students with disabilities, but as with the IDEA, Section 504 allows segregation only when students cannot be served adequately in more inclusive settings (Section 504 Regulations, 34 C.F.R. § 104.4(b)(3)). When educational programs are offered separately, facilities for students with disabilities must be comparable to those provided to students who do not have disabilities (34 C.F.R. § 104.34(c)).

Schools, too, must offer reasonable accommodations for otherwise qualified students with disabilities so that the students can participate in the schools' offerings. Reasonable accommodations may involve minor adjustments such as removing physical barriers, allowing extra time to take tests, permitting a student to bring a service dog to class, providing a sign language interpreter for a student with a hearing impairment, or giving extra time to travel between classes. Even so, school boards are not required to grant all requests for accommodations, especially those that would place an unreasonable financial or administrative burden on school districts.

AMERICANS WITH DISABILITIES ACT

The Americans with Disabilities Act (ADA), passed in 1990, extends the reach of Section 504 by prohibiting discrimination against individuals with disabilities in the private sector as well as the public sector. The ADA's preamble explains that its purpose is "to provide a clear and comprehensive national mandate for the elimination of discrimination against individuals with disabilities" (ADA, 42 U.S.C. § 12101). Basically, the intent of the ADA is to extend the protections afforded by Section 504 to programs and activities that are not covered by Section 504 because they do not receive federal funds (Russo and Osborne, 2008). Even so, public agencies are not immune to its provisions as the ADA also applies to public entities.

The ADA has five major sections, or titles, as they are known:

Title I covers employment in the private sector and is directly applicable to private schools. This section requires school authorities to make reasonable accommodations for otherwise qualified individuals once they are aware of the individuals' disabilities. Thus, to be covered by the ADA, students and employees need to inform the proper authorities of their impairments and needs.

Title II applies to the public services provided by state and local governments for both employers and providers, including transportation and education. Title II's mandates are similar to those found in Section 504.

Title III applies to public accommodations in both the private and public sectors. Thus, this title also expands the scope of Section 504.

Title III encompasses private businesses and a wide array of community services, including buildings, transportation systems, parks, recreational facilities, hotels, and theaters.

Title IV addresses telecommunications, specifically, voice and nonvoice systems.

Title V contains the ADA's miscellaneous provisions. This part of the law specifically states that the ADA cannot be interpreted as applying a lesser standard than that under Section 504 and its regulations and that qualified individuals are not required to accept services that fall short of meeting their needs.

The ADA is a comprehensive federal mandate designed to eliminate discrimination against individuals with disabilities and to provide "clear, strong, consistent and enforceable standards" (ADA, 42 U.S.C. § 12101(b)(2)) to help achieve this goal. The ADA is similar in scope to Section 504, particularly in its definitions. For example, the ADA also defines an individual with a disability as one who has "(a) a physical or mental impairment that substantially limits one or more of the major life activities; (b) a record of such an impairment; or (c) being regarded as having such an impairment" (ADA, 42 U.S.C. § 12102(2)).

By the same token, the ADA's requirements to provide reasonable accommodations to otherwise qualified individuals are almost identical to those of Section 504. Therefore, since schools are subject to nearly identical requirements under both the ADA and Section 504, compliance with the latter act should ensure compliance with the former.

In 2008 Congress passed the first, and to date, the only amendments to the ADA, largely in response to Congress's perception that the U.S. Supreme Court had not properly interpreted its intent. The ADA amendments broadened the definition of an individual with a disability and disqualified the effect mitigating measures have on the classification of persons as having disabilities. The ADA amendments essentially abrogated two Supreme Court decisions that had weakened the protections Congress had intended to provide for employees.

In those decisions, the Court proclaimed that individuals were not disabled under the ADA if they could mitigate their disabilities through the use of medications or other steps and that disabilities had to be permanent or long term before individuals could be protected under the statute (*Sutton v. United Air Lines* 1999; *Toyota Motor Manufacturing, Kentucky v. Williams* 2002).

The ADA amendments make it easier for individuals to prove that they are subjected to discrimination, especially if they suffer from epilepsy, diabetes, cancer, multiple sclerosis, or other ailments and are improperly denied protection because their conditions can be controlled by medications or other measures. The ADA amendments do provide an exception so that the mitigating effects of eyeglasses or other corrective lenses can be considered.

State Laws

Special education is governed by state statutes as well as federal law. Each state's special education statutes must be consistent with the IDEA, but differences do exist. Most states have legislation similar in scope to the IDEA, but several states have requirements that go beyond the IDEA's provisions. For example, some states have higher standards of what constitutes an appropriate education and/or stricter procedural requirements. In other instances, state laws establish procedures for special education program implementation that are not explicitly covered by federal law. For example, state laws often spell out details such as which school district is responsible for the special education costs of a student whose parents are divorced but have joint custody and reside in two different districts. Given the fifty separate state special education statutes, a comprehensive discussion of each is beyond the scope of this chapter.

CONCLUSION

During the past half century, three comprehensive laws have been passed that, combined, provide students with disabilities with access to public schools and entitle them to a FAPE. Although many strides have been made toward the goal of giving students with disabilities an equal educational opportunity, the goal has not been met fully. Insofar as the IDEA, as interpreted by courts, requires schools to provide students with disabilities with only a basic floor of opportunity, students with disabilities are not guaranteed an education that will help them to achieve their full potentials consistent with the opportunities provided to other students.

Congress has never lived up to its responsibility of funding its share of the costs of implementing the IDEA. Thus, the burden of providing special education programs has fallen largely on states and local school districts. The lack of adequate funding, particularly in an era when many deserving programs compete for scarce dollars, has thwarted efforts to provide students with disabilities with programs that will better meet their needs. Further, inasmuch as the IDEA does not give parentally placed private school students an individual entitlement to receive services, many students with disabilities whose parents have chosen to send them to private schools do not receive an education appropriate to their needs.

Although the IDEA's due process and dispute resolution provisions have given parents more clout in terms of advocating for their children, the limitations on their ability to recoup legal costs restricts their full access to the process and, in some cases, provides prevailing parents with a hollow victory. The practical effect of the *Buckhannon* decision is that parents who are forced to hire legal counsel to obtain an appropriate education for their children are not always able to recoup their costs if the school board agrees to settle the dispute short of a hearing. In addition, when disputes go to the hearing level, parents usually need the assistance of expert witnesses to counter the testimony of the school board's experts. As it now stands, the costs of these witnesses, which can be substantial, must be borne by the parents.

QUESTIONS FOR DISCUSSION

1. What are the most significant changes to the IDEA since its original enactment in 1975?
2. How do the IDEA, Section 504, and the ADA work together to protect the rights of students with disabilities to receive FAPEs in the least restrictive environment?
3. How has Congress's failure to fully fund the IDEA impacted the quality of education that students with disabilities receive?
4. What changes should be made to the IDEA the next time it is reauthorized?

REFERENCES

ADA Amendments Act of 2008, P.L. 110-325, 122 Stat. 3553 (2008).

Americans with Disabilities Act, 42 U.S.C. §§ 12101–213 (2006).

Arlington Central School District Board of Education v. Murphy, 548 U.S. 291 (2006).

Assistance to the States for the Education of Children with Disabilities, 34 C.F.R. §§ 300.1-818 (2006).

Board of Education of Hendrick Hudson Central School District v. Rowley, 458 U.S. 176 (1982).

Buckhannon Board and Care Home, Inc. v. West Virginia Department of Health and Human Resources, 532 U.S. 598 (2001).

Burlington School Committee v. Department of Education, Commonwealth of Massachusetts, 471 U.S. 359 (1985).

Civil Rights Act of 1871, Section 1983, 42 U.S.C. § 1983 (2006).

Civil Rights Act of 1964, Title IV, 42 U.S.C. § 2000c et seq. (2006).

Civil Rights Act of 1964, Title VI, 42 U.S.C. §§ 2000d et seq. (2006).

Dellmuth v. Muth, 491 U.S. 223 (1989).

Education for All Handicapped Children Act, P.L. 94-142, 89 Stat. 773 (1975), now codified, as amended, at 20 U.S.C. §§ 1400–82 (2006).

Education of the Handicapped Amendments, P.L. 99-457, 100 Stat. 1145 (1986), now codified, as amended, as Part C of the IDEA, 20 U.S.C. §§ 1431–44 (2006).

Florence County School District Four v. Carter, 510 U.S. 7 (1993).

Forest Grove School District v. T.A., 129 S. Ct. 2484 (2009).

Handicapped Children's Protection Act, P.L. 99-372, 100 Stat. 796 (1986), now codified, as amended, at 20 U.S.C. § 1415(i)(3) (2006).

Honig v. Doe, 484 U.S. 305 (1988).

Individuals with Disabilities Education Act, P.L. 101-476, 104 Stat. 1103 (1990), now codified, as amended, at 20 U.S.C. § 1400–91 (2006).

Individuals with Disabilities Education Act Amendments, P.L. 105-17, 111 Stat. 37 (1997), now codified, as amended, at 20 U.S.C. § 1400–91 (2006).

Individuals with Disabilities Education Improvement Act, P.L. 108-446, 118 Stat. 2647 (2004), now codified, as amended, at 20 U.S.C. § 1400–91 (2006).

Irving Independent School District v. Tatro, 468 U.S. 883 (1984).

Mills v. Board of Education of the District of Columbia, 348 F. Supp. 866 (D.D.C. 1972).

No Child Left Behind Act, 20 U.S.C. §§ 6301–7941 (2006).

Nondiscrimination on the Basis of Handicap in Programs or Activities Receiving Federal Financial Assistance, 34 C.F.R. §§ 104.1–39 (2006).

Osborne, A. G., and C. J. Russo. (2007). *Special education and the law: A guide for practitioners*. Thousand Oaks, CA: Corwin Press.

———. (2009a). *Discipline in special education*. Thousand Oaks, CA: Corwin Press.

———. (2009b). *Forest Grove School District v. T.A.*: The reimbursement rights of parents who unilaterally place their children with disabilities in private schools without having had them receive special education from public agencies. *Education Law Reporter* 250:1–17.

———. (2009c). *Section 504 and the ADA*. Thousand Oaks, CA: Corwin Press.

Pennsylvania Association for Retarded Children v. Commonwealth of Pennsylvania, 334 F. Supp. 1257 (E.D. Pa. 1971), 343 F. Supp. 279 (E.D. Pa. 1972).

Rehabilitation Act, Section 504, 29 U.S.C. § 794 (2006).

Russo, C. J., and A. G. Osborne. (2008). *Essential concepts & school-based cases in special education law*. Thousand Oaks, CA: Corwin Press.

Schaffer ex rel. Schaffer v. Weast, 546 U.S. 49 (2005).

Smith v. Robinson, 468 U.S. 992 (1984).

Sutton v. United Air Lines, 527 U.S. 471 (1999).

Toyota Motor Manufacturing v. Williams, 534 U.S. 184 (2002).

U.S. Constitution, Amendment XIV.

5

The Costs and Benefits
of Special Education

Bruce S. Cooper

INTRODUCTION

As the schools in the United States have risen to meet the needs of a larger, more diverse group of "children with disabilities," these special programs and services are expensive: these students may require extensive testing and re-testing, extra services, special transportation, intensive instruction, and personal counseling—all of which can be costly. Also, public school districts, responding to the needs of these special children, may be reducing their spending on other students to cover these increasing costs.

As Corbett (1999) explains:

> State and national studies, conducted over the past thirty years, show that the share of all spending received by general education declined from approximately eighty percent in 1967 to fifty-six percent in 1996. During this time, expenditures devoted to special education more than quadrupled from four percent to seventeen percent. (43)

Hence, the spending and level (and extent) of services have continued to increase—in costs and percentages of educational spending—and no ceiling is yet in sight. This is because the growth and complexity of the population of "classified" children continue to rise.

This chapter looks at the costs and percentages of spending on special education in the United States from three perspectives:

1. The raising of funds from federal, state, and local sources: these combined funds comprise the financial inputs for these services

2. The uses of these funds for student services: a variety of services and programs are provided at the district and school-site/classroom levels (as well as some outsourcing costs) for students with disabilities—the throughputs in the program

3. The results of these expenses for these children with disabilities, and others by implication: the outputs of special education funding are then related to treatment and service outcomes for these students

THE INPUTS FOR SPECIAL EDUCATION:

Raising the Money

The first steps in analyzing the financial process include tracing and analyzing the sources and uses of money for special education services in the United States. We want to learn how and why the nation decided to offer all children with disabilities full education services that are now required by law and policy and are publicly funded. Similar to other policies and funding, for example, are the following: (a) the extension and improvement of education to children of color, (b) those living in poverty, (c) students for whom English is not their first spoken language, and (d) the provision of services for children with disabilities.

This last category includes a growing number and percent of children (now nationally well over 13 percent of all students in pre-K through high school) who require special attention, testing, teaching, and a range of other services.

Since 1975, when Congress passed Public Law 94-142, the Education for All Handicapped Children Act—now codified as the IDEA (Individuals with Disabilities Education Act)—the services for the rising number of children with disabilities has expanded steadily.

The U.S. Congress thus determined that special education was primarily a state responsibility that would be stimulated by federal funding. However, "in order to receive federal funds, states must develop and implement policies that assure a 'free appropriate public education' (FAPE) to all children with disabilities." Similarly, in 1973, Section 504 of the Rehabilitation Act was legislation "that forbids organizations and employers from excluding or denying individuals with disabilities an equal opportunity to receive program benefits and services. It defines the rights of individuals with disabilities to participate in, and have access to, program benefits and services."

The Law

The Individuals with Disabilities Education Act (IDEA) is frequently described as a model of cooperative federalism (see *Little Rock School District v. Mauney*, 183 F. 3d 816, 830, CA8,1999). The law leaves primary responsibilities to the states for developing and executing educational programs for handicapped children, but imposes significant requirements to be followed in the discharge of that responsibility (see *Board of Education of Hendrick Hudson Central School District, Westchester County v. Rowley* 1982).

For example, the act mandates cooperation and reporting between state and federal educational authorities. Participating states must certify to the U.S. secretary of education that they have followed policies and procedures that will effectively meet the act's conditions. State educational agencies, in turn, must show that local schools and teachers are working to the state's educational standards. Local education agencies (for example, school boards or other administrative bodies) can thus receive IDEA funds only if they certify to a state education agency that they are acting in accordance with the state's policies and procedures.

Legal Action

Likewise, the federal court was active in a seminal case—requiring a free, publicly supported education for students receiving special education services. In *Mills v. Board of Education* (1972), "the United States District Court for the District of Columbia held that local school districts were required by the United States Constitution to provide a publicly supported education for all disabled children." In the *Mills* case, several disabled students brought suit against the Board of Education of Washington, D.C., because these children were denied a publicly supported education, being denied access to 193 public schools in the nation's capital.

Once the legal principle of "least restrictive" environment for children with disabilities was established, the funds followed the child, for "the Mills court held that this constitutional right of equal protection must be afforded despite the great expense involved" (Corbett 1999, 633). Thus, the courts ruled that denying children with disabilities an adequate education was a constitutional violation of both the Fourteenth Amendment's specifying equal protection under the law, and the Fifth Amendment's guarantee of the rights of due process.

Guaranteeing all children with disabilities an appropriate education, however, does not determine who will "pay" for these services and programs. Thus, the federal, state, and local governments were all involved; and the increased funding would come from all three: local funds mainly through property taxation, state resources from state income and other tax sources, and national funding from federal income and other taxes devoted to the education of special needs children.

Then, Congress reauthorized the law in 1990, creatively naming it the Individuals with Disabilities in Education Act (IDEA), making direct requirements on the states to fund special education. Lawmakers saw education as a constitutional responsibility of state governments, working with local districts in most states (Hawaii is an exception with one statewide public school district). The IDEA has worked to classify special students with a range of needs, as reported in Report 5 (Chambers, Shkolnik, and Pérez 2003):

Under the Individuals with Disabilities Education Act (IDEA), children served in a special education program are classified into one of 13 primary disability categories, that include: mental, physical, social, or behavioral impairments, and disabilities that impact the child's ability to learn or function in school. Four of the 13 categories (i.e., specific learning disability, speech/language impairment, mental retardation, and emotional disturbance) account for well over 80 percent of school-aged special education students. These are referred to as "high-incidence" disabilities since they represent the largest percentages of the special education population. The remaining categories are "low-incidence" disabilities.

In 2004, the law was reauthorized, and renamed, as President George W. Bush signed the Individuals with Disabilities Education Improvement Act on December 3, 2004. As the president stated, "The Individuals with Disabilities Education Improvement Act of 2004 will help children learn better by promoting accountability for results, enhancing parent involvement, using proven practices and materials, providing more flexibility, and reducing paperwork burdens for teachers, states and local school districts."

In part, the rising costs of special education were and are associated with the increased number of students classified. Table 1 shows U.S. students from ages six to twenty-one (eligible) served by schools in 2007, arranged into the thirteen groupings: (1) a national total of 6.44 million classified children; (2) the largest at 2.7 million being the category of learning disability (LD) category, followed by (3) the speech or language impairment (SI) with 1.16 million children so classified.

Table 5.1. Disability Students by Type of Disability

Disability Type (2007)	Number of Students	Percentage
1. Learning disability (LD)	2,710,476	44.6%
2. Speech or language impairment (SI)	1,160,904	19.1%
3. Other health impairment (OHI)	599,494	9.9%
4. Mental retardation (MR) (now known as intellectual disability)	523,240	8.6%
5. Emotional disturbance (ED)	458,881	7.5%
6. Autism	224,594	3.7%
7. Multiple disabilities	134,189	2.2%
8. Developmental delay	83,931	1.4%
9. Hearing impairment (HI)	72,559	1.2%
10. Orthopedic impairment (OI)	61,866	1.0%
11. Visual impairment (VI)	26,352	0.4%
12. Traumatic brain injury (TBI)	23,932	0.4%
13. Deafness & blindness	1,472	0.0%
Total children classified:	**6,081,890**	**100.0%**

And at the district level, local school boards and superintendents, who set and control the budgets, are under pressure to provide funding for a larger number of children with varying disabilities and needs. And in some communities (often those with a good reputation for serving special children), the costs can be close to 25 percent of local spending for about 8 to 14 percent of the children who are classified as having a disability. Some data indicate that middle-class families of children with disabilities will move into those jurisdictions (districts and neighborhoods) with good reputations for serving these children, raising the costs in those locations still more.

The total cost for special education, based on the rising number and percent of "classified" students, is a good place to start. In 1976–1977, for example, the United States had a total of 49.5 million children in K–12 public and private schools, with 3.7 million, or 7.5 percent, classified with a disability. By 2004, total K–12 school enrollment in the United States grew to 54.3 million students, an increase of 4.8 million, while students with disabilities increased to over 5.5 million classified (up 1.8 million for a total growth rate of 27 percent). Thus, by 2004, over 12 percent of all students in K–12 education were classified and were being serviced in a range of special education programs that operate both in district and out of district.

When inputs by government level are considered, the federal share for special education spending ranged from 4 to 21 percent, depending on the location and state, but averaged nationally about 8 percent. State-level inputs for special education were much more diverse, ranging from 90 percent to 3 percent of spending on special education. The state average nationally was around 45 percent of total special education spending. And locally, expenditures ranged from zero (in Hawaii) to 87 percent in other states, with an average nationally of 47 percent.

Thus, while the federal government passed legislation (such as Public Law 94-142) that increased the demand and level of services for special education nationally, the federal government pitched in only about 8 percent, or about $12 billion, to pay for all special education in the United States in 2008. Therefore, funding for special education is nationally balanced overall between local and state sources; but state and local spending varied widely—reaching $65 billion by 2008.

Recently, however, as the federal share in support of special education costs increases, some states and districts then reduced their percentage by "half of the federal levels," as explained in "What's Fueling the Redirection of Special Education Funding":

Essentially, the provision allows school districts that meet certain requirements—like those outlined in state academic performance plans—to reduce state and local spending on special education services by half of the district's increase in federal IDEA funds. For example, if a district received $500,000 in federal funds under IDEA in 2009 and $700,000 in 2010, it could lower its state and local shares of spending on special education by $100,000 (half of the difference between the 2010 and 2009 IDEA allocation) and use that money on general education purposes (i.e., non-special education purposes). For districts in great fiscal hardship, this provision could mean keeping a much needed math teacher or maintaining five-day bus services. (Cohen 2010)

THROUGHPUTS: SERVING STUDENTS WITH DISABILITIES IN SCHOOLS AND PROGRAMS

Looking next at decisions and practices of school boards, superintendents, and local school-site leaders and teachers, this section on *throughputs* examines the ways that school districts (1) control the services to children with disabilities, (2) cap the number of these students served under the IDEA, and (3) directly manage and control the costs of services these children receive in the district and school sites.

The rising costs of special education services affect the disparities among school districts. These differences often trigger local reactions of parents, school boards, and professionals in education (superintendents, principals, teachers, and specialists for children with disabilities). These professionals include psychologists, speech and physical therapists, and other personnel who serve and service these children—as they seek more local resources. These "throughputs" (services, testing, and teaching) are complex, changing, and expensive, as the numbers rise and needs grow for different types of children with disabilities.

State Expenditures: To cite one example, in 2007, New York State showed a total of 2.7 million general education students, and about 405,000 children were with disabilities. Thus, 15 percent of all schoolchildren in the state were being classified as in need of special education services. Also, New York spent $26 billion on all *general education* children, for an average of $9,485 per pupil, while *special education* costs were $9.7 billion, or $22,690 per student. The state was thus spending about two and a half times more per student for the special education than for the general education population.

CASE STUDIES

Each public school district has its own special education program, based on the needs and numbers of the "classified" children with disabilities—and the costs are thus associated with the location, staff, and programs that serve these children's complex, differing needs. Here are two case studies, to give some sense of the "local" throughput as each district must determine its own costs and provide special services for its children.

Local Case 1: Take the West Hudson School District (a fictitious title for a real New York district) as an example. It's a small exurban school district, with about

1,500 students, 200 of whom have been classified as children with disabilities. The school district is located in a terribly hilly region, and students with physical needs (using wheelchairs) have difficulty getting up to the schools and around in them.

Thus, West Hudson has spent large sums renovating the spaces to accommodate these children with disabilities. Out of its budget of $34 million in 2009–2010, West Hudson had about $5.59 million, or 18 percent, that went for special education. This spending ratio of 18 percent is well above the state or national average of about 12 percent and the New York State average of $3.6 billion for special education.

Table 2 shows the categories of cost that averaged $21,000 per student overall in 2007. The major categories were the students outplaced for special education services to other settings (special out-of-district schools and programs), which cost about $2.44 million out of total special education expenditures of $5.6 million, or 40 percent. Additional locally employed teachers, aides, and psychologists are the next most costly budget item, at nearly $1.9 million, with transportation at about a million dollars a year. As shown in table 2, other costs are much smaller, including those for secretarial and administrative support.

Income for Special Education: The revenues to West Hudson School District for special education (a Section 611 grant) are mostly from local taxes (e.g., on property), although outside and extra funding totals $1.73 million, of which only $249,000 is direct federal help under the IDEA.

Table 5.2. West Hudson SD Functional Special Education Budget: 2007 for Children with Disabilities

Type of Expense	Expense Amount
Major expenses	
Teachers, psychologists, and aides (instructional functions)	$1.87 million
Tuition (outplacements)	$2.44 million
Transportation	$1.00 million
Minor costs	
Materials and supplies	$32,000
Secretarial	$55,000
Administration	$155,000
Meeting expenses	$14,000
Salary of director	$134,000
Legal services	$10,000
TOTAL EXPENSES	**$5,590,000**

The following are reimbursements for out-of-district students:

- Public excess high-cost aid: $326,817
- Private excess cost aid: $34,156
- Public excess cost aid: $1,120,335

Total Special Education Aid: $1,481,308.

Thus, the cost for out-of-district placement for students from West Hudson SD totaled $75,886 per pupil ($1.73 million divided by the 20 students classified as in need of special education who received out-of-district placements). Of this amount, the per-pupil cost of $42,200 is drawn from local property taxes in West Hudson, with the rest coming from Section 611 grants from the federal government and also from additional state aid. Thus, overall the per-pupil costs for children served in district is $18,279, with income from local taxes averaging $15,598 per student.

Local Case 2: Taking another district in the state, Harristown Public Schools, we analyzed similar data for the percentage of students classified but with a slightly smaller gap at 9.4 percent (425 special education students, as compared to 4,475 students in general education). When we compare spending between general and special education, we see children classified with disabilities costing nearly $23,000 per student (or $9.75 million), while costs for students in general education were at around $12,000 per student ($53.4 million) total in 2008.

Table 3 shows a comparison of Harristown Public Schools with other upper-class districts in the state. First, we see that on a per-pupil basis, Harristown, with

Table 5.3. Comparative Public School Expenditures for 2002–2003

School/District	General Education	Special Education
Harristown Public Schools		
Total instructional expenditures	$53,402,120	$9,749,172
Number of pupils	4,475	425
Expenditures per pupil	$11,933	$22,939
Similar districts		
Total instructional expenditures	$3,500,041,555	$1,030,524,706
Number of pupils	391,930	49,598
Expenditures per pupil	$8,930	$20,778
All public schools in state		
Total instructional expenditures	$21,462,962,765	$7,108,485,134
Number of pupils	2,826,042	398,960
Expenditures per pupil	$7,595	$17,818

425 children with disabilities, averaged almost $23,000 per pupil for special education, compared to $20,778 per student in other districts of similar wealth. This district's spending on special education was well above the $17,818 per student that was the New York State average.

Likewise, as shown in table 3, Harristown expended nearly $12,000 per student overall in 2002–2003, compared to about $9,000 per student in other richer districts, and the statewide per-pupil average of $7,595.

Thus, we see how costs can be high at the "throughput" stage as districts spend large sums "outsourcing" the children with the most extreme disabilities, and serving the remainder in regular local schools with extra staffing and programming. Also, administrative costs, while low compared to the student services, still add additional costs to manage the testing, placement, financing, transportation, and instruction for these students.

OUTPUTS: WHAT WORKS?

Finally, this section looks at the results of special education spending—and the details of what works and how. Overall, costs have gone up and continue to do so, as Baker, Green, and Richards (2008) explain:

> The total national spending to provide a combination of regular and special education services to students with disabilities amounted to $77.3 billion in 2007, or an average of $12,474 per student. Students with disabilities for other special needs programs (e.g., Title I for poverty, ELL for poor English use, and gifted and talented students) received an additional $1 billion, bringing the per-student amount to $12,639. (197)

Overall, Baker, Green, and Richards (2008) determined that spending for children with disabilities was "1.90 times that expended to educate typical regular education students with no special needs" (2008, 197). And later estimates indicated that the cost of educating these special education students had risen to 2.08 times the amounts spent on typical/regular education pupils in schools by 2009.

The outputs—the results—of special education spending are complex and difficult to determine. Some states have moved to the concept of "weighted student funding" (WSF), and they find that spending on special needs children may be weighted up to eight times that of the regular/typical student. The Weighted Student Formula Yearbook (April 2009) found key principles that improve educational outcomes as well as the transparency and accountability of our schools:

> (1) Funding should follow the child to the public school of their choice; (2) per student funding should vary based on a child's educational needs, with children with disabilities, and others receiving larger amounts; and (3) funding should arrive at individual schools in real dollars, not in numbers of teaching positions or staffing ratios. (Snell 2009)

SCHOOL-SITE COST MANAGEMENT

Issues of finance, school board policy, and program development in special education all come together at the school site, where programs and services are delivered to children with special needs (Rothstein and Miles 1997). Legislation and litigation have sought to clarify the purpose and intent of the IDEA.

As federal and state legislation gives more and more direction to (and control of) school district school boards and administrators, the implementation of its provisions and the development of programs to educate children with disabilities have expanded—and become more costly and highly regulated.

However, different districts have implemented special education regulations and developed programs for children in different ways at the school level. The strategies that local school boards use are thus critical, as they help to determine

1. the funding levels of special education;
2. the control of actual services delivered to children with disabilities;
3. the capping of the number of students served under the IDEA; and
4. the management, manipulation, and control of all other aspects of educating children with disabilities.

Site-based costs are complex to determine, since children with disabilities receive general program help and aid, plus extra services, programming, and activities. Students may either be in a "regular classroom" with an aide, or be pulled out of class for special services. Districts may also set up special schools, or decide to outsource certain students to regional day-school programs, operated by the Bureau of Cooperative Educational Services (BOCES), a regional consortium of public school systems in New York. Likewise, students with serious disabilities may be sent to a regional or national boarding school, which can run over $70,000 per year. As Ellis (2010) explains:

> Nassau County BOCES offers a comprehensive array of special education programs for students who are moderately to severely disabled from three to 21. For each student, the Nassau BOCES program is the least restrictive environment. Each student is prepared to reach his or her potential and to become as independent and productive as possible. (Karen Ellis, Director, Board of Cooperative Educational Service, www.nassauboces.org)

The costs of the special education programs are complex, and regionalizing and sharing services across school districts saves dollars. Since children may have a range of disabilities and needs, sharing the programs regionally and countywide may be more practical than trying to serve all needs in a single district. As Nassau, New York, BOCES explains:

The results are in—thanks to a shared services initiative undertaken by Nassau BOCES, Nassau County and Nassau County school districts, hundreds of thousands of dollars have already been saved, and more savings are on the way. Funded by a $1 million 21st Century Demonstration Shared Services Grant, the initiative was charged with identifying key areas where savings could be realized and working together to make it happen. Its findings will be used as a model for similar multi-jurisdictional collaborations in New York state and nationally. Savings have been realized in several areas, including:

1. Lower pricing on out-of-district transportation for 28 school districts through regional bidding,
2. Savings on joint purchasing of goods and services by all participants, and
3. Lower costs for telecommunication services such as Internet, telephone and cellular for grant partners. (Nassau BOCES 2011)

In effect, the cost of and spending on children with disabilities have risen steadily and will likely continue to increase as the number of these children increases and the treatment and services for these children expands and becomes more involved.

Data also indicate that children with disabilities are receiving more and better services in the United States since the passage of the federal laws, with nearly 14 percent now identified and served. Often, it is difficult to measure all the results since these children differ greatly in their needs, education, support, and growth.

CONCLUSION

As this chapter has shown, the politics of special education—and the concomitant costs of providing these services—are closely related. Politics determined legally (in legislatures and courts) that children with disabilities were to be served and educated locally—and in a "least restrictive environment." Congress, the courts, and local legislative groups (school boards, state legislatures, county boards) all had a voice, as the funding has risen sharply and steadily. And as a result, the United States is serving a larger and larger group of children with more particular services.

Thus, in round numbers, of the some 55 million children in U.S. schools, about 6 million, or 12 percent, are classified with disabilities, and spending for special education is about $132 billion out of the approximate $550 billion in total spending on U.S. public education, levels K–12.

Politics occurs at all levels, as federal governmental agencies make demands and offer some, but little, financial help. States, meanwhile, continue to be major contributors to special education, while local boards and school leaders must decide what services to offer in the classroom or in a pull-out program—or even whether some students are best served in special local and regional programs and schools.

Recently, too, pre-referral special service costs have increased, as districts and schools realize that students can be diagnosed earlier, or retained as a means of their *catching up*. Some believe that early diagnosis and treatment will result in fewer students' being placed into special education, thus saving districts the costly, long-term special education costs and reducing the high number of children with disabilities where possible.

Giving students in kindergarten, first, and second grades extra time, help, and services might result in fewer students' being classified—meaning that children will catch up early and not be retained and classified. Consequently, the schools should benefit in reduced costs, and the children with disabilities may have a greater chance of keeping up in the regular classroom or getting referred for evaluation in a timely way.

THE FUTURE

The IDEA is frequently described as a model of cooperative federalism (*Little Rock School District. v. Mauney*, 183 F. 3d 816, 830, CA8, 1999). It leaves to the states the primary responsibility for developing and executing educational programs for handicapped children, but it imposes significant requirements to be followed in the discharge of that responsibility (*Board of Education of Hendrick Hudson Central School District, Westchester County v. Rowley*, 458 U. S. 176, 183, 1982).

For example, the act mandates cooperation and reporting between state and federal education authorities. Participating states must certify to the secretary of education that they have policies and procedures that will effectively meet the act's conditions. State educational agencies, in turn, must ensure that local schools and teachers are meeting the state's educational standards. Local education agencies (school boards or other administrative bodies) can receive IDEA funds only if they certify to a state education agency that they are acting in accordance with the state's policies and procedures.

Thus, the politics and the funding are intertwined and complexly related. Money reflects policies and programs; and programs are determined and expanded based on local, state, federal, and private funding—all to meet the needs of our children in their development and improvement.

The costs of special education have thus risen with more students who need help being identified, and with more services being provided for longer periods of time, from preschool through twelfth grade. In summary, the elaborate, costly process is mandated by the IDEA. As the law dictates:

> IDEA entitles every student to a free and appropriate public education (FAPE) in the least restrictive environment (LRE). To ensure a FAPE, a team of professionals from the local educational agency meets with the student's parents to identify the

student's unique educational needs, to develop annual goals for the student, and to determine the placement, program modification, testing accommodations, counseling, and other special services that the student needs. These choices are recorded in a written Individualized Education Program (IEP). The school is required to develop and implement an IEP that meets the standards of federal and state educational agencies. Parents have the option of refusing Special Education services for their child. (Wikipedia 2011)

Under the IDEA, students with disabilities are entitled to receive special educational services through their local school district from age three to twenty-one. To receive special education services, a student must demonstrate a disability in one of thirteen specific categories, including autism, developmental disability, specific learning disability, intellectual impairment, emotional and/or behavioral disability, speech and language disability, deaf-blind, visual impairment, hearing impairment, orthopedic or physical impairment, other health impaired (including attention deficit disorder), multiple disabilities, and traumatic brain injury.

Depending on the students' individual needs, their "least restrictive environment" may be placement in a regular classroom for all or part of the day, or placement in a special school. They may receive many specialized services in a resource room or a self-contained classroom. In addition to academic goals, the goals documented in the IEP may address self-care, social skills, physical or speech therapy, and vocational training.

A key issue for future research is the complex relationship between local special education costs and their relationship to spending on general education. In tight times, regular education spending will be limited as special education costs take away from general education resources. Baker and Green (2009) explain this interrelationship as follows:

That is, because local districts are obligated to comply with IDEA regardless of the level of state or federal support they receive, local fiscal capacity plays a significant role in determining the extent that districts can raise additional revenues to cover special education costs, or must reshuffle existing resources. Because fiscal capacity varies, and general education resource levels vary, the extent of encroachment also varies. (293)

Financially, richer districts like Harristown and West Hudson have more local resources (greater property wealth), and can provide higher-cost special education services, often without drastically reducing their general education spending. As such, the IDEA is a complex example of how federal regulations affect local districts—mandating expensive programs without financing them adequately.

States and districts, then, are mandated to provide a free and appropriate public education (FAPE) to all children with disabilities, meaning that federal program-required local spending will encroach on spending for regular education programs.

Changes in the number and percentage of children being classified may stabilize as school districts begin to use *Response to Intervention* (RTI) to reduce the number of students in special education programs and some of the costs of these services. As Baker and Ramsey (2010) explain,

> As RTI continues to be adopted, we might expect to see identification rates drop as more students are served through regular education interventions and not identified as children with disabilities. This service delivery model could significantly change the face of special education services and the costs associated with the services. (273)

QUESTIONS FOR DISCUSSION

1. What have been the major forces, legal and political, that have increased the services to children with disabilities and driven up the costs nationally and locally?
2. How can the costs of special education services be calculated locally, including the number of children with disabilities, their services, and how these expenses have changed in comparison to regular education costs?
3. What efforts have districts made to reduce the number and costs of special education, and how do they work?
4. What do you suggest to (a) determine the costs of special education, (b) control and make the best uses of these resources, and (c) ensure that all students are served with the best and most appropriate services, no matter the costs?
5. How do your school and district regulate and manage the funding and operations of education for children with disabilities, now and into the future, to ensure that all children reach their fullest potential in school and in community life?

REFERENCES

Baker, B. D., and M. J. Ramsey. (2010). What we don't know can't hurt us: Equity consequences of financing special education on the untested assumption of uniform needs. *Journal of Education Finance* 35 (3): 245–75.

Baker, B. D., P. Green, and C. E. Richards. (2008). *Financing education systems.* Upper Saddle River, NJ: Pearson Education.

Baker, B. D., and P. C. Green. (2009). Equal educational opportunity and the distribution of state aid to schools: Can or should racial composition be a factor? *Journal of Education Finance* 34 (3): 289–323.

Board of Education of Hendrick Hudson Central School District, Westchester County v. Rowley, 458 U.S. 176 (1982), 458 U.S. 176.

Chambers, J. G., J. Shkolnik, and M. Pérez. (2003). *Total expenditures for students with disabilities, 1999–2000: Spending variation by disability* (Report 5). Washington, DC: U.S. Department of Education, Office of Special Education Programs.

Cohen, J. (2010). What's fueling the redirection of special education funding? Ed Money Watch, New American Foundation. January 12. edmoney.newamerica.net/node/26213.

Corbett, G. F. (1999). Special education, equal protection and education finance: Does the Individuals with Disabilities Education Act violate a general education student's fundamental right to education? *Boston College Law Review* 40:633. lawdigitalcommons .bc.edu/bclr/vol40/iss2/4.

Ellis, K. (2010). Nassau Board of Cooperative Educational Services. Retrieved from www.nassauboces.org.

Hanushek, E. A., et al. (1994). *Making schools work: Improving performance and controlling costs.* Washington, DC: Brookings Institution.

Little Rock School District v. Mauney, 183 F. 3d 816, 830 (CA8, 1999).

Mills v. Board of Education, 348 F. Supp. 866 (D.D.C. 1972).

Mishel, L., and R. Rothstein. (1997). Measurement issues in adjusting school spending across time and place. Paper presented at the Summer Data Conference of the National Center for Education Statistics, Washington, D.C.

Nassau Board of Cooperative Educational Services. 2011. Retrieved from www.nassau boces.org.

Rothstein, R., and K. H. Miles. (1997). Where's the money going? Changes in the level and composition of education spending. In *Digest of education statistics*, 1–28. Washington, DC: Economic Policy Institute.

Snell, L. (2009). Examining the school districts using student-based "backpack" funding to improve results. Weighted student formula yearbook, Reason Foundation. April 30. reason.org/news/show/weighted-student-formula.

Wikipedia. (2011). S.v. "Special Education in the United States." Retrieved from en.wikipedia.org/wiki/Special_education, November 20.

6

❖ ❖

Kid in the Middle

A Case Study of an Impartial Hearing

Carol Strax and Marshall Strax

INTRODUCTION

The field of education is unclear and divided. Cultural and contextual borders (Giroux 2004)—such as race, ethnicity, and socioeconomic class, and the social contexts of psychological evaluations—stand as adversarial forces in dividing the energies, resources, and sense of community between stakeholders involved in the process of testing, classifying, placing, and developing Individualized Education Programs (IEP) for children with disabilities. No one wins a power struggle; costs are involved to the individuals on both sides.

As chapters 3 and 4 point out, the intent of the U.S. Congress when it passed the Individuals with Disabilities Education Improvement Act (IDEA) (2004) and earlier versions of this act was to remove the contextual and often supporting cultural borders between stakeholders in the education of children with disabilities (*Board of Education of Hendrick Hudson Central School District v. Rowley* 1982). However, the borders stand as strong as ever (*Schaffer v. Weast* 2005).

This chapter presents a case study to help understand (1) the source of these borders, (2) how they constrain discussions and amicable solutions to problems, and (3) how borders cause miscommunication and uncooperative behavior between school districts and people with disabilities. Suggestions to bridge cultural and contextual border crossings—to generate collective solutions to contextual and cultural issues that lead to adversarial legal battles instead of amicable negotiations—highlight the need for, and indicate the content of preservice education, sensitivity training, and school district policy changes.

THE MATTER OF ANGELICA B.

The Madison County Public School District found itself reeling from the expense of sending over 900 out of 14,000 eligible children with disabilities to out-of-district private placements at a cost exceeding $60 million a year. A new director of special education decided to legally challenge every child (minor children are represented by their parents) who she perceived would seek a private placement, even if outside law firms had to be hired by the district. Her goal was to discourage the parents from pursuing their idea of least restrictive environment by drastically increasing their legal and personal costs through the use of adversarial impartial hearings and the defense of verdicts against the district through the appeals process. Special education legal expenses for one school year exceeded $10 million.

Angelica Goes to School

Angelica was brought to the United States at the age of five. Upon arrival, Angelica, her sister, and her mother could not read or write in any language. They communicated verbally in Spanish. A black Hispanic native of Colombia, South America, she was enrolled in a kindergarten class at Big Timbers Elementary School. Because of her late entry and her lack of English fluency, Angelica was retained a year, completing kindergarten at age seven. Her sister was a successful, above-average student in the district. Angelica's mother continued to work full-time at minimum wage in a fast-food restaurant. She remains illiterate in Spanish and English with a limited command of the English language.

The district provided Angelica with an English for Speakers of Other Languages (ESOL) program for only one year during kindergarten. Angelica attended school, trying hard to meet teachers' expectations through grade three. During this time she was an outgoing, social, well-spoken child who gradually dropped below grade level in reading and math. Even though she sometimes became upset or behaved inappropriately, her teachers reported that she responded well to the behavioral program used in their classrooms.

Upon entering fourth grade, as academic tasks became more abstract and verbal and the classroom atmosphere was less nurturing, Angelica was unable to perform in the classroom. An Educational Management Team (EMT) reported that Angelica's performance was below average in basic reading skills, written expression, math calculation and reasoning, social studies, and science. She exhibited extraordinary art ability and earned a reputation as a hard worker who was eager to please. In district records this team noted that Angelica did not receive any academic support at home from her mother or sister. However, the team had no way of knowing anything about Angelica's home situation.

The EMT recommended certain teaching strategies and other program modifications that were implemented during Angelica's fourth-grade year. The goal of these prereferral strategies was to provide Angelica with grade-appropriate learning skills. However, her academic performance, in all subjects other than art and music, continued to fall further behind teachers' expectations as Angelica developed age-inappropriate expressions of anger at school.

Angelica Gets Evaluated

In April of Angelica's fourth-grade year, the school psychologist, Dr. Smith, formally referred her for an evaluation under the IDEA. Angelica's mother refused to consent to this evaluation even though through her adviser, Ms. Roth, she had Angelica evaluated by a well-respected psychologist in the community, Dr. Stanislowski. His extensive academic and behavioral evaluation (over ten hours of testing) and report (fourteen pages) indicated that Angelica exhibited a severe discrepancy between achievement and intellectual ability in written expression, basic reading skills, and math calculation.

When Angelica's mother submitted Dr. Stanislowski's report to the district and gave signed consent for an evaluation of Angelica, the district began its formal data gathering. Follow-up testing was done by the district psychologist, Dr. Smith; the district learning consultant, Ms. Gross; and the district speech pathologist, Ms. Fabiano. Even though the district's testing confirmed the severe discrepancies found by Dr. Stanislowski, the district, after missing three procedural timelines (IDEA 2004), rejected Dr. Stanislowski's recommendation that Angelica be classified as a child with a disability under the IDEA.

Angelica's mother, through her adviser, Ms. Roth, requested a copy of all district records concerning Angelica. Certain records crucial to the district team's argument that Angelica's learning and behavioral problems were due to cultural, economic, and environmental disadvantage were not received after three requests. The documents received were written in English, not Spanish, the family's preferred language of communication.

Angelica's mother and Ms. Roth found the district uncooperative, difficult to work with, and not fully candid in all communication. They had no intention of meeting with district personnel in a resolution session without representation. The mother requested an impartial hearing. The district responded by suggesting that a mediation session might bring both sides to an agreement (IDEA 2004). Ms. Roth hired a personal friend as an advocate on a pro bono basis to represent Angelica at this session. Ms. Roth and Angelica's mother could not afford an attorney and had no idea how to access a pro bono attorney.

Angelica Engages Due Process

At the mediation session, the district's representative offered to provide extremely limited services to Angelica under Section 504 of the Rehabilitation Act (1973). Her description of services indicated inappropriate use of Section 504 by offering special education services that were not available to students without disabilities. In addition, the one-page 504 education plan put forth stated that Angelica was a person with attention deficit/hyperactivity disorder. When asked for justification of this label, she stated, "I'm sorry. This must have been left on the computer from the last plan we typed."

The advocate requested that Angelica be classified as a student with a learning disability under the IDEA and suggested that both sides could meet after the mediation session to write an IEP for Angelica built around resource room and/ or consulting teacher services provided by the district. The mediator, who was a district employee, told the advocate and Ms. Roth that the district's offer was a generous one and to "take it or leave it." The advocate informed the mediator that Angelica's mother would accept the resource room services offered by the district in the inappropriate 504 plan, but she was requesting an impartial hearing to settle the matter of disability classification and the development of an IEP that included a full range of related services and accommodations for learning.

The district representative at the mediation session and the impartial hearing defense team leader, Ms. Casey, later stated that they believed the goal of Angelica's advocate was to have her placed in a private school at district expense. No one representing Angelica ever mentioned such a placement. Interestingly, the district chose to conduct a hearing without ever formally asking Angelica's representatives what placement they were requesting.

Angelica's Impartial Hearings

The impartial hearing at the local level lasted twenty-six hours over four days. The mediation session to the conclusion of the impartial hearing encompassed almost one year. Angelica's advocate called two witnesses (Dr. Stanislowski and Ms. Roth). The district called thirteen witnesses (ten teachers, Ms. Gross, one principal, and Dr. Smith).

Nine teachers of different levels and disciplines testified about Angelica's school-related problems. They did not believe her issues were due to a learning disability. Much of their testimony conflicted with the content of written documents put into evidence by the district. They were often evasive in answering questions designed to give evidence supporting Angelica's learning disability. One teacher and a principal called by the district gave testimony that supported Angelica's claim of a learning disability and minimized the effect of cultural, environmental, and economic disadvantage on Angelica's academic and behavioral difficulties. The principal stated that "Angelica is a fish out of water at Big Timbers Elementary School. It does not surprise me that she reacts to teasing from other children the way she does. I don't think the teachers understand her home situation at all."

Ms. Gross, the district learning specialist, confirmed Angelica's severe discrepancy in written expression in her report, but during testimony she tried to explain it as not being indicative of a learning disability. She made serious accusations about Angelica's home environment, including, "Angelica was not in an appropriate supportive environment, came to school without a coat, and had no help with her homework." On cross-examination she admitted to never having made a home visit and to not having any firsthand knowledge about the comments she was making.

Dr. Smith perjured himself several times while testifying. Several evidentiary district documents referred to a one-hour clinical observation, clinical interview, and testing protocols he conducted as part of Angelica's evaluation. The advocate could not find the appropriate reports in her records. After repeated requests from the advocate and the hearing officer, Dr. Smith refused to submit the documents that he testified to be in possession of. The hearing officer removed from the record that part of his testimony, claiming that environmental, cultural, and economic disadvantages were the cause of Angelica's learning problems.

Most of the school witnesses and Dr. Smith suggested that a child of Angelica's race, ethnicity, and socioeconomic status would exhibit learning and behavioral problems because of environmental, cultural, and economic disadvantages. These conditions would cause her to be ineligible for classification as a child with a learning disability under the IDEA (2004). While they agreed that Dr. Stanislowski correctly portrayed Angelica as a child at risk, they believed that he overstated the severity of her needs. The consensus among the district's witnesses was that Angelica could function well in a regular education classroom "provided she obtains accommodations and remediation" available to children not classified as students with disabilities under the IDEA.

Throughout this entire process, the district repeatedly failed to communicate with Angelica's mother in Spanish. Confidential written communication was regularly left in the mailbox or leaning against the front door. Written documents were in English, and an interpreter was usually not provided at meetings. Ms. Roth was not included in parent meetings even though Angelica's mother requested her attendance at all meetings in person or via telephone conference calls.

The hearing officer found in favor of Angelica. Stating that Angelica was eligible for special education and related services as a student with a learning disability, he ordered the district to implement an IEP within the time frame mandated by state regulations. In addition, Angelica was awarded five months of extended-year services in return for the district's behavior of delaying her evaluation five months past the legally mandated deadline (IDEA 2004) and reimbursement for expenses incurred in acquiring a private evaluation and hiring an advocate.

The district appealed the decision of the hearing officer and the case was heard by a state-level hearing panel. A private law firm represented the school district. The advocate assisted Ms. Roth in finding an attorney who, with him, would co-represent Angelica on a pro bono basis. The school district's attorney found reasons to delay hearing dates, causing the four-day, state-level hearing to last almost one calendar year. Transcripts indicate that the attorney for the district had a tendency to be crass and sarcastic. Surprisingly, the attorney chose experts with credentials inferior to the experts whom Angelica's team brought forward. The panel found in favor of Angelica and upheld the order of the local hearing officer.

Angelica Wins

This decision was not appealed. Both sides came together to write Angelica's IEP. Twenty-two months had passed since her mother refused to accept the district's decision that she was not a student with a learning disability, but a student with academic and behavioral problems due to environment or cultural, and/or economic disadvantage.

At the request of her mother, Angelica was seen for a psychological evaluation. The advocate recommended this testing to assist in the development of her IEP. He wanted the most up-to-date information on Angelica's levels of functioning to be available. After lengthy due process, she was finally identified by the school system as a student with a learning disability, having first been diagnosed almost three years earlier by Dr. Stanislowski.

Angelica had been receiving forty-five minutes a day of resource room special education services throughout the hearing process. When she went to an impartial hearing, her education program and placement were frozen until the case was settled (IDEA 2004). Her mother had accepted the district's offer of resource room services at the mediation session immediately before initiating the impartial hearing. Without the resource room placement, Angelica would have spent two years in school with no remedial services. The resource room teacher who provided the services was supportive of Angelica's case at the hearings. This turned out to be a lifesaver for Angelica.

This evaluation indicated that Angelica's reading skills were below her grade placement and her reading and writing performance continued to be affected by her weaknesses in auditory processing. She was a person with a disability in written expression and reading. Throughout the evaluation, Angelica demonstrated adequate attention and concentration. However, her haste in drawing conclusions lowered her scores. The tests also indicated that she had difficulty expressing anger, a lack of appropriate controls to manage her feelings, and a high level of depressed affect.

The evaluator, Dr. Stanislowski, recommended that Angelica continue to receive special education services as a student with learning disabilities in written language and reading. Related services such as speech and language therapy and accommodations for learning such as extended time and distraction-free settings for exams were requested. In addition, he recommended further consultation with a psychiatrist or other mental health professional to determine a course of treatment for the impulsive, emotional, behavioral, and other self-regulatory issues Angelica presented.

Angelica was represented at the IEP meeting by her mother and Ms. Roth. The district had a private attorney present at the meeting along with its educational team. Her mother's request for a resource room placement with other assorted related services and test accommodations was granted. No one requested a private school placement.

MOTIVATIONS AND BELIEFS OF THE STAKEHOLDERS

Dr. Stanislowski, who was involved with Angelica's needs throughout the hearing process, stated:

> I never thought she needed to go to the Private School. I don't know what gave the district that idea. Even though she benefited from the summer program her mom and Ms. Roth got the scholarship for her to attend at the Private School, I always thought she could get the services she needed at her local school. That's where she wanted to go anyway.

When asked why she chose to advise Angelica's mother and represent Angelica on this issue, Ms. Roth stated that she did it

> because it was the right thing to do. The school is just doing this because they think they can push her around because her mother is illiterate and has no money. She's black and poor and the school's like 99 percent white and upper middle class. I thought the new principal would help her because she's black, but either she can't or doesn't want to.

The advocate had different motivations. He stated:

> I always wondered what went on in an impartial hearing. When Ms. Roth called me and asked my advice, I advised her to get a private evaluation because from what she told me, she couldn't trust the district to do a fair assessment. After the mediation session I believed the district had an agenda bigger than just this child. By the second day of the hearing I was sure of it because they were losing bad but refused to discuss a settlement. Their key witnesses kept referring to the Private School even though we never brought it up.
>
> After reading the test results and meeting Angelica I firmly believed she was a child with a learning disability who needed to be in her local public school for her self-esteem and self-worth, preferably in regular classes with a consulting teacher, otherwise in a resource room. I also had counseling for her and her mom and language therapy in mind.
>
> I am glad I did the hearing because the district was so out of line. It bothered me to have to discredit teachers and the psychologist, but I believed they either lied to foster the district agenda or were organizational people who did not care about Angelica.

Angelica's pro bono attorney described his motivation in taking her case: "After I read the transcript of the impartial hearing and looked at her records, I thought if ever there was a case that begged justice, this one was. I couldn't believe the district took this case to a state hearing."

The impartial hearing officer could not believe that the district dragged the hearing on for four days, calling thirteen witnesses. He stated by day three that "this is an issue of poverty, illiteracy, ethnicity, and race rather than one of educational disagreement. . . . The district was neglectful of the child's needs and interfered with her federal rights."

Ms. Casey, when asked to negotiate a settlement, stated, "I asked the people upstairs and they said I had to follow the hearing through to the end. I was told that was my job and the district will not settle with any parent."

A local newspaper reporter wrote that this county school district hired prestigious law firms to lower the number of children with disabilities being placed in out-of-district schools and given damage awards and legal fees. The purpose was to give parents the message that any attempt to receive special education services would be met with an adversarial process designed to exhaust parents' financial and emotional resources.

Discussions with Angelica's advocate at the mediation session and local hearing, Angelica's pro bono attorney at the state-level hearing, and the impartial hearing officer would lead one to estimate that the district's expenditure for legal expenses would have paid for one-half of her tuition through grade twelve at the Private School. In addition, they believed the expenditure of political capital and development of ill will was not worth it.

APPLICABLE SPECIAL EDUCATION LAW

When the U.S. Congress passed the Education for All Handicapped Children Act (EAHCA) (1975), it sought to provide a just solution to a situation in American education where 17 percent of children with disabilities were not receiving a free public education in the United States, and 45 percent of children with disabilities were not provided any instruction, related services, or accommodations to remediate or address their special education needs. After hearing testimony from many educators and other experts in working with people with disabilities, parents of children with disabilities, and people with disabilities, Congress sought to eliminate some of the cultural and contextual borders that had led to the system of discrimination against children with disabilities.

Over the years, the terms used to identify various disabilities have changed and some expressions are considered to be politically incorrect. The reader will note that in some instances the original language of the courts is used. The terminology used here is that of the courts and not ours.

For example, children with emotional disturbances were excluded from public school in Washington, D.C. (*Mills v. Board of Education* 1972); and children with mental retardation, especially severe and profound retardation, were excluded from public education in Pennsylvania (*PARC v. Commonwealth of Pennsylvania* 1972). Children of color and poor children were overrepresented in existing classes of special education. The language used to evaluate children and communicate with parents was English, regardless of the language spoken by the children and parents.

In the arena of special education, local school districts did not meet children with disabilities and their parents with caring (Noddings 1984, 2005). Nor did their representatives open their hearts and minds to the potential of the children with a sense of what educated children could bring to their community and what the community could bring to the children and their families. Their behaviors did not maximize reciprocal relationships with stakeholders, maximize the potential of the children with disabilities, or consider the children to be the *end* of their decision making.

In creating the IDEA, Congress sought to provide a free and appropriate education in the least restrictive environment for all children with disabilities from three to twenty-one years of age. In addition, the IDEA provided for procedural due process to allow children whose educational needs were not met in school to pursue their rights under the law when special education services were denied by a school district. However, many children were forced to go through a long and costly judicial due process hearing procedure to receive their rights. For example, in *Honig v. Doe* (1988) the two children who brought suit had to wait over eight years to receive an offer of an appropriate education.

To comply with the IDEA, every state has regulations specifying the criteria to classify a child as a person with a disability for the purpose of providing special education services. A child is determined to be a person with a learning disability when a multidisciplinary evaluation team finds that the child has a disorder in one or more of the basic psychological processes involved in understanding or using spoken or written language that is not the result of an intellectual disability, emotional disturbance, or environmental, cultural, or economic disadvantage (IDEA 2004). A "child with a disorder in one or more of the basic psychological processes involved in understanding or in using spoken or written language" is often interpreted to mean a child with a severe discrepancy between his or her intellectual ability and academic performance.

When a child and a district disagree on any aspect of the testing, classification, and placement process and development of an IEP, either side can initiate due process to settle the disagreement. Systematic or unreasonable delays in the formulation of evaluations essential to the assessment of a child's eligibility violate procedural rights guaranteed by the IDEA. In the landmark Rowley case (*Board of Education of Hendrick Hudson Central School District v. Rowley* 1982), the U.S. Supreme Court stressed the importance of the procedural aspects of the IDEA. The Court pointed out that Congress placed as much emphasis on compliance as it did on the quality of the IEP. Parents and guardians were given opportunities to participate at every stage of the administrative process.

School systems must apprise parents of information relating to assessments concerning their children in a timely manner. When parents believe they have no significant role in the classification and placement of, and IEP preparation for, their children, parental participation will turn to acquiescence (*Hall v. Vance* 1985).

CULTURAL AND CONTEXTUAL BORDERS

Litigation of Angelica's case resulted in either high personal or monetary costs— or both—to all stakeholders: (a) Angelica in lost educational experiences and opportunities, academic frustration, and personal suffering; (b) Angelica's mother and Ms. Roth in time, money, emotional stress, and the insult of attacks on their personal integrity; (c) district personnel in attacks on their credibility and exposure of their professional shortcomings; and (d) the district in high legal costs and bad publicity. Further, the district was vulnerable to suits resulting from a breach of confidentiality stemming from the district's behavior of leaving confidential papers on the doorstep of Angelica's home.

Thirty-seven years after the passage of EAHCA (1975) and thirty-five years after its implementation, cultural and contextual borders still stand as adversarial divisions between parents, their children, and school districts. Children of color are classified as children with disabilities in higher percentages than white children. Children from lower socioeconomic status (SES) families are more likely to be found in special education settings than children from high SES families (U.S. Department of Education 2004). The percentage of litigation in education related to special education far exceeds the percentage of children evaluated or placed in special education (McCarthy 1988, 1991; Cuddy 2007).

As predicted by Zirkel (1990), the backlash against providing special education services for children with disabilities is increasing. Many school districts have resorted to legal, yet unethical, practices in an attempt to control special education cost by intimidating parents through legal action under the IDEA. The IDEA is becoming more district friendly (Cuddy 2007). The 2004 amendments allow school districts to bring actions against parents and attorneys for frivolous challenges under the IDEA.

In the case of Angelica B., educators working directly with children such as principals, teachers, psychologists, and learning disabilities specialists find themselves in the uncomfortable position of supporting an adversarial district policy or behavior. This results in the educators' developing an uncaring (Noddings 1984, 2005) prodistrict stance against children and parents who are members of their cultural, economic, and contextual communities.

For example, African American and Hispanic educators find themselves giving testimony to leading questions from an attorney representing their school district who is trying to stop a black Hispanic child from receiving services under the IDEA. A learning disabilities specialist—and parent of a child with a learning disability—is placed on the stand to declare that someone else's child's severe discrepancy between achievement and intellectual functioning is not the result of a learning disability but of economic, environmental, or cultural disadvantage. Education professionals from middle-class and wealthier communities are unable to relate to children of poverty and either misread issues of poverty as disability or misread issues of disability as economic disadvantage.

Sources of Borders

In 2004, Giroux sought to understand the source of cultural and contextual borders and how they constrain dialogue and problem solving in the educational community. In the case study of Angelica, the inability of educators to successfully negotiate border crossings is suggested in the writings of educators, philosophers, and a business scholar.

Morgan (1997) uses the metaphor of organizations as *living organisms* to describe how an organization will attack anybody threatening homeostasis in the same way a living organism fights off a virus or bacteria with all the strength it can muster. In the case of Angelica, the policy was to force a child who sought to receive special education services under the IDEA to accept whatever services the district chose to offer in an attempt to save money at the expense of meeting the educational needs of the child.

The district behaved unethically by using the child as a means to an end (Starratt 1991, 1994). District leaders in this case reveled in conducting trench warfare by using the legal avenues provided by the IDEA to be as adversarial as possible toward the child and her parent by perpetuating a costly legal battle that most parents would be unable to afford (Cuddy 2007). Her parent was met in battle at each step in the testing, classification, placement, and IEP development process. This war was fought to protect the district's construction of reality.

The district's reality might well be the result of elements put forth in Morgan's (1997) metaphor of organizations as psychic prisons. Plato, in book 7 of *The Republic*, was one of the first to intellectualize the predicament of human beings as prisoners of their thoughts and actions. More recently, many critical theorists, including those of the Frankfurt school, such as Horkheimer (1972), Horkheimer and Adorno (2004), Habermas (1972), and Marcuse (1955, 1964), have pointed out how human beings have become trapped by images and ideas, needing a radical critique of their situation. This critique would require an understanding of the hidden purposes of daily language used and the power-based reality of organizational life. This critique could build on the idea that person-made society dominates its members through complex systems of organizational control.

In an attempt to control the spiraling local costs of providing services to children with disabilities, the district sought to meet all parents, especially parents believed to be seeking private school placements for their children, in an adversarial manner. Any sense of caring and community was replaced with logical, objective reasoning based on the district's construction of reality. The burden to prove this reality as false was placed on the parent.

For example, the district defined a document it created as a 504 plan—purported to provide greater educational services to Angelica and to offer greater due process than an IEP. The district created a list of tests that were the only tests district personnel were allowed to use in the assessment of children. A mediation session had a district employee defined as an impartial mediator. All parents were suspected to be considering private school placement for their children. The hearing team could not settle with parents but had to battle the parent to the end.

THE PROBLEMS WITH BORDERS

Critical theorists such as Apple (2004) would suggest that the district's construction of reality, using everyday words to define procedures and programs, is simply a vehicle to control significant discourse affecting the assessment, classification, placement of, and IEP preparation for children with disabilities. For example, the purpose of the testing and classification process was not to assess the strengths and weaknesses of Angelica, but, in the inappropriate words of Ms. Casey, the district hearing team leader, and hearing witnesses, to *code her*. Angelica's legal representatives first placed her picture into evidence and later had her briefly meet people at the impartial hearing in order to humanize the district's reality of objectivity by showing that this case was about a living, feeling, and sensitive child.

The district emphasized objective use of statistics to explain its interpretation of psychological testing. This incorrect use of statistical analysis of test results had to be pointed out by the defense. The district team had created its own reality, the 504 plan. They attempted to bring this plan into evidence and testimony. The hearing officer had to remind the district hearing team that issues under Section 504 could not be heard in a hearing conducted under the IDEA (2004).

The idea that people are often prisoners of their own thoughts might explain why so many educators were able to show a lack of caring for Angelica (Noddings 1984). For example, Ms. Gross, the district learning disabilities specialist, and a parent of a child with a learning disability, interpreted results of her own testing indicating a learning disability as cultural and environmental disadvantage. A Spanish-speaking elementary school teacher who recommended Angelica's sister for an advanced program testified that Angelica's learning problems were the result of economic and environmental disadvantage. An African American principal and several African American hearing team members were unable to articulate how a poor child of color would have difficulty making friends in an upper-middle-class and white elementary school.

Perhaps, as Rist (1970) discovered, educators such as the principal and hearing team members identify with the upper middle class to which they belong and prefer to look down on poor people of color. Angelica and her sister, one and a half years apart in age, were raised together their entire lives. One wonders what the Spanish teacher was thinking when she claimed that one child was the victim of economic and environmental disadvantage and the other child was not. The learning disabilities specialist chose an individualistic interpretation of the situation by supporting the district's contention that Angelica was not a child with a learning disability. She managed to block out the commonalties between her situation and those of Angelica's mother and Ms. Roth.

BRIDGING BORDERS

The key to bridging cultural and contextual borders and bringing together all stakeholders involved in the process of testing, classifying, and placing children with disabilities and developing their IEPs is to build an ethical child study team using Starratt's (1991, 1994) multidimensional ethical framework to implement the mandates of a just IDEA.

To critique current structures in the testing, classification, and placement of students with disabilities using alternative belief systems, stakeholders must first free themselves from what Morgan (1997) refers to as their *psychic prison*. They should be able to see the learning potential of children with disabilities and look past the constraints of resources to find ways to maximize this potential. Their minds should rise above the status quo and perceive the many issues of power, domination of one group over another, and resource control that are inherent in the hierarchy of special education. Stakeholders must be willing to critique these structures in daily action with students and colleagues and be advocates for their flock, who are often the vulnerable and powerless members of society.

The legal road to justice and opportunity for people with disabilities parallels the legal road to justice and equality of earlier civil rights struggles. Only through an active critique of the structures that are understood to be the cause of the subordinate position of people with disabilities can a dialogue develop that may gradually lead to a more just and equal education system for students with disabilities through the established legal system of the social order.

Stakeholders should

- be caring persons who can perceive the potential of every student as a possibility for development and strive to develop this potential;
- have a vision of who the student can be, not just who that child is today;

- grasp the social and intellectual possibilities in children with disabilities and develop these possibilities by recognizing the children's unique value as human beings who can better the whole of society;
- strive to bring learning above the literal level through unique and creative approaches.

The spirit of the IDEA allows district personnel and parents to meet cooperatively. The IDEA created a system that enables parents and school districts that grasp the spirit of the law to work together in a reciprocal relationship to meet the needs of children with disabilities. District professionals can pursue a course of collaboration with parents to provide the best evaluations of children. Stakeholders can then meet to classify, place, and develop educational programs.

In the long run, the development of children enhances the microcommunity from which they come and the larger community of our nation and world (Committee for Economic Development 1985). The Committee for Economic Development has shown the tremendous savings inherent in investing in the education and development of children. To maximize their investment, stakeholders will need to understand the nature of contextual and cultural borders as scientifically managed systems (Taylor 1911), categorically grouping people in hopes of controlling which groups succeed and which groups reproduce themselves as subordinate in American society (Apple 2004).

CONCLUSION

This chapter explored many factors that lead to miscommunication and uncooperative behavior between school districts and people with disabilities and provided a clearer understanding of problems of communication and cooperation between educators and children with disabilities and their representatives.

Suggestions to facilitate cultural and contextual border crossings highlight the need for, and content of, preservice education, sensitivity training, and school district policy changes. Educators should meet to think about changes they can implement in their district IEP planning process to make it into an ethical one. As Mooney (1986) suggests, a spirit of inclusion and discussion would bring together stakeholders in cases under the IDEA to focus on their common interests instead of going into litigation.

QUESTIONS FOR DISCUSSION

1. Do you think there was prejudice involved in the district's decision to refuse to classify Angelica? Why or why not?
2. What cultural and contextual borders have you confronted in your education? How were you able to cross these borders?

3. If you were planning the sensitivity training workshops for the district personnel involved in this hearing, what would the content of the workshops be?
4. Does the teacher education program you attend contain adequate content to negotiate the border crossings described in this chapter? What is this content?
5. What policy changes would you recommend to the board of education of the Madison County Public School District?

REFERENCES

Apple, M. W. (2004). *Ideology and curriculum*. 3rd ed. New York: Routledge.
Board of Education of Hendrick Hudson Central School District v. Rowley, 458 U.S. 176 (1982).
Committee for Economic Development. (1985). *Investing in our children: Business and the public schools*. New York: Author.
———. (1989). *Children in need: Investment strategy for the educationally disadvantaged*. New York: Author.
Cuddy, A. (2007). *The special education battlefield: A guide to the due process hearing and other tools of effective advocacy*. Dryden, NY: Ithaca Press.
Education for All Handicapped Children Act, P.L. 94-142, 89 Stat. 773 (1975), now codified, as amended, at 20 U.S.C. §§ 1400–82 (2006).
Giroux, H. A. (2004). *Border crossings: Cultural workers and the politics of education*. 2nd ed. New York: Routledge.
Habermas, J. (1972). *Knowledge and human interests*. London: Heinemann.
Hall v. Vance, 774 F. 2d. 629, 634 (4th Cir. 1985).
Honig v. Doe, 484 U.S. 305 (1988).
Horkheimer, M. (1972). *Critical theory: Collected essays*. New York: Herder.
Horkheimer, M., and T. Adorno. (2004). *Dialectic of enlightenment*. Trans. J. Cumming. New York: Crossroad.
Individuals with Disabilities Education Improvement Act, P.L. 108-446, 118 Stat. 2647 (2004), now codified, as amended, at 20 U.S.C. § 1400–91 (2006).
Marcuse, H. (1955). *Eros and civilization*. Boston: Beacon Press.
———. (1964). *One-dimensional man*. Boston: Beacon Press.
McCarthy, M. (1988). The public school's responsibility to serve severely disabled children. *Education Law Reporter* 49: 453–467.
———. (1991. Severely disabled children: Who pays? *Phi Delta Kappan* 23 (1): 66–71.
Mills v. Board of Education of the District of Columbia, 348 F. Supp. 866 (D.D.C. 1972).
Mooney, C. F. (1986). *Public virtue: Law and the social character of religion*. South Bend, IN: Notre Dame Press.
Morgan, G. (1997). *Images of organization*. 2nd ed. Newbury Park, CA: Sage Publications.
Noddings, N. (1984). *Caring: A feminine approach to ethics and moral education*. Berkeley: University of California Press.

————. (2005). *The challenge to care in schools.* 2nd ed. New York: Teachers College Press.

Pennsylvania Association for Retarded Children v. Commonwealth of Pennsylvania, 334 F. Supp. 1257 (E.D. Pa. 1971), 343 F. Supp. 279 (E.D. Pa. 1972).

Plato. (1892). *The republic.* Trans. B. Jowett. New York: Oxford University Press.

Rehabilitation Act, Section 504, 29 U.S.C. § 794 (2006).

Rist, R. (1970). Student social class and teacher expectations: The self-fulfilling prophecy in ghetto education. *Harvard Educational Review* 40 (3): 411–51.

Schaffer ex rel. Schaffer v. Weast, 546 U.S. 49 (2005).

Starratt, R. J. (1991). Building an ethical school: A theory for practice in educational leadership. *Educational Administration Quarterly* 27 (2): 185–202.

————. (1994). *Building an ethical school.* New York: Falmer Press.

Taylor, F. W. (1911). *Principles of scientific management.* New York: Harper & Row.

U.S. Department of Education. (2004). *Twenty-sixth annual report to Congress on the implementation of the Individuals with Disabilities Education Act.* Washington, DC: Author.

Zirkel, P. (1990). "Backlash" threatens special education. *Education Week,* August, p. 64.

III

POLITICS OF THE PRESENT: REALITY ON THE GROUND

In this part of the book, chapters will explore the politics currently involved in the delivery of services to children with disabilities. Competing constructions of the popular term *inclusion* and the politics behind implementing inclusive education for children receiving special education services will be presented. Attention will be given to the issues behind providing a least restrictive educational environment for children with severe disabilities. Tommy—first introduced in chapter 2—is revisited. His education in the present is explored.

Chapter 7, "Common Confusions with Inclusion," discusses the politics behind the practical dilemmas involved in implementing inclusive education. Among these dilemmas are the placement of children in the least restrictive environment, the classroom ratio of children to teachers, and the successful collaboration between special and regular educators. Since its inception, the IDEA has mandated the education of children with disabilities in the least restrictive environment.

Children with disabilities are to be educated in schools and classrooms to the greatest extent possible, based on their individual needs, with all other children. School districts' personnel, parents, and most other stakeholders refer to this mandate as the *inclusion* of children with disabilities. Because the term *inclusion* does not appear in special education legislation or regulations, it has no clear definition. Wherever one goes, services are implemented in different ways, many of which seem to thwart the congressional intent of integration.

Chapter 8, "Don't Ask, Don't Tell, Don't Pay: Services for Children with Severe and Chronic Disabilities," gives a frank and thorough discussion of a family's experiences with the special education establishment. Students with severe and chronic disabilities tend to be oppressed and discriminated against to a greater degree than other children with disabilities. Usually their least restrictive environment is found to be placement in a school or classroom segregated from peers with mild or no disabilities. Over the years, attempts have been made to exclude them from IDEA services by changing the description of children covered by the act and by court challenges to not fund the host of services required to meet their educational needs.

In chapter 9, "Schooling Tommy in the Present," we revisit Tommy—whom we met in chapter 2—and explore three scenarios about educating him in the present. With the legal protections of the IDEA, one would assume Tommy would have easy access to a free appropriate education in the least restrictive environment. However, this may not be the case. Chapter 9 will discuss: (1) The cultural and contextual borders that still exist; (2) the political issues that continue to arise in educating Tommy; and (3) the political and power struggles needed to negotiate border crossings.

7

❖ ❖

Common Confusions with Inclusion

David J. Connor

INTRODUCTION: MUDDY WATERS

The inclusion of children and youth with disabilities alongside their nondisabled peers in general education classes is a simple concept. However, the idea continues to evoke a wide range of responses from various stakeholders, many of whom are at odds with one another. In brief, this simple concept gives rise to complicated issues that touch our core values, including: In a democracy, who has the right to decide about the schooling of others? What are the civil rights of young citizens in relation to their schooling? What constitutes access to a quality education for all students? And in what ways is being separate, paradoxically, considered to promote equality among citizens?

The preceding questions point toward one of society's most complicated and contested terrains: how best to educate all its children. In a rapidly changing world based on competition among citizens, where access to resources is limited, and education is perceived as being key to success in life, those who support or oppose inclusion realize that much is at stake.

This chapter describes some of the complexities involved in conceptualizing, creating, and sustaining inclusive schools. From the tangle of laws, court cases, opinions, rights, policies, belief systems, and traditions, I shall discuss various knotty issues that have served to confuse families and educators alike about inclusion. First, six tenets of Public Law 94-142 (Education for All Handicapped Children Act of 1975) are described, including the original legislation that ensured access to education for all students with disabilities, and illuminating ways in which these policies continue to cause contentions that mark the contemporary landscape of inclusion.

Second, I look at issues pertinent to eight different stakeholders: parents, teachers, administrators, school districts, state policymakers, teacher education programs in universities, the field of special education, and children and youth with disabilities. The issues of constituents all intertwine with one another, creating conflicts, tensions, paradoxes, and arguments about what constitutes *progress*, resulting in complications when schools are required to respond to the challenge of inclusion. Third, in the desire to counter the many areas of confusion experienced by various stakeholders, the findings of a recent study indicate some effective qualities of successful inclusive schools. Finally, the chapter closes with some thoughts on the lessons we have learned so far about inclusion.

EDUCATION LAWS: IMPLEMENTATIONS, INTERPRETATIONS, AND OPINIONS

The history of inclusion is one of slow, but steady, progress. While changes have occurred that increased integration of students with disabilities into mainstream education, we still have a long way to go. In many respects, from its inception, the growth of inclusion could be characterized as taking three steps forward and two steps back, in a constant tug-of-war between competing forces.

Importantly, the impetus for the inclusion movement is rooted in the civil rights struggles of the 1950s, pioneered by African Americans who mobilized to protest their marginalized status and actively sought greater access to all that society offered to its European American citizens. Subsequently, women and homosexuals were united into distinct groups that called attention to oppression based on their gender and sexual orientation. Likewise, citizens with disabilities have gathered strength and momentum from unifying and applying political pressure on society to recognize injustices with a view to changing them (Fleischer and Zames 2001).

From the start, parents were integral to the disability rights movement, aggressively seeking to forge a better quality of life for their children with disabilities, starting with access to a quality public education. Indeed, through the actions of parents, Congress passed the landmark federal legislation of P.L. 94-142. In addition, parents have been an integral force in subsequent reauthorizations of the law now known as the Individuals with Disabilities Education Act (1990, 1997) and later, the Individuals with Disabilities Education Improvement Act (2004).

The following six tenets of the original law have been crucial in moving the rights of children with disabilities forward. At the same time, the interpretation and implementation of the policies have equally proven cause for concern, as they have contributed to inhibiting the inclusion of all children, regardless of their disabilities.

Tenet #1: A Free and Appropriate Public Education

A major tenet of the new law guaranteed a free and appropriate education to all citizens with disabilities. Incredibly, until the mid-1970s, local education authorities (LEAs) were not required to provide a public education to children and youth with disabilities. In other words, it was an acceptable practice to deny children entry to schools by claiming not to have the right available expertise, personnel, or specialized resources for them. After the passage of the law, LEAs were suddenly required to provide a public education to students with disabilities that was *free and appropriate*. Little, if any, confusion is generated by the word *free*. In contrast, the term *appropriate* soon came to serve as one of the bones of contention when making decisions about children with disabilities—and it remains so until this day. Some argue that "appropriate," and its counterpart "inappropriate," are sophisticated forms of what is considered "right" and "wrong."

Discerning what is the appropriate (or "the right") education for a child with a disability is essentially an interpretive act. *Who* is interpreting the nature of the disability, and its educational implications, is therefore a complicating factor, related to the historic marginalization of people with disabilities by those without them (Stiker 1999). This pervasive marginalization includes how society permits or prevents access to people with disabilities, and includes notions of *where* to place them for their own good. In sum, P.L. 94-142 ensured the provision of an education to students with disabilities, but the term "appropriate" was interpreted mainly as providing that education in a separate setting. Thus, special classes, special floors, and special schools began to flourish. That children with disabilities were even in the regular school building signaled progress, but still being largely segregated from their nondisabled peers was problematic.

Tenet #2: In the Least Restrictive Environment

Another tenet within P.L. 94-142 that has been subject to many interpretations is the clause known as the least restrictive environment (LRE). In this, the law states:

> To the maximum extent appropriate, children with disabilities, including children in public or private institutions or other care facilities, are to be educated with children who are not disabled, and that special classes, separate schooling, or other removal of children with disabilities from the regular educational environment occur only when the nature or severity of the disability is such that education in the regular classes with the use of supplementary aids and services cannot be achieved satisfactorily. (IDEA §300.114 (a)(2))

In other words, the concept of LRE states that children with disabilities should be educated with their nondisabled peers, unless unsatisfactory evidence of their educational growth—even with additional support—is available. Clearly, the intent of the law was (and remains) to maximize the inclusion of children with disabilities. However, the concept of LRE inspired the growth of a complex, multilayered continuum of placements ranging from general education classrooms with no support (LRE), to services provided at home and in hospital settings (the most restrictive environments). Once this array of options grew exponentially, they were used by LEAs to place a burgeoning number of students with disabilities into segregated environments (Salend 2004).

Supporters of inclusive practices have always raised a constellation of questions around the supposed neutrality of the LRE concept. One serious concern is how LRE has served as a loophole in the education system to remove problematic students—those who do not conform academically or behaviorally to grade-level and teacher expectations (Lipsky and Gardner 1997). Indeed, others have charged that LRE has been used to siphon off students of color into more segregated settings (Losen and Orfield 2002), a way of maintaining segregated racial privileges and inequities that undeniably still exist over half a century after the passage of the court decision *Brown v. Board of Education* (1954). Furthermore, the environment to which LRE refers evokes an idealized generic classroom in our collective (and perhaps nostalgic) minds without considering how the orchestration of the environment can actively enable or disable a student's academic, behavioral, and social development and success.

In addition, the "supplementary aids and services" that are needed to ensure the opportunity of student success vary enormously among districts according to their priorities, wealth, policies, and available resources. After all, determining *who* decides *what* is a supplementary aid and/or service needed by a child—and the feasibility of providing such aids and services—can complicate notions of consistency within the operationalization of law.

Indeed, some argue that concepts such as LRE have exacerbated some inequities by well-heeled and well-educated parents (with their attorneys present), evoking legal rights and requiring specialized equipment, services, and accommodations for their children (Brantlinger 2003). In contrast, poorer and less-educated parents usually do not know their rights as guaranteed by law; and if they do, they often cannot afford an attorney, and are more likely to be refused their requests for supplemental aids and services (Valle and Aponte 2002).

Interestingly, the concept of LRE has been used in many landmark court cases seeking to advance the inclusion of children with various disabilities. For example, in the case of *Oberti v. Board of Education of the Borough of Clementon School District* (1993), the parents of a son with Down syndrome gained national attention in their fight to have him included, eventually going all the way up to the U.S. District Court. The crux of their argument rested on the *interpretation* of P.L. 94-142.

Cases such as *Oberti* raise important questions: Does a child have to earn the right to be with nondisabled peers? To what degree should the value of social growth for both nondisabled and disabled students be weighed along with their academic growth? Why were some states able to provide inclusion of children with Down syndrome (such as New Hampshire) while others (in this case, New Jersey) were not? What does it mean when young citizens within the same country have the very same disability, but one receives services while the other is denied? Who decides who gets which resources, and what criteria are used?

Tenet #3: Due Process

The new legislation to protect the educational rights of children and youth with disabilities also included due process procedures, serving as checks and balances between institutions and families of students with disabilities. In brief, all information regarding decisions about the education of a student with (or suspected of having) a disability must be provided to the parents in their first language; this includes the procedural safeguards. In addition, students are encouraged to participate in this process when appropriate, and parents have the right to bring their child to any meetings pertaining to the child's education.

Given the nature of what is at stake during due process procedures, any initial disagreements between parent and institutions are attempted to be ameliorated through a guaranteed process of mediation. However, although only a minority is aware, parents are power brokers within due process procedures. They have the right to refuse consent to have a child evaluated or reevaluated, and can prevent major decisions such as labeling, placement, accommodations, and services (or lack thereof). Unfortunately, space limitations here do not permit a thorough analysis of this complex aspect of the law, except to say that while well intended, due process subsequently evolved into an enormous bureaucratic endeavor that often focused on compliance of documentation versus the actual well-being of families and children with disabilities (Skrtic 1991).

Tenet # 4: Parental Participation

Although parental participation is often presented within legislation, school personnel who are required to operationalize the law can place parental concerns in the background. Instead of informing parents about their rights, and inviting them into the process of determining options for their child, the process has historically alienated a majority of parents, even misleading them. One result is that school systems frequently label and place children with disabilities as they please, typically fitting them within the limited existing school organization.

A major, and underexplored, dilemma is the sidestepping of parents' having input into choices, signifying schools' virtually dictating a fait accompli in decision making about children (Valle 2009). Issues of social class, race, ethnicity, language, education level, and parental disability, along with cultural understandings of school, authority, and disability, significantly affect how parents are informed, addressed, and given options (Harry and Klingner 2006).

Tenet #5: Nondiscriminatory Identification and Evaluation

The misidentification of linguistically diverse children as having disabilities was a pervasive practice within LEAs until the passage of P.L. 94-142. Previously, *Diana v. State Board of Education* (1970) documented how Spanish-speaking children had been labeled "mentally retarded" based on IQ tests administered in English. With this case, the misuse of testing practices and procedures was openly acknowledged. The law therefore now guarantees nondiscriminatory identification and evaluation of children with disabilities. However, all assessments—from the commonplace to the specialized—can be questioned on many levels. The notion that intelligence can be quantified into a specific number representing a fixed entity is highly problematic in its implications (Gould 1996).

Furthermore, much has been written about cultural biases of assessments, including the impossibility of assessors to be value free in their interpretations (Giordano 2005). Of great importance is the subjectivity involved in assessing categories such as learning disability (LD), emotional disturbance (ED), speech and language (SL), and cognitive impairment/intellectual disability (CI/ID). Together, these categories approximate 85 percent of all disability labels of children identified in schools (Hehir et al. 2005). As has been noted, students of color continue to be overidentified in comparison with European American counterparts, indicating ongoing institutional biases (Losen and Orfield 2002). Finally, regardless of the law's stating that being a second language learner and/or immigrant does not equate with having a disability, this group also continues to be subjected to high rates of identification (Artiles, Rueda, Salazar, and Higareda 2002).

Tenet #6: The Individualized Education Program (IEP)

A cornerstone of P.L. 94-142 was the required creation of Individualized Education Programs (IEPs) for all children and youth with disabilities. The IEP documents the specific disability of each student, along with the supports and services needed, and annual goals for academic and social growth. IEPs, varying in format, length, and complexity among states and LEAs within each state, are designed as "living" documents that change according to the progress made by the child, and continuous monitoring by the IEP team, including parent members. However, of interest is that the term "inclusion" is not written into educational law, and subsequently is not considered a legal category. In other words, IEPs are not required to include the word "inclusion." They do, however, include a "least restrictive environment" (LRE) statement justifying the placement of a child in the specific setting.

MIXED MESSAGES OF INCLUSION:
OPERATIONALIZING THE LAW

Not coincidentally, this law refrains from using the actual word "inclusion" in its expectations of educating all children. Inclusion has been, and will likely remain, a political hot potato for many of the reasons raised in this chapter and book. Some argue that the law, by *not* using inclusion explicitly, allows degrees of latitude in considering the contextual concerns expressed by local LEAs and the families within them. However, like Pandora's box, once the "lid of choice" is lifted, many other ill-suited options also circulate throughout the educational world, often becoming habitual practices. On the other hand, *not* to have a choice seems antithetical to the culture of Americanism, flies in the face of working collaboratively with parents, and opens the possibility of endless litigation among stakeholders.

As mentioned earlier, interpreting to the principle of LRE is not necessarily straightforward, consistent, or predictable. For example, a mother of a child with a mild learning disability may seek a special class with a lower teacher–student ratio and specialized reading instruction. In contrast, the father of a child who is paraplegic and cognitively impaired, and talks via a personalized communication board may seek full inclusion for the child. These two scenarios reveal that the type and degree of disability can be immaterial to the placement sought by parents and confirmed within the IEP team—as both instances can be justified through existing laws. In sum, laws that govern students with disabilities—including Section 504 of the Rehabilitation Act of 1973, in addition to P.L. 94-142 and its reauthorizations—do not mandate inclusion; but they do convey the need for LEAs to exert a genuine effort to find the most inclusive placement of children with disabilities.

What's in a Word?

Terminology used in relation to inclusion can also serve to confuse many people's conceptualization of what inclusion actually is, along with their responsibilities toward inclusive practices and policies. Three terms that contribute to the confusion are *mainstreaming, inclusion*, and *full inclusion.*

First, traditionally, the word *mainstreaming* has been applied to the practice of placing students with disabilities in general education when they are able to succeed in such classes for part of their program. For example, a student who struggles with reading, but who excels in math, can feasibly participate in a general education math classroom with no specialized support. The premise of mainstreaming rests on the belief that a student must earn the right to be in general education by proving him- or herself able to perform (academically, behaviorally, and emotionally) within generally accepted levels of "normalcy."

Second, in contrast, the concept of *inclusion* begins with the notion that every child with a disability belongs with his or her nondisabled peers. Instead of special education being understood as a place, it is seen, rather, as a service—a service that can and should be provided within general education. A child, therefore, does not have to approximate what is deemed as "normal" in terms of academics or behaviors to receive instruction with nondisabled peers. This acceptance of diversity means that children with disabilities may work on different skills and/or content information, in addition to receiving whole-class instruction. Admittedly, this flexibility requires a significant shift in how teachers prepare and deliver instruction, as well as how they primarily respect differences among students.

The term *full inclusion* is the belief that all students, no matter the type and severity of their impairment(s), belong in a general education classroom all the time. This concept in particular has raised the ire of many traditional special educators who believe the ideal is not only impossible, but dangerous, propagated by a radical faction within special education led by parents of children with severe and multiple disabilities (Fuchs and Fuchs 1995). Its supporters, on the other hand, advocate the concept of full inclusion that should be first viewed as a philosophy rather than an issue of placement. Villa and Thousand (1995) describe it as "a way of life, a way of living together, based on the belief that each individual is valued and does belong" (11).

To confuse matters regarding the three important and very distinct notions of *mainstreaming, inclusion,* and *full inclusion,* the terms are often used interchangeably. For example, some educators mistake inclusion for mainstreaming, and mainstreaming is understood as a form of "low-maintenance" inclusion. Opponents of inclusion, in general, tend to focus on the concept of full inclusion to point to a philosophical premise that cannot be operationalized, and openly deride any attempts to cultivate this change (Kauffman and Hallahan 1995). In doing so, they tend to blur the lines of inclusion (to the maximum extent possible) with full inclusion, viewing the integration between general and special education as a loss of their own power, influence, resources, and by extension, professional identity (Kauffman 1995).

Separation Anxiety?

One consequence of the passage of P.L. 94-142 was the need for teachers to become qualified through master's degree programs and officially certified by the state to teach students with disabilities. As a result, teachers became divided into two models, subcategorized into *general* and *special* educators. This professionalization of educators into subcategories contributed to the evolution of two separate systems that, despite legislation, inhibited their effective interaction. Unfortunately, this bifurcated system generated a form of separatism, enculturating teachers to think in terms of "my kids" and "your kids," based on commonly shared notions of (dis)ability (Friend 2005).

This trend is still alive and well today, evident when inclusion classes are initially planned. Confusion arises when thinking of who is responsible for teaching *all* students within inclusive classrooms, since labels of "special" and "general" have created what some educators see as two distinct types of children.

Many schools of education at the university level continue to struggle in apportioning responsibility about who teaches what information to which college students in their segregated departments (Young 2008). Some argue that many educational institutions are fairly conservative and passive rather than proactive. In my own school of education, for example, relatively little interest in inclusion is expressed by the Special Education Department. Ironically, a recent mandate from New York State has created a single compulsory class for teaching students with disabilities to be taken by students in all education programs (beginning in spring 2012) that spurred our department to create a course for *all* teacher candidates. Clearly, resistance to, and confusion about, who is responsible for inclusive education are still manifest at the university level.

In schools and universities, some special educators view their profession as providing valuable support and services to people with disabilities in specialized settings, often separate from the mainstream. Other special educators see the flaws inherent in how special education currently functions and seek significant changes in where and how some of the most marginalized children in society are educated. Thus, the field of special education has been divided for decades about many contentious areas, including the purpose of special education (Andrews et al. 2000).

The issue of inclusion has, perhaps, reinforced existing ideological divisions both within special education itself and between general and special education. Each educator, regardless of self-identified affiliation with notions of special or general education, is required to think in terms of: To what degree do I support inclusion or contest it? Is special education without the valid option of inclusion a service or a disservice? When children are being included, what exactly are they being included into? In sum, the shift toward effective inclusion means that roles of all teachers must be rethought and redefined.

PERSONAL BELIEFS AND PRACTICAL DILEMMAS OF STAKEHOLDERS

The broad focus of this chapter so far has been on areas of potential confusion around the interpretation and operationalization of legislation to ensure the rights of children and youth with disabilities. This section now gives further details of potential uncertainty about inclusive educational practices by examining the perspectives of various stakeholders. Each featured group has a vested interest in seeing how inclusion continues to grow or becomes inhibited. However, these groups are far from homogeneous, containing both proponents and opponents of inclusion, as well as individuals who move in the vast middle zone of "it depends." Given the multiple factors involved in each educational context, including personal experiences, professional influences, and district policies, all people have the potential to shift their views.

One of the overall commonalities that all stakeholders have is their individualized understanding of disability in relation to how society conceptualizes human difference. Special education has been predicated largely on the medical model of disability, namely, that cognitive, emotional, physical, and sensory differences need to be treated, fixed, cured, or at the very least, made to approximate normalcy as much as possible. Throughout history, nondisabled people have largely demonstrated a low threshold for tolerating people with various impairments (Stiker 1999). School settings in contemporary America are no exception.

The inclusive education movement is fueled, in part, by a significant challenge to the current concepts of the "norm" that are used in oppressive ways to delineate criteria for being accepted or rejected by the majority group. In contrast to the medical model, the social model of disability, embraced by inclusionists, recognizes that the structures, practices, and processes of society can actively disable people based on their impairments (Davis 1997). Scholars who call attention to disabling customs, including those in schools and classrooms, seek to "widen the circle" of normalcy so society is inclusive of all people (Sapon-Shevin 2007).

Perhaps to state the obvious, individual beliefs influence what each person thinks about inclusive education. Yet we must ask, from where do these influences about disability come? In truth, they have surrounded us all from birth. The history of people with disabilities has only recently begun to be excavated (Kudlick 2003). So what we do know are stories of indifference at best and oppression at worst (Linton 1998), even to the point of death (Terry and Urla 1995). Although television and film are saturated with portrayals of disability, few are deemed accurate, and instead, many reinforce stereotypes and limited tropes (Haller 2011). Likewise, classic literature reflects characteristics of people with disabilities who are usually limited in their humanity, serving as a "narrative prosthesis" to the story (Mitchell and Snyder 2000).

In addition, the charity industry that campaigns for various disabilities still revolves around playing on pity and fear (Charlton 2000). Furthermore, until recently, schools themselves have traditionally sifted and separated children into various placements, preventing the nondisabled from coming personally to know their peers with disabilities, and vice versa (Lipsky and Gardner 1997). All in all, a bleak picture emerges of how disability is still (re)presented as a personal tragedy, rather than simply a form of human diversity. That said, much of the negativity circulating within society at large is challenged by everyday interactions within actual families who demonstrate—without the use of experts—how inclusion can exist. In families, members are understood in all their personal complexity, rather than being viewed primarily through the lens of their ascribed label.

The purpose of calling attention to these multiple forces within our society, culture, and history is that they have shaped us from an early age and continue to influence our individual beliefs and understandings about human difference. As schools are microcosms of society, they reflect our collective belief of who belongs where. However, our collective belief is one not of harmony but rather contention, with each group having a particular interest in the degree to which children with disabilities are included and how they are taught. The following sections reflect selective views and concerns of various micropolitical constituents to demonstrate the multiple perspectives through which inclusion is viewed.

Parents

Understandably, parents want what is best for their children. Yet what is considered the "best" placement for a child with a disability depends on many factors including:

- Services provided in various settings
- Supports available
- The receptivity of human difference by teachers and administrators
- The proximity of school to home
- The option of a child attending school with his or her nondisabled siblings and/or peers

Families who identify as culturally Deaf often prefer separate programs; and parents of students with blindness or visual impairments have also expressed concern, as well as parents of children with learning disabilities, about what they believe are the limitations of inclusion (Kauffman and Hallahan 1995). In some cases, parents perceive inclusion as a loss—rather than a transfer, or gain—of hard-earned services. In contrast, as previously noted, other parents have pushed the inclusion envelope all the way to the federal courts for their children to participate in a general education environment.

More often than not, parents of children and youth with disabilities advocate for their child to maximize their connection to general education classrooms (Habib 2008). However, experiences of parents vary enormously in accordance with their cultural capital, based on social class, gender, race, ethnicity, and nationality (Valle 2009). For example, many parents who have not graduated from high school themselves are overwhelmed by aspects of due process and feel powerless in making specific requests concerning placement (Ong-Dean 2009).

Teachers

Successful teachers in inclusive classrooms work collaboratively with other adults. Teacher collaboration is essential, as an inclusive classroom requires the combined skills of two teachers, and possibly one or more paraprofessionals, depending on the nature of students' needs in relation to their disabilities (Murawski and Dieker 2008). Being required to co-teach does not appeal to some teachers, while others enjoy working in partnership with fellow professionals. There have been developed several models of co-teaching that incorporate a variety of formats to match the objectives of lessons (Friend 2005).

Clearly, teachers in partnerships, who understand the premise of inclusion, who collaboratively plan instruction, and who share the responsibilities for teaching all children, can effectively support their students and one another. In contrast, teacher partnerships that do not see the value of inclusion, or who express cynicism toward its goals, influence inclusion's degree of success (or failure) because in effect, much is within their locus of control. Another factor that influences teachers' disposition toward the effectiveness of inclusion is how much they have been educated in ways to collaborate, a responsibility of both their college preparation programs and subsequent school or LEA in-service training (Mastropieri et al. 2005). In sum, since the teaching force has never been universal in its beliefs—and probably never will be—each school throughout the country contains educators, both special and general, with a wide variety of opinions that reflect support of, or resistance to, inclusion.

Administrators

School administrators are often caught in the cross fire between the rights of children with disabilities and the managerial system-based demands of the LEA. School bureaucracies, by their nature, have evolved into an interlocking apparatus that responds to human diversity in a primarily managerial manner or as a technical endeavor. Enormous tensions exist between the establishment (i.e., school, curriculum, educational policy, laws, and rules) and the population mandated to comply with the demands of the establishment. Principals must carry out the following:

- High-stakes testing at the bidding of local and state authorities
- Ascertaining and monitoring the academic levels of all students
- Providing evidence of student growth in different areas

The standardized expectations of all students, the assigning of their academic performance (for example, from low to high as a 1, 2, 3, or 4), and uniformity of a lockstep curriculum appear at odds with educating a multicultural, diverse population in every sense of the word (including students with disabilities). Because a standard practice for principals is to be rewarded or disgraced publicly based on their school's scores, they view inclusion with mixed concerns—as poor scores pose a very real risk of their removal. Such systemwide practices indicate that some principals are vigilant about low-scoring students in their schools, which translates to decreased access for students with disabilities (Sweet 2006). In contrast, other principals prefer to include students with disabilities as much as possible to provide them access to the general education curriculum and the chance of attending college (Lagares 2010).

On a related note, when programming collaborative teachers and students in inclusive classrooms, principals have the power to create "responsible" or "irresponsible" combinations of people. For example, by scheduling approximately 15–20 percent of students with IEPs into a class, the principal reflects the natural proportion of disabled to nondisabled students in the population. However, when allotting 40 percent of students with IEPs in a class and culling the other 60 percent from high-risk or chronically absent students, a principal may be implementing inclusion according to LEA guidelines, but is actually creating what could easily be interpreted as a larger special education class.

School Districts

Local education authorities must juggle multiple — even conflicting—demands. The juggernaut "standards movement" can potentially clash with issues within other reform efforts such as multiculturalism and the inclusion of students with disabilities. The desire for uniformity in schools often emphasizes long-standing and much-valued cultural norms of what constitutes acceptable levels of thought, expression, behavior, and knowledge. When the importance of scores appears to supersede the general well-being and comfort of students, inclusive education can easily be de-emphasized and placed on the back burner.

District responses to inclusion can be bureaucratic and formulaic, with prescriptions such as 40:60 (disabled:nondisabled ratio) coming to be employed across New York City. Within the same LEA the placement of students in District 75 (one of the few districts in the nation exclusively for students with moderate and severe disabilities) into programs that are called "inclusion"—but do not accurately reflect the principles of inclusion—represents the reality that students are housed in a general education school while attending segregated classes. Such misnomers serve to further confuse the concept of inclusion.

State Policies

Positioned between federal mandates and the LEAs, states must guide and monitor from a distance, so they are also a factor in the success or failure of inclusion. Each state's response to both categorizing students with disabilities and including them in general education classes varies enormously. For example, in Nebraska an African American student is over six times more likely to be labeled emotionally disturbed (ED) than his European American counterpart; four times more likely in Iowa; twice as likely in Colorado; and about the same in Michigan (Parrish 2002). However, the inclusion of students with different labels varies widely among states. For example, in terms of the ED label, New Hampshire leads the way at just over 60 percent of its students being included for more than 79 percent of their school day, while neighboring Massachusetts brings up the rear with 15.5 percent (Smith 2010).

These two instances reveal major state-level discrepancies about states' responsibilities toward the inclusion of students with disabilities, thus highlighting great inconsistencies across the nation. Although states have autonomy in how they manage federal regulations, their labeling and placement practices indicate the level of subjectivity involved in special education decisions, showing that the "hard science" of finding disabilities is largely culturally determined. Finally, states have the power to decide the format and content of high-stakes tests, as well as to provide a safety net for students with disabilities in the form of alternative assessments. Who takes which mandated exams is an interesting phenomenon.

In New York State, for example, students with severe and multiple disabilities can participate in highly customized assessments based on their IEP goals. However, students with LD may also sit for a different set of examinations less academically rigorous in nature, but only *in addition* to standard examinations. Ironically, students who struggle the most academically are expected to take twice as many examinations.

Teacher Education Programs

As mentioned earlier in this chapter, inclusive education as a content area has evolved as a distinct program in some degree-granting programs, such as Syracuse University and Teachers College, Columbia University. At the same time, inclusive education has been minimally integrated into traditional special education programs such as the one in which I work. All over the country, schools of education have had to decide whether general and special education departments should be integrated or remain separate entities that graduate separately certified students.

Young (2008) has chronicled ways in which a school of education responded to the challenge in apparently superficial ways of disrupting existing ideologies and power structures. Her study suggests that universities, looked to for leadership in matters of inclusive education, are more like the school systems where they are being asked to help change. When, for example, is an inclusion class about collaborative teaching actually taught by two university instructors who earnestly explore the issues from multiple perspectives? The answer, sadly, is "rarely." Student teachers, therefore, often leave their programs with abstract notions of team teaching in inclusive classrooms, perhaps feeling that it is a good idea, but it is unrealistic in practice.

The Field of Special Education

The field of special education has grappled with the concept of inclusion for several decades, causing acrimonious debates (Kauffman and Sasso 2006; Gallagher 2006), outraged diatribes (Kauffman 1995), accusations that a radical few are hijacking the special education agenda of the many (Fuchs and Fuchs 1995), and attempts at internal reconciliation (Andrews et al. 2000). What became evident in these exchanges was that anything pertaining to disability and education had become automatically placed into the default box of "special education." In fact, special education seemed to monopolize any discussions about inclusion. However, as disability studies scholar Barton (2007) notes, "Inclusive education is not a sub-branch of special education." Rather, special education is an artifact of society's response to disability, and a highly limited one at that.

Over the last decade, a network of critical special educators have emerged, united in their common desire to seek a different framework through which to look at the issues of disability, education, and the need to increase access to all aspects of society for people with disabilities, including schools. Disability studies, an interdisciplinary field that evolved since the 1970s in a similar vein to women's studies, black studies, gay and lesbian studies, and so on, offered ways in which to highlight social interpretations of disability usually eschewed within traditional special education.

Disability studies in education (DSE), therefore, grew largely in opposition to the foundational knowledge valued and taught within special education, including its persistent resistance to inclusion. Tenets of DSE advocated for inclusive classrooms as a way to forge social change toward a more inclusive world, and openly challenged the hegemony of positivism within special education research, evident in the field's obsession with "scientifically proven" practices that rarely reach classrooms (Connor, Gabel, Gallagher, and Morton 2008). By calling for a plurality of perspectives within the broad field(s) of education about dis/ability, including within special education, DSE supports inclusion as a fundamental civil right—and is interested in finding new ways to move forward in creating, maintaining, and improving inclusive classrooms (Valle and Connor 2010).

Students with Disabilities

Interestingly, relatively little attention is paid to students with disabilities and their experiences with, or their opinions about, inclusion. Overall, findings have veered toward favoring their receiving education in general settings as much as possible, but not necessarily all the time, suggesting a small but important degree of ambivalence. In studies of elementary students, children indicated some satisfaction with receiving individualized support outside the general education classroom, but felt that their academic and social needs were better met in general education (Elbaum 2002). In addition, students were upset that they missed academic work, running the risk of being teased and stigmatized, causing embarrassment and pain (Reid and Button 1995). In several secondary school studies, students labeled as LD and ED performed higher academically and experienced greater social acceptance (Forgan and Vaughn 2000; Rea, McLaughlin, and Walther-Thomas 2002).

Narratives of students with disabilities reveal their sense of isolation experienced in segregated settings. As a young man in Stussman's (1996) study shared,

I began to realize I was separated from the "regular kids." I can remember that during lunch the special education kids and the "regular kids" ate at separate tables, and all the special ed. kids were herded onto the G-12 bus. (15)

Time after time, students who spent prolonged time in segregated settings described how much that experience negatively affected their sense of self, making them feel inferior to nondisabled peers (Connor 2008; Keefe, Moore, and Duff 2006; Mooney 2008; Rodis, Garrod, and Boscardin 2001). In one account, Phillip, a student with cerebral palsy who had spent his school career in special education, was serving as a peer educator, making presentations about his disability to general education classes. He poignantly recalls,

Even though I got excited before each presentation, I would sometimes get sad, too. I used to look around and wish I could be in there with them. I wanted the chance to get to do all of the things they were doing in there, like reading interesting books, conducting science experiments, or even just hanging out. One time when I was giving my lecture I wondered . . . if I'm good enough to speak to the kids in these classes, why can't I be in these classes? No one had a good answer to explain why I wasn't allowed in there. I was always just told that my skills weren't high enough or that I needed to be in a class where I could learn how to live in the community. (Contreras 2006, 136)

This quotation sums up the need for inclusive classrooms as Phillip would have benefited enormously from stimulating peer interactions and having access to more interesting work. Conversely, his peers would have come to know him as a person and have had a greater understanding of cerebral palsy, and perhaps disability in general. Phillip was not granted his wish, nor was he provided with a good enough reason to justify his segregation.

BEYOND CONFUSION: CONTEMPLATING WHAT WORKS

The issues above illustrate how the simple concept of inclusion can cause confusion for many of the constituents involved in its design and implementation. If inclusive classrooms are created purely because of district policies—administered by principals concerned about scores more than children, and taught by teachers with little or no background knowledge of disability history or preparation in collaboration—these settings are more likely to cause everyone involved frustration and failure ("We're doing inclusion, and it doesn't work!"). In these situations, we have to be honest and admit that without certain elements, the effectiveness of inclusive classrooms—or rather, what is being done in the name of inclusion—is significantly compromised. Knowledge of how to create and maintain effective inclusive schools exists. Much has been written about what makes inclusion work, including:

- The use of universal design in creating classrooms (Hitchcock, Meyer, Rose, and Jackson 2002)
- Building class and school community (Sapon-Shevin 2007)
- Promoting professional collaboration (Friend 2005)
- Examining educator beliefs and values (Villa and Thousand 1995)
- Challenging ableism (Hehir 2005)

In a recent study, Hehir (2011) analyzed the factors that helped principals envision, develop, and sustain successful inclusive schools in the Boston area. Using the four frames of leadership developed by Bolman and Deal (1997)—symbolic, structural, political, and human resources—Hehir captures the complexities of inclusion in action. Each frame is worth briefly examining, as all four provide different windows into how inclusive practices can and do work.

1. *The Symbolic Frame* asserts that values and culture matter. Successful inclusive schools have a strong mission statement in which children and youth with disabilities are represented. Principals recognize and support the belief that the mission(s) of the schools are very complex, and their efforts are part of a larger change effort to remake education reflect a society that is more equitable and inclusive. The principals of these schools are value driven, and their values have been formed within, or influenced by, the civil rights movement. Furthermore, the mission statement is promoted through ceremonies that celebrate evidence of growth and success, so the purpose is always within people's minds as a "real" force.

2. *The Structural Frame* focuses on organization, resources, and policies. Successful leaders are found to be highly entrepreneurial and creative in reaching their vision. Collaboration with staff, parents, and the community is considered essential. Creating consciously collaborative team-teaching partnerships, and providing ongoing support are also considered essential. Viewing teachers as fellow problem solvers, and creating opportunities for them to come together and share thoughts about specific children, curriculum, and methodologies, acknowledges the value of educators.

In such a respectful environment, teachers can self-sustain and usually stay in their schools, ultimately serving as stable and dependable forces in these settings. All staff in these schools share the goal of designing classrooms founded on the principles of universal design, integrating technology in both high (screen readers) and low (pencil grips) forms. Interacting with community resources also provides schools with public recognition and support. Interestingly, a strong incorporation of the arts occurs in these schools, verifying their use in providing various forms of expression.

3. *The Political Frame* addresses how an organization deals with issues of power. Principals are keenly aware of politics both in and out of their buildings, and they must cultivate the support of faculty and community members, including political backing to obtain resources they deem necessary for their schools. In

many ways, principals who promote change operate within an "insider-outsider" role, balancing their professional knowledge and responsibilities with a countercultural awareness that propels them in pursuit of social change. Finally and importantly, racial and ethnic diversity is also recognized and valued in these institutions.

4. *The Human Resource Frame* looks at how individuals within the organization are treated, supported, and developed. In successful inclusive schools, all persons agree with the mission and participate in distributed leadership. In particular, teacher leadership is encouraged and supported; being active problem solvers is expected. For example, to help address the significant lag in reading levels by entering freshman students, one high school adopted a policy in which all teachers were self-defined as "teachers of reading" within their subject matter. At the same time, expertise in certain areas is respected (such as working with students who have severe disabilities) as all staff members respect one another's strengths. Another feature that helps sustain strong, inclusive classrooms is the focus and quality of ongoing professional development recognized as integral to school culture. In sum, the norm is that all professionals are clearly expected constantly to improve their ability to work with diverse learners.

When integrated, the practices described in the four frames interlock to provide pictures of actual schools that succeed in creating inclusive environments that are welcoming of and respectful toward all students. Instead of being "egg crate" models in which everyone is separated and viewed as independent, these schools are organized around collaborative problem solving and interdependence. Echoing the sentiments expressed earlier by Barton (2007), Hehir's work conveys that inclusion is not merely an appendage, but is rather a shift in structure, values, and operations. In sum, inclusion requires fundamental, not merely surface, change.

CONCLUSION: KEEPING A CLEAR FOCUS

This chapter has focused largely on what muddies the waters about inclusion, for the tangle of laws, opinions, rights, policies, belief systems, practices, and traditions—and how they are interpreted—can easily cause confusion for stakeholders. However, the final part of the chapter consciously presents qualities and practices within schools that help create and sustain inclusive environments. As a supporter of inclusive education, one cannot help but bristle when naysayers point out that inclusion does not work. It does. It can. And it is also perhaps most useful to think in terms of degrees of success. I have worked in schools and visited others in which inclusive education is a worthy ideal to work toward, not a policy that is begrudgingly and halfheartedly implemented without real investment.

Like the desire to eliminate racism, sexism, classism, and heterosexism, inclusion seeks to promote equality, provide access to all aspects of society, and be welcoming of diversity that was once viewed as far from the norm. In challenging ableism (Hehir 2005), inclusion confronts traditional practices within education that have historically excluded a large segment of the population. As such, inclusion in education is a work in progress for all. Because it materializes differently in different contexts, inclusion will always be a work in progress. Despite forces that seek to muddy the waters with their own self-interests, we must keep a clear focus on those who can benefit from expanding inclusive practices. That is all of us.

QUESTIONS FOR DISCUSSION

1. Why might inclusion be viewed as a simple concept that can be complicated to implement?
2. What are some ways in which teachers can support all students in their classes?
3. In what ways does ableism affect the lives of all people?
4. What are supporting beliefs and arguments in inclusion as held by (a) parents, (b) administrators, (c) students, and (d) school political leaders?
5. How do you define inclusion? Do you support it? Why or why not?

REFERENCES

Andrews, J. E., D. W. Carnine, M. J. Coutinho, E. B. Edgar, and S. R. Forness, et al (2000). Bridging the special education divide. *Remedial and Special Education* 21 (5): 258–60, 267.

Artiles, A. J., R. Rueda, J. J. Salazar, and I. Higareda. (2002). English-language learner representation in special education in California urban school districts. *Racial inequality in special education*, ed. D. J. Losen and G. Orfield, 117–36. Cambridge, MA: Harvard Education Press.

Barton, L. (2007). Inclusive education and disability studies. Observations and issues for debate. Paper presented at the 7th Annual Second City Conference on Disability Studies in Education, Chicago.

Bolman, L. E., and T. E. Deal. (1997). *Reframing organizations: Artistry, choice, and leadership.* San Francisco, CA: Jossey-Bass.

Brantlinger, E. (2003). *Dividing classes: How the middle class negotiates and rationalizes school advantage.* New York: Routledge.

Brown v. Board of Education of Topeka, 347 U.S. 483 (1954).

Charlton, J. I. (2000). *Nothing about us without us: Disability, oppression and empowerment.* Berkeley: University of California Press.

Connor, D. J. (2008). *Urban narratives: Portraits in progress: Life at the intersections of learning disability, race, and social class.* New York: Peter Lang.

Connor, D. J., S. Gabel, D. Gallagher, and M. Morton. (2008). Disability studies and inclusive education—implications for theory, research, and practice. *International Journal of Inclusive Education* 12 (5–6): 441–57.

Contreras, P. (2006). We can do more things than we can't do. In *Listening to the experts: Students with disabilities speak out*, ed. E. B. Keefe, V. M. Moore, and F. R. Duff, 135–39. Baltimore, MD: Brookes.

Davis, L. J., ed. (1997). *The disability studies reader*. New York: Routledge.

Diana v. State Board of Education CA 70 RFT (1970).

Education for All Handicapped Children Act, P.L. 94-142, 20 USC 1401 et. seq (1975).

Elbaum, B. (2002). The self-concept of students with learning disabilities: A meta-analysis of comparisons across different placements. *Learning Disabilities Research & Practice* 17 (4): 216–26.

Fleischer, D., and F. Zames. (2001). *The disabilities rights movement: From charity to confrontation*. Philadelphia: Temple University Press.

Forgan, J. W., and S. Vaughn. (2000). Adolescents with and without LD make the transition to middle school. *Journal of Learning Disabilities* 33 (1): 33–43.

Friend, M. (2005). *The power of 2*. DVD. www.nprinc.com/co-teach/vpw2r.htm.

Fuchs, D., and L. S. Fuchs. (1995). Inclusive schools movement and the radicalization of special education reform. In *The illusion of full inclusion*, ed. J. M. Kauffman and D. P. Hallahan, 213–43. Austin, TX: ProEd.

Gallagher, D. (2006). If not absolute objectivity, then what? A reply to Kauffman and Sasso. *Exceptionality* 14 (2): 91–107.

Giordano, G. (2005). *How testing came to dominate American schools*. New York: Peter Lang.

Gould, S. J. (1996). *The mismeasure of man*. New York: Norton.

Habib, D., producer. (2008). *Including Samuel*. DVD. www.includingsamuel.com/home.aspx.

Haller, B. (2011). *Representing disability in an ableist world: Essay on mass media*. Louisville, KY: Advocado Press.

Harry, B., and J. Klingner. (2006). *Why are so many minority students in special education? Understanding race and disability in schools*. New York: Teachers College Press.

Hehir, T. (2005). *New directions in special education: Eliminating ableism in policy and practice*. Cambridge, MA: Harvard Education Press.

———. (2011). Universally designed schools that work. Presentation at the 26th Annual Learning Differences Conference, Harvard School of Education, Cambridge, Mass.

Hehir, T., R. Figueroa, S. Gamm, L. I. Katzman, A. Gruner, J. Karger, and J. Hernandez. (2005). *Comprehension management review and evaluation of special education submitted to the New York City Department of Education*. Cambridge, MA: Harvard School of Education.

Hitchcock, C., A. Meyer, D. Rose, and R. Jackson. (2002). Providing new access to the general curriculum: Universal design for learning. *TEACHING Exceptional Children* 35 (2): 8–17.

Individuals with Disabilities Education Act, P.L. 101-476 (1990).

Individuals with Disabilities Education Act, P.L. 105-17 (1997).

Individuals with Disabilities Education Improvement Act, P.L. 108-446 (2004).

Kauffman, J. M. (1995). Commentary: Today's special education and its messages for tomorrow. *Journal of Special Education* 32 (4): 244–54.

Kauffman, J. M., and D. P. Hallahan, eds. (1995). *The illusion of full inclusion: A comprehensive critique of a current special education bandwagon.* Austin, TX: ProEd.

Kauffman, J. M, and G. M. Sasso. (2006). Toward ending cultural and cognitive relativism in special education. *Exceptionality* 14 (2): 65–90.

Keefe, E. B., V. M. Moore, and F. R. Duff. (2006). *Listening to the experts: Students with disabilities speak out.* Baltimore, MD: Brookes.

Kudlick, C. J. (2003). Disability history: Why we need another "other." Available at www .historycoop.org/journals/ahr/108.3/kudlick.html.

Lagares, C. (2010). Personal communication. October 15.

Linton, S. (1998). *Claiming disability.* New York: New York University Press.

Lipsky, D. K., and A. Gartner. (1997). *Inclusion and school reform: Transforming America's classrooms.* Baltimore, MD: Brookes.

Losen, D. J., and G. Orfield, eds. (2002). *Racial inequality in special education.* Cambridge, MA: Harvard University Press.

Mastropieri, M. A., T. E. Scruggs, J. Graetz, J. Norland, W. Gardizi, and K. McDuffie. (2005). Case studies in co-teaching in the content areas: Successes, failures, and challenges. *Intervention in School and Clinic* 40 (5): 260–70.

Mitchell, D., and S. Snyder. (2000). *Narrative prosthesis: Disability and the dependencies of discourse.* Ann Arbor: University of Michigan Press.

Mooney, J. (2008). *The short bus: A journey beyond normal.* New York: Henry Holt.

Murawski, W. W., and L. Dieker. (2008). 50 ways to keep your co-teacher: Strategies before, during, and after co-teaching. *TEACHING Exceptional Children* 40 (4): 40–48.

Oberti v. Board of Education of the Borough of Clementon School District, 995 F. wd. 1204 (1993).

Ong-Dean, C. (2009). *Distinguishing disability: Parents, privilege, and special education.* Chicago: University of Chicago Press.

Parrish, T. (2002). Racial disparities in the identification, funding, and provision of special education. In *Racial inequality in special education*, ed. D. J. Losen and G. Orfield, 1–13. Cambridge, MA: Harvard Education Press.

Rea, P. J., V. L. McLaughlin, and C. Walther-Thomas. (2002). Outcomes for students with learning disabilities in inclusive and pullout programs. *Exceptional Children* 68 (2): 203–22.

Reid, D. K., and L. J. Button. (1995). Anna's story: Narratives of personal experience about being labeled learning disabled. *Journal of Learning Disabilities* 28 (10): 602–14.

Rodis, P., A. Garrod, and M. L. Boscardin, eds. (2001). *Learning disabilities and life stories.* Needham Heights, MA: Allyn & Bacon.

Salend, S. (2004). *Creating inclusive classrooms: Effective and reflective practices for all students.* 5th ed. Upper Saddle River, NJ: Pearson.

Sapon-Shevin, M. (2007). *Widening the circle: The power of inclusive classrooms.* Boston: Beacon Press.

Skrtic, T. (1991). *Behind special education: A critical analysis of professional culture and school organization.* Denver: Love.

Smith, P. (2010). Trends for including students with intellectual disabilities in general education classrooms. In *Whatever happened to inclusion?* ed. P. Smith, 38–60. New York: Peter Lang.

Stiker, H. J. (1999). *A history of disability.* Ann Arbor, MI: Love.

Stussman, B. (1996). *Inclusion: It's not all academic.* ERIC Clearinghouse, 4, 3. www .eric.ed.gov:80/PDFS/ED403874.pdf, accessed March 27.

Sweet, K. (2006, October). *Small schools, few choices: How New York City's high school reform effort left students with disabilities behind.* Parents for Inclusive Education, New York: Author.

Terry, J., and J. Urla, eds. (1995). *Deviant bodies.* Bloomington: Indiana University Press.

Valle, J. W. (2009). *What mothers say about special education: From the 1960s to the present.* New York: Palgrave.

Valle, J. W., and E. Aponte. (2002). IDEA: A Bakhtinian perspective on parent and professional discourse. *Journal of Learning Disabilities* 35 (5): 469–79.

Valle, J. W., and D. J. Connor. (2010). *Rethinking disability: A disability studies approach to inclusive practices.* New York: McGraw-Hill.

Villa, R. A., and J. Thousand. (1995). *Creating an inclusive school.* Alexandria, VA: Council for Supervision and Curriculum Development.

Young, K. (2008). Physical and social organization of space in a combined credential programme: Implications for inclusion. *International Journal of Inclusive Education* 12 (6): 477–95.

8

❖ ❖

Don't Ask, Don't Tell, Don't Pay

Services for Children with Severe and Chronic Disabilities

Arnold B. Danzig

INTRODUCTION

This chapter discusses the politics of serving children with severe and profound disabilities. Children with multiple handicaps and severe or profound disabilities tend to receive fewer services and are discriminated against to a greater degree than other children with disabilities. At school, their least restrictive environment is often in a site or classroom segregated from their peers with mild or no disability. Alternatively, these children are placed in less segregated or more mainstreamed settings with few or limited services.

Over the years, attempts have been made to exclude them from IDEA services by changing the description of children covered by the act and/or court challenges to not fund the host of services required to meet their educational needs. There exists a small body of research literature on understanding how chronic illness and severe disabilities are related to equity and service delivery. This chapter also discusses the absence of literature that explores family relations, particularly related to multiple siblings, and implications for understanding growing up in a family with a child with a chronic illness and developmental disabilities.

BEGINNINGS

Over a career as a college professor, I have been engaged in research, scholarship, grants, and professional development related to leadership and administrative practices. The current chapter applies some of the insights that I have gained from working with principals and other school leaders to understanding how education and social services are provided for children with severe and chronic disabilities.

This chapter explores a deeply held interest in understanding the connections between the personal and professional experience that has happened across my career. The discussion looks at the ways in which a family with a child who has severe and chronic disability participates in educational, social, medical, and legal decision making; it extends the argument in new directions, by referencing the social learning and behavioral actions that are part of family relationships, and how these actions spill over into professional life.

My personal experiences as the father of a child with severe disabilities and chronic illness provide an opportunity to experience events firsthand, and describe the resulting insights into the politics of special education along with its problems, promises, and progress. Focusing on the personal—and the ways that at least one family has experienced "the system" and advocated for services—stands as a case study, entitled "Don't Ask, Don't Tell, Don't Pay: Services for Children with Severe and Chronic Disabilities."

PARENT INVOLVEMENT IN SCHOOLS— BENEFITS AND COSTS OF PARTICIPATION

In other places I have written about the ambivalence that schools and other agencies exhibit when working with parents who advocate for their children, especially for children with severe special needs (Danzig 1992, 1994, 2003). Essentially, my argument is:

- There have long existed disputes and conflict between parents and educators (teachers and administrators) over educational decisions and practices related to children's educational experiences (Waller 1932/1965).
- Family participation and parent involvement are not one-dimensional concepts, present or absent, but understood as complex interactions with costs and benefits (Lareau 1987, 1989; Gonzalez, Moll, and Amanti 2005).
- No single best way exists to serve all families and children. The interests of parents and children with severe and chronic disabilities are not the same across their disability, ethnicity, social class groups, or family configurations. Parents want and expect different things from the educational experiences of their children (Danzig 2003).
- The language of professionalism distances parents from articulating the need for services for their children. Professional discourse gives higher status to professional knowledge that is represented as neutral or objective. Whereas specialists are invited to present their largely technical reports free from interruption, the information from parents (and teachers) is more often *elicited*, with interruptions and questions regarding clarification of meanings (Mehan 1983; Turnbull and Turnbull 1985).
- Current educational and service delivery models fragment services to children and families, which lead to: (1) isolating problems, (2) labeling children

and families, (3) providing conflicting goals and services, (4) failing to bring existing resources to bear on problems, and (5) disempowering children and their families (Kirst and McLaughlin 1990; Danzig 2003).

- Schools and other organizations undervalue and blame actors outside the local system for a lack of individual progress and program failures. Everyone blames "the other" without recognizing systemic failures in which the "ball gets dropped" and a child with severe and chronic disabilities goes under- or unserved (Danzig 2003).
- A more detailed and richer description of the lives and the circumstances that children bring to school is needed for educational and other service providers to improve the availability and quality of services needed for children with severe and chronic disabilities (Danzig 2003).

Social Class as a Context for Understanding Family Life

Social class provides a context for understanding parents' values (Kohn 1969, 1976). This view is especially obvious for parents with children with severe disabilities, in how parents think about the family, and in how they engage with the institutions that serve them and their children. Lareau's (1987, 1989) study of first- and second-grade students and their families points to difference in the quantity and quality of family–school interactions. While the middle-class parents in her study participated in schools only slightly more than the working-class parents, when a child was identified as needing special services, the participation of middle-class parents increased dramatically.

Middle-class parents, to a greater degree than working-class parents, were more willing to challenge core practices of the school (teaching and learning) and the authority of the teacher. Lareau (1989) also found that teachers and administrators at schools serving middle-class families faced greater scrutiny and challenges over their professional competence than did teachers serving working-class families and students. She explains:

> Social class appears to influence the content of the "battles" and, at least in upper-middle-class schools, the intensity and frequency with which parents take the offensive in trying to control the teacher and their children's education. Parents are less willing to grant teachers a "backstage" and automatically defer professional expertise. (Lareau 1989, 164)

Social class also provides unequal resources and dispositions, which in turn affect what parents ask for, how they ask, and what they receive.

The Challenges of Parent Involvement

On the one hand, parents are recognized as critical contributors to their children's social and academic achievement (Dauber and Epstein 1993; Henderson and

Berla 1994; Kreider 2002). We also see a growing appreciation that parents and families participate in school at a number of levels—through basic parenting, communicating with children and school personnel, volunteering, supporting a home learning environment, participating in school governance, and through collaboration (Epstein et al. 1997; Valdés 1996). On the other hand, parents whom professionals perceive as too involved risk the following: (1) alienating the professionals working with their children, (2) having their parent advocacy interpreted as distrusting professional judgment, and (3) getting in the way of educators doing their jobs.

A related set of challenges is faced by parents who are viewed as lacking involvement in the education of their children. Keeping children at home to care for siblings is considered abuse. Missing school to participate in family events is seen as "ill advised" and risks the child's "academic achievement." Children are penalized at school for not keeping up with assignments, for missing class or school time, and for not participating in school events. Since few teachers, however, are explicitly trained in working with families (Garcia 1990), teacher preparation in family engagement is needed to work effectively with families (Chavkin 1993; Shartrand et al. 1997).

THE DOUBLE BIND FOR PARENTS OF CHILDREN WITH SEVERE AND CHRONIC DISABILITIES

Parents and families of children with severe and chronic disabilities face a double bind. The challenges of raising a child with severe disabilities places increased time demands on the whole family, including the child with disabilities, the parents, and other children. Stress and fatigue limit time flexibility, and families have to choose among competing priorities, such as education, medical services, and social services. Sometimes, what happens at school or in a classroom is a lower priority for them (in the family scheme of things) than it is for education professionals.

Considering the current requirements related to testing and reaching needed thresholds of participation, we are not surprised that conflict results from parents' deciding that testing days are less relevant for their children while school authorities require 95 percent participation in all nonexempt categories. Schools risk not meeting Adequate Yearly Progress (AYP) and being labeled as a "failing school." The rational actions of parents, which prioritize family ahead of schooling, risk being interpreted in negative ways, as "uninvolved, uncommitted, or overcommitted."

The second bind is that parents who strongly advocate for their children risk being accused of being "in denial," "unrealistic," "overcommitted," and "too aggressive" in their advocacy. On the one hand, since parents see themselves as experts about their own children, the parents see their children in contexts unavailable to the school and independently assess the strengths and weaknesses of their own children. Parent knowledge and expertise are important sources of understanding for any educational or service delivery model. And, research points to a congruence of parent and professional assessments of children's abilities and disabilities (Stotland 1984; Turnbull and Turnbull 1985).

On the other hand, getting families and service providers, with different disciplinary assumptions and class backgrounds, to work together as a team requires greater appreciation for the authority of the gatekeepers and payers of last resort. The decision to provide services, to pay or not, usually resides outside the purview of parents, and it is the responsibility of the school or agency to budget and provide payment for services.

THE MISMATCH BETWEEN SERVICES NEEDED AND SERVICES PROVIDED

The final decisions regarding services are ultimately made by the person (s) with the authority to approve payment. Regardless of how this authority is presented, the result is a gap between the requests of parents and the willingness of providers to meet them. This gulf manifests itself in a mismatch between the services parents' request and options that schools and service providers make available. This chapter explicitly argues that unacknowledged power arrangements result in lost services and missed opportunities, justified by the rational decisions of providers and experts. Decisions are made that are detrimental to families and children with severe disabilities in ways that are little understood and barely explored.

The following examples are taken from my own experiences getting services for my multiply handicapped daughter. These cases illustrate the distance between services that are needed by children as articulated by families, and what is actually provided. The first example reports on the family's experience with the integrated preschool located at a regional state university in the southwestern United States. The example is taken from a transcription of an Individualized Education Program (IEP) meeting among the parents, the teacher, staff, and director of an integrated preschool in which disagreements occur among stakeholders over whether the school will provide a feeding program for the preschool child with multiple disabilities. The mother says that it is unreasonable for her to get her daughter up, fed, dressed, and off to school, only to have to pick her up two hours later and then have to feed her again. She asks that the school feed her daughter lunch, a task that takes an hour or more to do.

The transcript captures the mother's frustration at the program's decision not to feed her daughter; it shows a failure on the part of a program manager to even acknowledge the importance of feeding to the overall well-being of the child, let alone the mother's general need to care for her young family with two other younger children (two and a half years and six months in age).

> Mother: *We need for you to feed Sidney. It's not fair that you have to get her up and dressed, and by the time you've finally got her off to school, you have to pick her up again.*
>
> Preschool Director: *Well, I choose not to have a feeding program. We are a vendor, and I don't have to offer feeding if I don't want to. And, I don't choose to offer a feeding program.*
>
> Mother: *Then you have a lousy program. And, we'll complain to everyone that the integrated preschool is lousy.* (Transcription from IEP videotape)

In this example, the family's needs and the services that are provided are mismatched, resulting in anger, frustration, and bad feelings all around.

WHOSE OPINION COUNTS? FURTHER ELABORATION ON WHAT IS REQUESTED AND WHAT IS RECEIVED

The next section provides examples of actual requests for services, goods, and equipment, what was actually provided, and the largely unreported results. The cases illustrate a slightly different ending to the Jagger and Richards (1969) song "You Can't Always Get What You Want"—*you get what someone else thinks you need.*

1. **Feeder seat.** Child has become bigger and cannot sit in a high chair. The child is also too big to be held and fed at the same time.
Services Provided: An older and used feeder seat, with no safety straps, provided by state agency.
Result: On two occasions, the child fell out of the chair, face-first onto the floor, resulting in emergency room visits. The cost of these hospital visits was more than the cost of a new feeder seat with the appropriate safety straps. The result is injury to child falling face-first on the floor, without protective reflexes to cushion the fall.

2. **Wheelchair.** Parents ask state agency to provide a safe and appropriate wheelchair to assist with carrying and moving their young daughter.
Services Provided: No wheelchair ever provided by the state. Parents carried the child around until she was five, when private insurance paid for a wheelchair.
Result: Chronic back pain for mother, and difficulty sitting for long periods of time.

3. **Wheelchair Lift for Family Automobile.** Parents request wheelchair lift for their car.

Services Provided: None. State agency declined coverage.

Result: Mother and father put wheelchair in and out of car every time they go someplace, increasing time to lift their child and wheelchair in and out of car.

4. **Diapers.** As child becomes older and larger, adult-size diapers become an extra expense and financial burden.

Services Provided: Six cloth diapers were provided by state agency. Agency rejected purchasing and paying for disposable diapers for ecological reasons.

Result: Cloth diapers were not allowed at the child's preschool because of health codes. Diapers were of infant size and child quickly grew out of them. Mother was also required to wash six diapers every day and soon threw them away.

5. **Preschool.** Parents and especially mother felt that half-day preschool program would not only benefit the four-year-old child's social needs, but also mother's need for respite and time to participate in the lives of her other children. Since feeding child every meal took one to two hours, the mother also requested that the lunch meal be given at school, as part of the child's education. Spending more than six hours a day hand-feeding her child was extremely wearing on her energy, and her request was to be relieved for one of the feedings so she could keep up her strength. A private Montessori preschool agreed to enroll daughter and manage her program and feeding if the state would pay for an aide to accompany and feed her at school.

Services Provided: State agency denied her request and recommended alternative placement in the integrated preschool; the program met for two hours per day, with no feeding.

Result: School agreed to provide "educational services" but would not agree to feed in the classroom at the integrated preschool. In the parents' view, the teacher "didn't want to get the carpet dirty." An aide to feed the child was hired separately but had limited training and no supervision. Lunch feedings for daughter were largely unsuccessful, with lunches coming home uneaten and the mother being required to feed the child again.

6. **Transportation.** Parents requested assistance getting child to and from preschool. With getting in and out of the car, parents spent approximately sixty minutes getting their child to and from preschool, where she was to participate in a two-hour preschool program. Parents felt that time could be better spent with other children.

Services Provided: None; transportation denied by preschool program.

Result: Mother, father, and two younger siblings spent many hours in a car driving their daughter to school, therapies, doctors' visits, and so on.

7. **Home Health Aide.** The preschool opted out of feeding or supervising the feeding of their daughter at school, and an external aide was requested to feed daughter at home after preschool.

Services Provided: State agency paid for an aide to come to the house to feed daughter. The aide was not trained to feed a multiply handicapped child with eating and swallowing problems.

Result: The aide spent up to two to three hours per day trying to feed the daughter lunch. Aide also brought to the house her own daughter, who had acting-out problems. Since the child (and aide) needed to be supervised, the goal of relieving the mother of workload and stress was not met. The mother was still unable to spend one-on-one time with her other children or get respite time for herself.

8. **Respite.** Parents were under strain and constant stress of caring for child with special needs, without a break. Mother requested respite (a few hours away from the house and children, for example, some time to go to a movie) on several occasions from list of respite providers provided by the state.

Services Provided: List of potential respite providers given to the family by state agency, Department of Developmental Disabilities.

Result: Over four years, the family was able to locate a respite provider on only three occasions. Each time, the state-sponsored respite providers brought along another child with disabilities in their care.

9. **Peer Support (Another Parent with a Child with Disabilities).** This support was not a requested service, but was offered by the state agency and the family agreed to it.

Services Provided: A person came to the house about once a month to "visit" the family.

Result: Mother was unaware that the support person coming to see her was being paid. The mother assumed that this person was simply another parent with a child with a disability who lived in the same neighborhood and sought friendship. The peer-support person would also bring her child with disabilities to play with the other children in the family.

10. **Housekeeping.** This service was not a high priority, but it was requested and offered.

Services Provided: Several different housekeepers were sent by state agency.

Result: One housekeeper stole the father's tools from the garage. Another stole all of the mother's jewelry and an iron. The last provider brought her husband with disabilities to the home, and both of them often reeked of alcohol. They never took anything, but mother was uncomfortable having them in her house.

11. **Music Therapy.** Mother felt that music provided a particular sense of joy to the child, and family identified music therapy as a priority. The mother requested music therapy above all other therapies.

Services Provided: Denied by state agency. Family request for music therapy was denied on two separate occasions.

Result: Opportunity for the child to experience pleasure was missed. Mother felt an access route to internal state for child was lost and this was an indication that her life was less valued.

12. **Formula.** As the child moved to tube feeding, she received special formula to keep her nutrition well balanced. Formula was costly and a financial burden for the family.

Services Provided: None; denied by state agency.

Result: Parents had to pay for costly formula themselves.

13. **Bath Chair.** As child got older and became too big to be bathed without great difficulty, parents request bath chair for body support and to prevent child from slipping all over the tub.

Services Provided: None; state agency acknowledged the need for bath chair, but it was never provided.

Result: Parents continued to bathe their child, with two people needed for safety and support with added back pain and strain for both.

14. **Special School Placement.** At public school, the child was physically dropped on her face (no protective reflexes) on two separate occasions. One time, she was left unattended on a table, and the other time an ambulatory child climbed on her wheelchair and tipped it over. Parents determined that school was neither prepared nor equipped to care for child's safety needs, and requested placement in private school.

Services Provided: Public school argued that their program was "defendable." Parents filed formal grievance and threatened litigation. School district agreed to private school placement for two years only.

Result: Two years elapsed and public school system refused to support outside placement in private school.

15. **Extended Summer School Program.** While the public school agreed that summer program was needed, it declined to pay for summer program in a private school. State agency also denied payment. While the IEP recognized the benefit of school and summer school program, neither the school district nor the state agency came up with funds required for participation.

Services Provided: None. Funding was denied by school district and state. Private provider was unwilling to provide educational services during summer months.

Result: The daughter did not receive summer school programming, thus increasing the fatigue factor for her family.

16. **Residential Care.** Family requests residential care for their daughter.

Services Provided: Residential care was denied by state agency. Agency philosophy is that the child belongs at home with her natural family. State offers foster care as option, until family agrees to bring daughter home.

Result: Parents placed the child in residential setting and care was provided through private resources, supported by insurance, under a limited and uncertain time frame. No state agency or public school offered any plan of service or care for child, which accounted for the combination of medical, educational, and social services needed by the child.

INTERPRETATION OF FINDINGS

These examples describe a pattern in which parents' requests for services are ignored, denied, or reinterpreted; the outcomes reported meet the requirements and interests of providers instead of serving the interests of children and families. This mismatch between the parents' identified needs for their child with chronic and multiple disabilities and what educational, social, medical, and other providers have to offer has been the basis of countless hours of conflict, meetings, and even litigation. Ultimately, I argue that the quality and context of family life are largely unseen and unrecognized by professionals and service providers. As a result, a significant gap appears between service providers and recipients, and between the services needed and the services received.

The costs of services are rarely discussed or even referenced as the determining factor—whether services are provided or not. The child's needs are the defining criteria; and when services are rejected, costs are not recognized as the reason. Instead, the provision of services is based on a determination that the need threshold has not been met. Too often, this disingenuous strategy leads to conflict and adversarial relationships that never address the real issue, *money.* Money dictates whose definition of the problem will be adopted and which services will be provided.

The conflict is also exacerbated by the state's position that the state is required only to provide a minimum or "standard" level of services to all eligible clients. Parents generally, and highly educated middle-class parents in particular, attempt to customize services to meet the individual needs of their child and family. Schools and state agencies rarely talk about optimal or customized services for a child. Instead, providers adopt a factory model of services in which families either take what is offered or risk getting nothing. The alternative—that of customizing services and the systems to serve the particular needs of one child and family—is rejected as inefficient and cost prohibitive. Exceptions require significant commitments of time, energy, and resources to put together. Developing a customized approach that combines public and private resources, however, is rejected for multiple reasons: as too costly, too difficult, too time consuming, and too resource intensive.

Better Options and Strategies

A better strategy would include more open discussion of the realities of family life and the realities of funding, and how both should drive thinking about options, availability, and payment. The costs of providing services for a child with severe disabilities are enormous and require a more nuanced understanding of the implicit factors that are weighed by the various decision makers and their representatives. For example:

- Providers apply two competing cultural norms for serving their clients: an equal share of the pie to all versus each according to his or her need. Parents are more focused on both according to need.
- In the face of limited resources, one way of limiting services is to make them less user friendly and hope that self-selection will reduce demand. This strategy masks the true availability of services and satisfies the government (bureaucratic) requirement of serving all eligible clients, as cheaply as possible.
- Social class differences between parents and providers are also a source of disconnect. Teachers, therapists, doctors, clinicians, case managers, social workers, and agency managers, for example, bring their own class assumptions to interactions, with potential mismatch up and down the class hierarchy. The social class assumptions of gatekeepers in schools, state agencies, and private practice affect the expectations of what services can be "legitimately" requested and what services are made available.
- Financial resources of parents are a double-edged sword. On the one hand, independent resources provide options that allow parents to demand more from institutional providers, seek more family-friendly private service providers, bring in advocates to press their case, and hire legal counsel to support their demands. At their worst, however, financially independent parents can use their resources to create mutually fatiguing adversarial relations that result in less flexibility (or even push-back) from providers and greater resentments.
- Child and family needs are not uniform across the disabilities, although there exists a tendency to lump many categories of disability together. This categorizing then triggers certain services and eligibilities, rather than building individual service plans.
- Access to services is often decided by people who may not have children, and likely do not have children with severe and chronic disabilities. Inevitably, value judgments are made as to how to serve clients without a deep understanding of the experience of having a child with a severe and chronic disability, and the multiplier effects on family life.
- Recommended service providers are sometimes recipients of state services themselves; they become providers for the state (and thereby earn income). This situation means that the quality of provider is balanced by a secondary goal, that of providing employment and additional work for the state agency's clients.
- The provider system can also be out of balance in the other direction, where only squeaky wheels get oiled. This happens when highly educated parents

with additional resources can leverage what they want over the objections of the service providers. With legal advocacy, these parents can break a system that is underfunded and reduce options for those who are less vocal or demanding.

A Caution about Equity

From my perspective, it would have been much simpler and better for someone to say, "Here is a voucher for you to purchase or customize whichever services you deem necessary and beneficial for the short- and long-term care of your child. Do what you think is best for your child and your family." In practice, public providers do not trust families to use resources wisely, let alone follow necessary rules to document the proper allocation and effective use of funds.

Should the state pay for costly services for the wealthy? This question raises an important equity concern. Obviously, some parents have much greater resources than others; therefore, the ability to supplement and customize services is not equally available, even if funds were allocated with few strings attached based on the principle of "each according to one's needs." I am sympathetic to this argument, and also recognize that families with significant financial resources have greater options to supplement what the state provides. The recommended course of action is not to reduce options for those with greater resources but rather to increase options and flexibility so those with fewer resources could in fact customize the services received and achieve greater flexibility in designing a system to meet their family's needs.

Tapping New Sources of Understanding

In an article in the *New York Times* (May 8, 2011), Roger Rosenblatt reviews a book by journalist Ian Brown that describes his experiences raising a son with multiple disabilities and chronic illness, having been diagnosed with a rare medical condition called cardiofaciocutaneous syndrome (CFC). Brown's son is tube fed, cannot speak, walk, or dress himself, and is completely dependent on caregivers (his parents) for his daily survival. "In the first eight years of Walker's life, neither parent slept two uninterrupted nights in a row" (Rosenblatt 2011, 1).

Brown's experiences of caring for a son who is chronically ill with multiple disabilities raises many questions about one's humanity and about society's willingness and capacity to care for the weakest and most vulnerable among us. Brown ponders whether it is a measure of man to provide for the "survival of the weakest." Rosenblatt in his book review explains:

> Walker has made the Browns greater people. He has alerted them to the value of living in the here and now. He has helped to enlarge their ethical nature. He has made them aware that in most important things—war, love, death—we are as helpless as

Walker. Nonetheless, for all that and then some, would we assume the care and feeding of Walker Brown? (Rosenblatt 2011, 8)

In talking publicly about our daughter, I recall my wife saying (and my repeating) that the measure of a person's life is less about one's individual accomplishments and more about the ways one person's life affects the lives of others. In this regard, my wife would always say our daughter was not handicapped; rather, she was gifted because she changed the people around her—parents, siblings, teachers, caregivers, bureaucrats—with great ideas concerning social responsibility, chronic care, the meaning of vulnerability, the limitations of medical practice, and so on.

While I have never fully described my own journey as a father, I think that the challenges of the impacts of raising and providing care for a child with severe and chronic disabilities extends beyond my own case, and is much more a story of family, and in particular, a narrative that includes the understanding of how the siblings of a child with severe and chronic disabilities are affected as well.

Why look at siblings as a source of information? "Sibling relationships serve as important contexts for individual development and family functioning" (Kramer and Bank 2005, 483). "The issue of sibling influence, whether on antisocial behavior . . . or on positive development, is far from simple" (Dunn 2005, 655), and researchers are just beginning to explore social processes within the family by which sibling influence is exerted. The significance of these studies is in its potential for understanding what happens in families (Dunn 2005; Kramer and Bank 2005). Lobato, Kao, and Plante (2005) report:

> The impact of child's illness or disability on sibling emotional and behavioral functioning is multilaterally determined, influenced by characteristics of the sibling and sibling dyad, the nature and demands of the child's condition, and parental and family functioning . . . siblings of children with chronic illness and disability are more likely than their peers to experience emotional or internalizing symptoms such as depression and anxiety. (625)

Others report that interactions among siblings are affected by the type of disability and the onset of the disability (Seltzer, Greenberg, Krauss, Gordon, and Judge 1997). For example:

> It was found that siblings of adults with mental retardation were significantly more likely than siblings of adults with mental illness to perceive that the brother or sister had a pervasive influence on their life decisions and to evaluate their sibling experience as mostly positive. In addition, siblings of adults with mental retardation had a closer relationship with the brother or sister with the disability than siblings of adults with serious mental illness. Finally, siblings of adults with mental retardation had better psychological well-being when they had a close relationship with the brother or sister. In contrast, siblings of adults with serious mental illness had more favorable psychological well-being when they perceived a less pervasive impact of the brother or sister on their life. (395)

The authors conclude that "structurally similar family roles—in this case, being a sibling to an adult with a lifelong disability—have markedly different effects depending on the specific features of the care giving context" (404).

Important and unexplained effects of disability and chronic illness on families and particularly on siblings are needed to understand more fully the implications for services (Dyson 1991; Sharpe and Rossiter 2002). The significance of siblings' relations in families points to one added source of understanding for service needs, and more detailed descriptions of how chronic disabilities are experienced by a sibling or among multiple siblings growing up in a family with a brother or sister with a chronic illness and developmental disability are needed. I would argue that with multiple siblings, different social and psychological responses are possible and even likely between or among siblings.

Sibling relationships are thus an important context for understanding individual development and family functioning (Kramer and Bank 2005). Little research, however, has examined these sibling interactions within families in connection to severe disability and chronic illness. I would suggest that having a sibling with a lifelong disability is a double-edged sword: siblings are likely to receive less parent time and fewer resources because of what is required in the care of a disabled brother or sister; at the same time, siblings gain a new potential for understanding themselves and expressing their humanity.

CONCLUSION: FINAL THOUGHTS ON SERVING CHILDREN WITH SEVERE DISABILITIES

I have spent most of my career thinking and writing about education and leadership. I have worked in schools, colleges, and state government, as a teacher, professor, administrator, and bureaucrat. I assist in the preparation of future administrators, and I structure professional development for novice and experienced administrators. In my experience, practitioners are expected to be in control of actions and events under their purview and responsibility. School administrators expect to be held accountable for school-site stability and control. Teachers expect to be in control of their classrooms. Government workers expect to be in charge of their programs and services.

Without powerful incentives, stakeholders resist collaboration so they can preserve their individual control over their respective domains. The boundaries between family and provider, and among school, social service agency, and medical practitioner, make it difficult to introduce a norm that looks at the whole picture. Educators are often unfamiliar with what goes on at other levels of the school system as well as in the community; we see an inevitable undervaluing of the contribution of others to the greater welfare of children. Parents and providers must overcome these tendencies in order to interact effectively to serve children. All must recognize that the welfare of a child with severe and chronic disabilities requires efforts greater than any single person, institution, or agency can provide.

Administration is more than simply managing existing arrangements or keeping fires from burning out of control. If professional practices around service to children with severe and chronic disabilities are to move forward, compliance and control must be replaced with concern for the betterment of the institutions that serve children and families. Political leadership is required to translate guiding ideas into educational practices that engage multiple constituents with different interests and resources. The image of leader as community builder encourages a view of leadership that is deeply distributed among these multiple constituents of services.

This chapter argues for increased interaction among parts of multiple-provider systems based on a better and more complete view of the lives and the circumstances that children and families bring to their requests for services; it advocates for including multiple perspectives on children's lives such as the lives of parents and siblings, and a more complete understanding of the variables that shape the interactions among participants. This strategy recognizes the overlapping responsibilities of parents, teachers, administrators, and other service professionals.

By dealing openly with class and cultural differences, involving parents in decision making and building relationships, adopting respectful practices, and building trusting relationships among all the relevant actors—children, parents, teachers, administrators, and providers—trust can be developed. Trust influences services across providers and recipients (Bryk and Schneider 2002; Tschannen-Moran 2004).

A second recommendation that affects program quality and the usefulness of services is to build user-friendly road maps of the multiple systems engaged in serving children with severe and chronic disabilities. Research already points to the importance of building road maps for parents who have been traditionally underrepresented in order to understand key entry, transition, and exit points (Delgado-Gaitan 2004; Oakes, Quartz, Ryan, and Lipton 2000; Valdés, 1996). For families with children with severe disabilities and chronic illness, building effective plans requires an understanding of the system in four ways: (1) what services are available, (2) how they are accessed and paid for, (3) how success is evaluated, and (4) how these areas articulate within and across multiple providers, agencies, and institutions.

From my experience, the knowledge that grows from professionals' training *and* the wisdom that comes from the experiences of parents and families are both necessary to the crafting of effective road maps that all parties can use to navigate the system, and neither is sufficient by itself. Parents want to learn and they need to know many things: (1) ways that others look at child development, (2) ways to support a child's development, regardless of path taken, (3) ways to communicate with people in positions of authority and control of resources, (4) ways that systems track data and evaluate services, (5) when to seek help or assistance, and (6) what resources are available to their children and family members.

Professionals need to know that the lived experiences of families affect how services are actually utilized in the larger context of family and relationship, and how people share their personal stories. Personal narratives delineate some of the multiple perspectives that parents bring, and they give meaning to their experiences. By writing and sharing examples of their experiences and the experiences of children, siblings, and families at home and in school, parents become teachers as well as learners. These stories present an opportunity to connect the explicit and tacit knowledge associated with family life to the formal ways knowledge is represented in institutional settings.

As people become more aware of the beliefs and assumptions underlying their actions, they are more likely to recognize when their beliefs are unfounded versus when their theories lead to consequences that they did not want or could not explicitly espouse. Stories illustrate the "practical theories," focusing on people in context, how people actually do things, and the changes that result. People's willingness to share their experiences through written narratives and stories depends on the culture of sharing that is developed in a school and the basis of partnership among parents, teachers, and administrators. This knowledge can be used to bridge home and institutional settings. This view argues for a discourse that is respectful of the expertise and wisdom of parents, and thus is one that bridges the personal and the professional. Ultimately, behind all social science explanations and theory lives a personal biography.

QUESTIONS FOR DISCUSSION

1. What assumptions about services for children with severe and chronic disabilities did you bring to your reading of this chapter? How have your understandings and assumptions changed as a result of the reading?
2. Serving children with severe and chronic disabilities often magnifies the conflicts between parents and providers (schools and other service providers). What have you learned from reading the author's perspective, which helps better understand how these conflicts work in actual situations?
3. How do you explain the multiple failures in the delivery of services that are explored in the chapter? Does any specific example resonate with you? If yes, what does this tell you about yourself as an educator, service provider, or advocate?
4. Who is ultimately responsible for providing services to children with severe and chronic disabilities? How do you separate medical, social, and educational needs? Who is responsible for payment? Who is responsible for coordinating medical, social, and educational needs and services?

5. What happens when parents' stated needs for their child are unmet and providers are unwilling to accommodate those needs? Whose judgment should determine which services will be provided?

REFERENCES

Bryk, A., and B. Schneider. (2002). *Trust in schools: A core resource for improvement.* New York: Russell Sage Foundation.

Chavkin, N., ed. (1993). *Families and schools in a pluralistic society.* Albany: State University of New York Press.

Danzig, A. B. (1992). Basil Bernstein's sociology of language applied to education: Deficits, differences, and bewitchment. *Journal of Education Policy* 7 (3): 285–300.

———. (1994). Parents versus professionals: Social class and services to children and families. *People and Education: The Human Side of Schools* 2 (3): 296–319.

———. 2003. Schooling as an embedded institution: Challenges to parent-school-community connections. *Journal of School Public Relations* 24 (Spring): 124–41.

Dauber, S. L., and J. L. Epstein. (1993). Parent attitudes and practices of involvement in inner-city elementary and middle schools. In *Families and schools in a pluralistic society,* ed. N. F. Chavkin, 53–71. Albany: State University of New York Press.

Delgado-Gaitan, C. (2004) *Involving Latino families in schools: Raising student achievement through home-school partnerships.* Thousand Oaks, CA: Corwin Press.

Dunn, J. (2005). Commentary: Siblings in their families. *Journal of Family Psychology* 19 (4): 654–57.

Dyson, L. L. (1991). Families of young children with handicaps: Parental stress and family functioning. *American Journal on Mental Retardation* 95: 623–29.

Epstein, J. L., L. Coates, K. C. Salinas, M. G. Sanders, and B. S. Simon. (1997). *School, family, and community partnerships: Your handbook for action.* Thousand Oaks, CA: Corwin Press.

Garcia, D. C. (1990). *Creating parent involvement: A manual for school children and parents interacting program.* Miami: Florida International University, School of Education.

Gonzalez, G., L. Moll, and C. Amanti. (2005). *Funds of knowledge: Theorizing practice in households, communities, and classrooms.* Mahwah, NJ: Erlbaum Associates.

Henderson, A., and N. Berla, eds. (1994). *A new generation of evidence: The family is critical to student achievement.* Washington, DC: National Committee for Citizens in Education, Center for Law and Education.

Jagger, M., and K. Richards. (1969). You can't always get what you want. Recorded by the Rolling Stones. On *Let it bleed.* LP. London: DECCA Records.

Kirst, M., and M. McLaughlin. (1990). Rethinking policy for children: Implications for educational administration. In *Educational leadership and changing contexts for families, communities, and schools,* ed. B. Mitchell and L. Cunningham, 69–90. Chicago: University of Chicago Press.

Kohn, M. (1969). *Class and conformity: A study in values.* Homewood, IL: Dorsey Press.

———. (1976). Social class and parental values. Another confirmation of the relationship. *American Journal of Sociology* 41: 538–45.

Kramer, L., and L. Bank. (2005). Sibling relationship contributions to individual and family well-being: Introduction to the special issue. *Journal of Family Psychology* 19: 483–85.

Kreider, H. (2002). Getting parents "ready" for kindergarten: The role of early childhood education. Cambridge, MA: Harvard Family Research Project. www.gse.harvard.edu/hfrp/projects/fine/resources/research/kreider.html.

Lareau, A. (1987). Social class differences in family-school relationships: The importance of cultural capital. *Sociology of Education* 60 (2): 73–85.

———. (1989). *Home advantage: Social class and parental intervention in elementary school.* London: Taylor & Francis.

Lobato, D., B. Kao, and W. Plante. (2005). Latino sibling knowledge and adjustment to chronic disability. *Journal of Family Psychology* 19 (4): 625–32.

Mehan, H. (1983). The role of language and the language of role in institutional decision making. *Language and Society* 12: 187–211.

Oakes, J., K. Quartz, S. Ryan, and M. Lipton. (2000). *Becoming good American schools.* San Francisco: Jossey-Bass.

Rosenblatt, R. (2011). The unknowable. Review of Ian Brown's *The boy in the moon: A father's journey to understand his extraordinary son. New York Times*, Book Review, May 8, pp. 1, 8.

Seltzer, M., J. Greenberg, M. Krauss, R. Gordon, and K. Judge. (1997). Siblings of adults with mental retardation or mental illness: Effects on lifestyle and psychological well-being. *Family Relation* 46: 395–405.

Sharpe, D., and L. Rossiter. (2002). Siblings of children with a chronic illness: A meta-analysis. *Journal of Pediatric Psychology* 27: 699–710.

Shartrand, A. M., H. B. Weiss, H. M. Kreider, and M. E. Lopez. (1997). New skills for new schools: Preparing teachers in family involvement. www.gse.harvard.edu/hfrp/pubs/onlinepubs/skills/overview.html, accessed May 3, 2006.

Stotland, J. (1984). Relations of parents to professionals. *Journal of Visual Impairment and Blindness* 78: 69–74.

Tschannen-Moran, M. (2004). *Trust matters: Leadership for successful schools.* San Francisco: Jossey-Bass.

Turnbull, H. R., and A. Turnbull. (1985). *Parents speak out: Then and now.* Columbus, OH: Charles E. Merrill.

Valdés, G. (1996). *Con respeto: Bridging the distances between culturally diverse families and schools.* New York: Teachers College Press.

Waller, W. (1932/1965). *The sociology of teaching.* New York: John Wiley & Sons.

9

Schooling Tommy in the Present

Catherine Hall Rikhye

INTRODUCTION

Things have certainly improved for individuals with disabilities since the 1940s when Tommy was born. The law is now decidedly on Tommy's side. Only a fraction of children with mild disabilities attended public schools in the years prior to the passing in 1975 of the Education for All Handicapped Children Act, Public Law 94-142 (P.L. 94-142). Based on civil rights decisions in the U.S. courts during the 1950s, 1960s, and early 1970s—such as *Brown v. the Board of Education of Topeka, KS* (1954), *Mills v. D.C. Board of Education* (1972), *Pennsylvania Association for Retarded Children v. Commonwealth of Pennsylvania* (1971)—P.L. 94-142 mandated *a free appropriate public education* (FAPE) for all children with disabilities. Following the passing of that law, access to public education became a right for all.

The expansion of P.L. 94-142 in 1990, under the new title of the Individuals with Disabilities Education Act (IDEA), reaffirmed and broadened the mandates, now offering service to children from birth to three years of age and to students transitioning out of school, through the age of twenty-one (IDEA 1990). The IDEA was reauthorized in 1997, and again in 2004, and focused more and more on issues beyond access. Increasingly, the focus for education of children with disabilities became the *quality of education*. The standards movement of the 1990s pressed for higher expectations for all students, that is, those with and without disabilities. In 1997 the IDEA highlighted, among other issues, the alignment of special education with general education standards and expectations.

The 2004 reauthorization of the IDEA went even further, requiring that the IDEA align with the No Child Left Behind Act, the federal general education law. Now all students with disabilities are expected to follow a course of study that aligns with the general education curriculum and take assessments that will be published and reflected in data of the schools they attend. Students with disabilities have at last become visible. Beyond these students' merely attending public schools, their outcomes at school would be held up to the light; schools would be explicitly accountable for the students' educational success as defined by assessments and by graduation rates.

Further, all the education laws that focused on students with disabilities from 1975 onward stressed the significance of placing students in the least restrictive environment (LRE). The IDEA defines LRE as follows:

> To the maximum extent appropriate, children with disabilities including children in public or private institutions or care facilities, are educated with children who are *non*disabled; and special classes, separate schooling or other removal of children with disabilities from regular educational environment occurs only if the nature or severity of the disability is such that education in regular classes with the use of supplementary aids and services cannot be achieved satisfactorily. (20 U.S.C. Section 1412 (5)(B))

Thus, the mandate requires that children attend schools with their able-bodied peers and, to the degree possible, participate in general education classrooms with supports and services that would assist them in accessing the general education curriculum. The first choice for placement of students with IEPs (Individualized Education Programs) is always the general education classroom with more restrictive placement coming afterward. Oversight for putting LRE into practice is left to individual states and local districts.

It would appear, then, that if Tommy were born today, he would be in a good position to participate fully with his typical peers in the demanding curriculum of an age-appropriate general education classroom, receiving the related services and other supports necessary to ensure his success in that classroom. According to the law, Tommy could succeed without the substantial personal supports he had received from his family in the 1940s. At that time, and in the absence of mandates ensuring educational access, the family's vision and advocacy had ensured Tommy's success. He had internalized their expectations for his success despite physical disabilities.

The fact that individuals in the education system were reluctant to welcome Tommy or simply to educate him ultimately could not deter him. He had internalized a vision of his own capacities and of his future that could not be suppressed. Thus, Tommy's own strength of character and personality certainly played a role in his eventual success. But of course it did. His personal qualities were of enormous significance in his challenge of prevailing norms and in his achievements that went so far beyond common expectations.

However, there is no doubt that the family he was born into—its financial resources and attitudes toward his achievement—played a significant role in his ultimate success. Unsupportive, insulting teachers and bus drivers who refused to allow him onto the school bus were, in the end, no match for the strength of purpose his family had fostered in him and that he had internalized.

The question now is: Have things changed so much since the 1940s that whatever family Tommy had been born into, given the overwhelming changes in laws and the assurances provided by the mandates, the educational system itself would assure him access and support to optimize his potential? Let us consider three scenarios that could inform the answer to this question.

SCENARIO 1: AN URBAN SETTING

Tommy is born into an urban lower-middle-class family with restricted resources. He grows up under the mandates of the IDEA. He is identified with physical disabilities shortly after his birth while he is still in the regional hospital. Tommy is identified as requiring special services for infants born with disabilities. Under Part C of the IDEA, he and his family are provided with early intervention services including physical therapy, occupational therapy, and a Special Education Itinerant Teacher (SEIT). Services are provided at home, at the early childhood developmental center at the hospital and, later, at his integrated preschool. As he approaches his fifth birthday and nears kindergarten age, Tommy is seen by a team of evaluators at the Committee for Preschool Special Education (New York State Department of Education 2001, 32).

He is classified as having orthopedic impairments and multiple disabilities. The team considers available placement options and, although aware of the LRE requirement, finds that Tommy will require a number of support services that can be most easily provided in a self-contained setting where access to related service providers is more easily achieved. Thus, the evaluation team recommends that Tommy attend a self-contained classroom where he might receive the intensive related services that would benefit him and that are available at the site, as well as the one-to-one attention the team believes would support him optimally.

Tommy's parents are pleased that he will continue to receive services at school and are relieved he will be in a safe and secure environment. Both parents hold two jobs, switching off night and day shifts to attend to Tommy and his siblings. Tommy attends classes from kindergarten onward. His teachers present material that aligns with the general education curriculum. Tommy is in a classroom with seven other children who have been determined to have similar needs. He does not have access to nondisabled peers and the vast quantity of incidental learning that comes from being around typically developing children.

He receives much support from one of the three paraeducators assigned to the class who helps above and beyond his need for assistance (Giangreco, Luiselli, and MacFarland 1997). The paraeducator who supports him is eager to help Tommy and perceives his position as providing maximum help to Tommy. The paraeducator does not realize, nor has he received professional development to help him recognize, the importance of fostering independence in the students he serves. The special educator who manages this instructional team is equally focused on caring for her students rather than supporting their independence.

Tommy's third-grade teacher notices that he has a substantial understanding of concepts in math. Informally, she asks her friend, a general education third-grade teacher, if she would mind if Tommy attended math lessons in her class as long as the paraeducator accompanies him. He is welcomed into the third-grade math class and does very well. He loves being there.

In subsequent years, Tommy's teachers are not inclined to integrate him into general education classrooms; and, as it is determined that he cannot take standardized assessments, he remains in self-contained classrooms through high school. When he reaches transition age, a meeting is held with United Cerebral Palsy and his IEP team during which a transition plan is designed for Tommy.

From 2007 to 2009, an increase from 74 percent to 91 percent occurs in the number of students with disabilities that actually had an IEP in which the "Transition Page in the IEP is not Left Blank" in this urban district. In 2007, 4 percent of IEP meetings for students of transition age had "Outside Agencies [are] Included in Planning Meeting" in keeping with the IDEA mandates; in 2009, this number went down to 1 percent (Advocates for Children 2011, 4). Thus, it is considered a bonus that Tommy has a transition plan in place and that an adult service agency participates in the IEP meeting.

His parents decide that upon graduation at the age of twenty-one, Tommy will attend a day-habilitation program, with busing to bring him back and forth to the day program location. His program there will focus on functional academics, skills of daily living including grooming and hygiene, nutrition, simple cooking, shopping and budgeting, community experiences with supports, first aid, and other topics considered age appropriate. Outreach will be made to group homes in the area, and his name will be placed on a waiting list. Since it often takes ten years or more on the waiting list for a space to become available at group homes, by the time Tommy is in his late twenties, he will hopefully obtain a place.

Analysis

The IDEA supports Tommy in pursuing an education in the least restrictive environment, alongside his nondisabled peers where he might best access general education curriculum and where expectations for him might be optimal. However, in the absence of an advocate, Tommy's already overburdened parents do not negotiate for a change of program for him. Throughout the classification and placement sequence, Tommy's family or informed public school professionals would have to advocate for the most suitable placement for Tommy. Such a placement would depend on the knowledge base of Tommy's family and school personnel as well as their willingness to understand and then to challenge the system.

Committees on special education often place students on the basis of existing programs and available seats, rather than on the optimal appropriateness of the placement. At times, since committee members are not aware of all available placements and supports, they are concerned with finding a seat in a school before the legal timeline runs out; then they are held liable for not adhering to the established timeline for placement, enabling the family to seek private school placement at the Department of Education's expense (Advocates for Children 2001).

Multiple pressures prevent the stakeholders from searching for the best placement for Tommy. If the family had the resources or the time to identify legal counsel, they could argue for a different placement. However, overwhelming responsibilities and unawareness of the variety of programs available limit their ability to identify such a program. The Committee on Special Education has similar limitations.

In a large urban center, the Committee on Special Education is responsible for placing large numbers of children in school seats. In addition to what may be their limited knowledge base about all available programs, restrictions include the amount of time they have to make a workable decision about a student's placement (New York City Department of Education 2002). All stakeholders in Tommy's educational choices are, to some degree, at the mercy of the system and the systemic limitations within which they operate.

Once Tommy is in school, his path is largely prescribed and he is unlikely to access the opportunities available to—but not necessarily always exploited—by families who have greater means or greater access to or time for advocacy.

SCENARIO 2: A SUBURBAN SETTING

Tommy is born into a comfortable upper-middle-class household in a thriving suburban school district. Tommy's father is an attorney and his mother is a homemaker. During his early development, Tommy is supported by the mandates of the IDEA and receives a rich array of therapies with Special Education Itinerant Teacher (SEIT) services provided in the home. A special educator works with Tommy's mother and is able to teach her successful strategies and techniques to ensure that even in the absence of direct services, supportive strategies are in place and maintained.

For example,

- the occupational and physical therapists work together to find optimal lying and sitting positions for Tommy;
- they teach Tommy's mother massage techniques to relax Tommy so he can better attend to and interact with his environment;

- the speech therapist works with the occupational and physical therapists and Tommy's mother to achieve the best position for Tommy to breathe and vocalize;
- the team develops optimal positioning and strategies that will support Tommy's oral-motor skills better to ingest food and to speak.

Role release has been described as the "assigning of specific tasks and methods usually performed by one person on a child's team to other team members" (McEwen 2000, 67). The SEIT and the occupational and physical and speech and language therapist who support Tommy implement the practice of role release. They teach Tommy's mother key strategies and assign her specific tasks, using their recommended strategies to employ throughout the week at times when they are not present (Bowser and Roberts 2003). Thus, the practices that the related service providers recommend can be extended to support Tommy during all his waking hours beyond the time the therapists give direct services to support him. The luxury of time allows for remediation on an ongoing and uninterrupted basis.

Tommy is enrolled in a private inclusive early childhood program where he begins to interact with his nondisabled peers from a very early age. He enjoys participating in their celebrations and parties and is invited to their homes for playdates. Tommy forms friendships with the children in his class, and many of them will follow him into elementary school.

Before he is enrolled in his local elementary school, Tommy's parents meet with his preschool general and special education teachers, his SEIT leader, and his related service providers to discuss the best alternatives for supporting Tommy as he enters public school. After determining with the team the optimal scenario for Tommy's entry into kindergarten, Tommy's parents meet with the Committee on Preschool Special Education where the family is ensured that Tommy will attend a general education kindergarten and receive integrated related services and Special Education Teacher Support Services.

Thus, Tommy's parents and the team that supports him have already determined the services he will require as he enters public elementary school. The Committee on Preschool Special Education is eager to assist them in obtaining services. They have a manageable number of children entering public school in need of review and thus can do a thorough analysis of Tommy's needs well within schedule.

Tommy will attend a well-funded school. According to the U.S. Census Bureau, New York State—with the highest per-student expenditure of the fifty states (United States Census 2006, issued 2008, 8)—had per-student expenses in 2006 that varied from approximately $11,000 to $17,000 (U.S. Census Bureau 2006, issued 2008, 104). For a class of twenty-five students, this per capita difference would amount to $125,000 per class per year, depending on where a family lives and where a school is located. Utah, the state with the lowest per capita student expenditure, varied from a low of $4,918 per student to $6,386. Again, when this difference of $2,532 per student is multiplied in a class of twenty-five students, it amounts to a sizable $63,300 per classroom per annum.

Further, state sources of support account for 46.6 percent of funding for public schools whereas local sources of support amount to 44.4 percent of funding. Of this sum approximately 38 percent is provided by local taxes (U.S. Census Bureau 2006, issued 2008, ix). In locales with high local taxation, where local district decisions favor a large percentage of local taxes being devoted to public education, schools will benefit significantly from the differences in public school funding that persist across the United States.

Hence, the district in which Tommy's family lives is well known for the litigiousness of its families. School district administrators for the schools serving these families understand that services must be provided or they will be engaged in expensive and protracted legal battles. Most often, school district administrators are eager to preempt litigation. Thus, Tommy's family is looking forward to having a special education teacher who will support Tommy for two hours a day and provide related services per his IEP in the classroom. A technology evaluation has also been recommended.

Tommy thrives in elementary and secondary school, being fully included in all aspects of curricular and extracurricular life. When he reaches adolescence, a transition plan is put in place for him with his instructional team and United Cerebral Palsy, the agency that will support him in postschool years. The plan addresses postschool options as stated in the IDEA, including college education, living arrangements and needs, vocational sampling during the summer months, transportation, related service needs, and technological supports.

Tommy's school uses resources including a college counselor and an onsite test-preparation course to prepare him to take the Scholastic Aptitude Test (SAT) required for application to colleges that he would like to attend. He joins a student focus group whose members practice responding to college interview questions; they work together to develop their applications and their application essays. Tommy's family also obtains the services of a private college counselor who assists him in formulating a list of potential colleges and helps him refine his college essay. Since Tommy receives acceptances from a number of his college choices, his options are open. He is on his way to a rich and positive life.

Analysis

Tommy's parents are well informed about their rights and options at Tommy's birth. They have the perspective, the means, and the time to engage in proactive advocacy on behalf of Tommy. The IDEA supports Tommy in pursuing an education from the time of his birth and enjoying the supports of related therapies and educational services in the home. Because Tommy's mother is able to participate in his services, she can act as team manager, and she learns from the specialists the strategies and techniques that will best support Tommy's access to his environment and his ability to respond optimally to it.

The law supports Tommy's pursuit of education in the "least restrictive environment" alongside nondisabled peers, where he might best access the general education curriculum and where expectations for him might be optimal. Tommy's parents use the law to its fullest potential in advocating for the most suitable placements for Tommy as he moves from preschool to elementary and secondary school. They are savvy consumers and knowledgeable about using the education system to optimize Tommy's learning experiences.

The Committee on Special Education in his well-to-do suburban environment is ready to support Tommy's receiving all required services in a general education classroom. They agree with the decisions that have already been discussed by the instructional team where Tommy will be attending school. Further, in a relatively small community, Tommy's family is friendly with the families of his schoolmates, many of whom they already know from preschool. All the stakeholders in Tommy's educational choices are knowledgeable about the mandates of the law. Further, with a difference of approximately $100,000 per annum per classroom, considerable resources are devoted to Tommy's needs and to those of his classmates. Once Tommy is in school, his path is largely prescribed. He will access the opportunities available to families who have greater means and/or greater access to or time for advocacy.

SCENARIO 3: A RURAL SETTING

Tommy is born to a family living on a subsistence income from farming in a rural area far from any urban center; he is born at home with a local nurse providing assistance. Issues of atypical development are noted at birth. Tommy stays at home during his preschool years, playing in his family's yard and being watched over by his mother and older siblings. Until he begins to attend school, he is not identified as requiring any particular supports. His parents and siblings provide him with a great deal of attention and enjoy his company, as he does theirs, and they include him in all family activities.

Tommy's father states that he had "seen many of God's creatures born on the farm who were different," and he believes Tommy is one of God's creatures. Tommy's parents see him within the range of a normal continuum of atypical to typical, and view diversity as part of a fact of life (Mierendorf 1996). Tommy never receives early intervention services per the mandates of the IDEA, nor do his family and the early intervention team develop an Individualized Family Support Plan (IFSP) or, later, an Individualized Education Program (IEP).

When Tommy reaches school at age six, he is sent to first grade in the single-room schoolhouse closest to his home that serves students from first grade through high school. The school is located ten miles from his home, and a bus passes by on a road down the hill from his parents' farm daily to pick him up and transport him to and from school. Tommy is first identified as having disabilities when he arrives for the first day of school in September.

He continues to attend class while the school's teachers and administration try to contact the state Department of Education to request services for Tommy in the way of a physical and speech therapist. After they wait for several months, a physical therapist who serves this part of the state is identified. The physical therapist spends many hours per week traveling all over the state to provide services to children identified as needing support. He is able to come once a week to support Tommy directly and to provide suggestions to Tommy's teachers on how best to position Tommy for optimal learning.

The search for a speech and language therapist is less successful. Very much in demand, a therapist becomes available only as Tommy attends third grade. In this case too, the therapist serves a large geographic area and comes once a week for a half-hour period to provide services and make recommendations to Tommy's teachers. Role release, or the "assigning of specific tasks and methods usually performed by one person on a child's team to other team members" (McEwen 2000, 67), is a desirable strategy. Role release, ensuring that multiple team members can carry out recommended supports and that no one individual has sole control over any aspect of the child's development, is one of several recommended strategies for the appropriate provision of integrated related services (Haggart 2001; Hazelgrove 1998). However, in this case, role release occurs partly as a result of the scarcity of available therapists rather than by design.

Tommy attends class with all the other children in his catchment area and proceeds from grade to grade along with them. His attending a self-contained special education environment is not considered as this separate service is not available in his school. Tommy participates with his classmates in all curricular and extracurricular activities that the transportation schedule for the school bus service permits. He is viewed from the outset as a valuable member of the community and he enjoys friendships throughout his years at school. While his physical condition is not optimal and his muscles contract to some degree, Tommy excels in basic academic skills and is diligent in completing school tasks. His siblings help him complete assignments and his family massages him regularly to make him feel more comfortable.

In approaching graduation, Tommy looks forward to his life on the farm, helping out with chores and interacting with family and community members. It is taken for granted that some member of his family will always be there to support him and that he will continue to live on the farm with his parents and siblings. He has a clear adult role as a member of his family and his community.

Analysis

Tommy's parents are well aware of Tommy's differences from the time of his birth. They welcome Tommy into the family and see his disabilities as part of nature. Although Tommy does not benefit from early intervention services or from the ongoing services of related service providers, he does profit from being part of a close-knit family and a vibrant community. Supports are provided by his family and are seen as an integral part of ongoing life on the farm.

When Tommy begins to attend school, the instructional team is aware of needed services. However, while the team seeks out and is able to access services, they can be delivered only as part of the state education department's efforts to supply therapy across a broad geographic area. Service professionals are few and far between and provide only itinerant services to students widely spread across the region.

Although Tommy does not receive optimal supports because of the logistic issues of service provision in sparsely populated rural areas, Tommy obtains many other benefits from attending school. He is part of an inclusive classroom with ongoing access to the general education curriculum and to positive peer interactions. With natural supports from peers and teachers in the context of the ongoing curriculum, Tommy learns the standard curriculum along with his typical peers. He also participates with his peers in all of school life including extracurricular activities.

By virtue of living in an area that has few special services for students with disabilities, Tommy shares busing and all other school activities with his peers. He is able to learn many skills spontaneously through his peers as well as from his teachers. Most significantly, he is a valued member of his community both at home and at school.

After Tommy graduates from high school, he is expected to live on the farm with his family and participate in agricultural work. This path is in keeping with that of the majority of his peers, many of whom will also continue to live with their families and find work locally on the family farm or in small local businesses. It is anticipated that Tommy will assist with work on the farm and will continue to live on the farm, and that his parents and his siblings will continue to support him as needed. His future seems largely prescribed, as is that of most of his peers. They live in a close-knit community with secure, reliable, interdependent social ties, and Tommy is very much one of its integral members.

CONCLUSION

We return now to the question posed earlier in this chapter: given the overwhelming changes in laws and the assurances provided by the mandates, can the educational system itself assure Tommy access and support to optimize his potential no matter what the circumstances of location, context, family support, and resources?

A consideration of the three scenarios suggests that laws and mandates that have been put in place during the last three decades of the twentieth century and the beginning of the twenty-first century ensure equal access for all students, including those students with a disability, to a free appropriate public education (FAPE) with the provision of supports and services necessary to access the general education curriculum.

Tommy is certainly better off at the beginning of the new century than he was in the middle of the past century. Increasingly, but not unfailingly, Tommy and his family do not have to suffer the vagaries of teachers who are unwilling to teach him and bus drivers who refuse to transport him to and from school. So parents can demand better services and, held to the dictum of the law, they will receive better services.

The national movement toward more inclusive classrooms has also helped provide Tommy's family with models of and options for integrated learning opportunities. Tommy can now learn alongside his nondisabled peers in general education classrooms. Here, he will have greater access to the general education curriculum and will benefit from a rich interactive environment in which he can learn from his peers and they from him.

In all three scenarios, instructional teams were aware of the potential benefits of related and specialized services to improve Tommy's learning environment and the facilitation of his access to that environment. Further, there was a burgeoning appreciation for the benefits of teaming and collaboration among general and special education teachers, administrators, related service providers, and Tommy's family. The legal and systemic infrastructures exist to provide Tommy with the sum of needed services and supports, access to curriculum, the possibility of a wide circle of relationships, and the potential to develop the skills needed for transition to a productive postschool life.

While major advances have been made in ensuring Tommy access to a better education than he had in the 1940s and 1950s, significant gaps among individuals and among systems still prevent equal access to appropriate education. The three scenarios highlighted a number of factors that could influence the participation in and access to a free and appropriate public education by an individual with disabilities.

Resources and Equity

Without question, personal and community wealth make a difference in the provision of and access to services. Family resources also provide time for families to utilize the available services optimally. We have seen how the difference of a few thousand dollars per student can multiply significantly when these dollars are considered per classroom per annum.

Personal wealth also provides the expectation of service delivery, as families with greater personal resources have the money to obtain legal and educational expertise and counsel to support their children and maximize their use of the mandates to the advantage of their child. Families who do not have the time or the means to explore options and ensure the best services are in place for their child are at a distinct disadvantage. Structures must be developed at all levels of education systems to help families understand service options and to support them in accessing services to support their child.

Advocacy

Knowledge of the mandates and of available services and programs is essential for both the family and for the professionals who serve a child at every level of the system. It is vital for service providers to know the law and to have a broad understanding of existing programs and of new programs that need to be developed to best support students with disabilities across the age span. Further, both the family and the educational professionals should advocate for developing a quality of life and of learning that will most benefit the student.

This goal can be accomplished only if all stakeholders are knowledgeable about desirable educational options, services, and supports, and by encouraging them actively to demand the needed services. Self-advocacy skills must also be taught to students so that they can become active participants in and architects of their present and future life course and quality.

Related and Other Support Services

Families and professionals need to know about available services in order to use these services to best advantage by ensuring they are delivered. Instructional team participants should collaborate and, together, learn and plan the most effective strategies and techniques to use with a particular student. We have seen scenarios in which services are (1) present but not well integrated into a meaningful and holistic educational program, (2) only intermittently available but used maximally, (3) available in compliance with the law but not well integrated into a well-rounded instructional program, and (4) used to exploit every possible advantage for a student.

Inclusive Classrooms

Significant differences exist among states and districts regarding the availability of inclusive schools. Some school systems are far behind others in providing any kind of inclusive classrooms. School districts vary greatly in the kinds of inclusive classrooms and inclusive supports they provide and in how successful they are in delivering educational services to all students.

The three scenarios explore very different practices and philosophies regarding inclusive education. However, in all three scenarios, students with and without disabilities benefit from learning together. In all three scenarios Tommy gains both academically and socially.

Professional Quality

The issue of professional quality and expertise is one of the foundations of the No Child Left Behind Act. Certification has long been the standard by which professional quality is defined, with teacher evaluation recently coming to the fore as another gauge of professionalism. The three scenarios present teachers with very diverse levels of professional quality and knowledge.

Unquestionable needs exist to provide sufficient preservice and in-service professional training and development to level the playing field in terms of professional instructional skills and to achieve a more unified philosophical orientation toward inclusive education to ensure implementation across the diverse communities of this country.

Community Supports

Building a sense of community and belonging is essential to the well-being of all students and of all instructional team members. A sense of a cohesive vision, shared goals, and alignment of purpose is vital for all school communities and all stakeholders participating in the school community. The three scenarios present very different pictures of joint purpose and of the valuing of individuals within the system.

What the rural community lacks in resources is offset by its strong sense of person-centered supports, civic-mindedness, and common purpose. Many reasons can explain why this might be easier to manage in a small, homogeneous society than in a large, diverse, and disparate municipality. However, within a single school, regardless of its location, building community and interdependence as well as valuing individual constituents must be a primary and core objective.

SUMMARY

The six components that emerge as significant in the three scenarios should be considered as we develop supportive instructional systems for students with and without disabilities. Tommy and his classmates, as well as their families and the instructional teams that support them, would all benefit from greater equity in accessing educational resources. To exploit the powerful mandates of existing laws, families and instructional teams should be able to activate them more equitably. Tommy and his family have enjoyed great advances in accessing supports and services from the 1940s and 1950s to the turn of the twenty-first century. Important, too, in the coming decades, is that we should work to ensure that Tommy and his family can look forward to greater parity of participation in a rich educational experience, whatever their income, context, or community.

QUESTIONS FOR DISCUSSION

1. Based on these three scenarios, how is special education linked to resources and funding?
2. What are the benefits and drawbacks to a person with a disability living in an urban setting? A suburban area? A rural community?
3. How do the IDEA mandates support families of and children with disabilities? What are the limitations of the IDEA as seen in these three scenarios?
4. How is disability defined in these three scenarios? How does that definition shift depending on context?
5. What is the role of legislation and advocacy, and family and community, in supporting students with disabilities?

REFERENCES

Advocates for Children. (2011). *Out of school and unprepared: The need to improve support for students with disabilities transitioning to adulthood.* New York: Author.

Advocates for children special education questions. (2001). www.advocatesforchildren .org/resource/specialfaq08.php3.

Bowser, G., and D. Roberts. (2003). Aspects of role release in the provision of services to young children: A concept paper offered by the Collaborative Teaming Work Group. Oregon Early Intervention and Early Childhood Special Education Programs. www.rsoi.org/Documents/Aspects%20of%20Role%20Release%20in%20the%20Provision%20of%20Services%20to%20Young%20Children.PDF.

Brown v. Board of Education of Topeka, KS, 347 U.S. 483 (1954).

Giangreco, M .F., T. E. Luiselli, and S. Z. C. MacFarland. (1997). Helping or hovering? Effects of instructional assistant proximity on students with disabilities. *Exceptional Children* 64 (1): 7–18.

Haggart, A. G. (2001). *Integrated therapies.* Hampton, NH: AGH Associates.

Hazelgrove, J. (1998). *What is integrated therapy?* May/June. education.wm.edu› Articles › Consultation/ Collaboration.

Individuals with Disabilities Education Act, P.L. 101-476, 104 Stat. 1103 (1990), now codified, as amended, at 20 U.S.C. § 1400–91 (2006).

Individuals with Disabilities Education Act Amendments, P.L. 105-17, 111 Stat. 37 (1997), now codified, as amended, at 20 U.S.C. § 1400–91 (2006).

Individuals with Disabilities Education Improvement Act, P.L. 108-446, 118 Stat. 2647 (2004), now codified, as amended, at 20 U.S.C. § 1400–91 (2006).

McEwen, I., ed. (2000). *Providing physical therapy services under Parts B & C of the Individuals with Disabilities Education Act (IDEA)*. Oklahoma City, OK: American Physical Therapy Association Section on Pediatrics.

Mierendorf, M., producer. (1996). *Without Pity*. DVD. Films for the Humanities & Sciences.

Mills v. D.C. Board of Education, 348 F. Supp. 866 (D.D.C. 1972).

New York City Department of Education. (2002). *Standard operating procedures manual*. New York: Author.

New York State Department of Education. (2001). *Part 200 regulations*. Albany, NY: Author.

No Child Left Behind Act of 2001, 20 U.S.C. Secs. 6301 et. seq. (2001).

Pennsylvania Association for Retarded Children v. Commonwealth of Pennsylvania, 344 F. Supp. 1257 (E.D. Pa.1971).

U.S. Census Bureau. (2006, issued in 2008). *Public education finance report*. Washington, DC: Author.

IV

POLITICS OF THE FUTURE

Part IV provides a vision of special education in the future as the personal perspectives of providers and consumers in the arena of special education are juxtaposed and compared. With competition for scarce resources always on the minds of stakeholders in the process of educating children with disabilities, this book will end with a description of the best system to educate them. We observe how Tommy, whom we met in chapters 2 and 9, fares in this ideal system.

Chapter 10, "Voices from the Field: Students Speak Out," explores the stories of students with disabilities. These narratives focus on the types of special education that consumers and ex-consumers of the current system experienced. As stakeholders who were often challenged, turned away, or intimidated by the cultural and contextual borders in the special education system and sometimes coerced into accepting mediocre solutions that did not fulfill their needs, their perspectives are especially important.

Chapter 11, "Voices from the Field: Parents Speak Out," delves into the stories of parents of children with disabilities. These accounts, in the parents' own words, describe their encounters navigating the special education system. Often challenged, turned away, or intimidated by school district personnel into accepting inadequate solutions to their children's learning difficulties, these parents offer essential perspectives.

Chapter 12, "Voices from the Field: Education Professionals," investigates stakeholders' professional experiences with, and personal beliefs about, educating children with disabilities. Their professional and personal ideas about future directions in educating children with disabilities—both practical and ideal—including those to improve or replace the IDEA, are explored. The politics involved in removing the cultural and contextual borders that divide stakeholders involved in the education of children with disabilities are discussed. Stakeholders include school administrators, other professional school personnel, attorneys, advocates, professors, and others who provide direct service to children and their parents.

Chapter 13, "Schooling Tommy in the Future: The Ideal," reflects on the narratives of the stakeholders participating in chapters 10, 11, and 12. Their voices focus on the types of special education system consumers and ex-consumers of the current system experienced and would like to experience in the future. A new model for creating the ideal future of special education is introduced—which draws on humanistic educational psychology, an ethic of caring, and a critical analysis of the political issues raised in previous chapters—to create an ideal system to educate children with disabilities. Last, we observe how Tommy, whom we met in chapters 2 and 9, should fare in the ideal system of the future.

10

Voices from the Field

Students Speak Out

Carol Strax

Chapters 10 and 11 are stories told by children with disabilities and parents of children with disabilities who speak out in their own voices on the subject of special education. As stakeholders in the system, they were often intimidated, forced to accept inappropriate solutions to education placements, and placed in adversarial positions to get services to which they were entitled.

With the advent of all the special education laws, considerable progress has been made in the education and treatment of children with disabilities. For example:

- 1942. A baby is born blue, not breathing, and has obvious weakness of his right arm and leg. There is blood in his cerebral fluid. The father *has to insist* that everything be done to save the baby. Down the hall in the waiting room is the grandmother. As the obstetrician speaks to her, she experiences joy, excitement, dismay, and horror. He states, "The parents are young and healthy. They can have more children. The baby is better off dead."
- 1947. A little boy bounces up and down excitedly on the sidewalk. He waits for the school bus to pick him up on his first day of school. The bus pulls up to the curb, the door opens, and the bus driver says, "I'm not taking a cripple on my bus." The little boy has cerebral palsy.
- 1955. An adolescent boy with cerebral palsy enters high school. He has to rely on teachers' being supportive and kind—giving him a few extra accommodations. These are personal acts of kindness, not services they are obligated to provide.
- 1959. A young man enters college as the only person on campus with a physical disability. He encounters a small group of people who go out of their way to stop what they consider to be unacceptable—the boy in college.

Society has certainly advanced from those days. But how far have we really come? For example:

- 1987. Parents take their child to a pediatric neurologist for diagnosis. Without interviewing the father or siblings of the child, the psychologist looks at his paperwork and states, "I see that you fit the criteria of *refrigerator mother*: overeducated and lacking emotion."
- 1988. A mom suggests that it doesn't make any sense to get her daughter up, dressed, and off to preschool, only to have to pick her up two hours later because the school won't feed her. It takes an hour or more to feed her lunch. The program director's response: "I don't have to offer feeding if I don't want to and I choose not to."
- 1990. A child has become bigger and cannot sit in a high chair. The child is too old to be held and fed at the same time. An older and used feeder seat with no safety straps is being used. A new chair will not be provided. The child falls on two occasions, face-first onto the floor, resulting in emergency room visits and injury to a child who has no protective reflexes to cushion the fall (a chair would cost less than the emergency room visits).
- 1998. A man said, "I adopted my son from Poland. When we got home I began to realize there was something wrong. He was diagnosed with autism. I called the agency and asked them if they had known, to get some information." They said, "If you can't handle it, send him back and we'll send you another one. Or if you keep him we'll send you another that's OK for free. You just have to pay the airfare." I responded, "Send him back like a shirt that doesn't fit? Like a commodity?" They responded, "It's your choice."
- 2006. A resource room teacher tells her students the reason they are in her class is that they "don't function like regular kids"—their biggest achievement in life would be "working at a grocery store. So sit down and shut up."
- 2009. A mother and her child are eating in a fast-food restaurant. The child, a young adult, has autism. The child is getting louder and louder—repeating words and yelling—while sitting there eating. A woman from the table behind taps the mother on the shoulder and asks, "Do you have other children?" "Yes I do," the mother responds. "Are they older or younger?" the woman asks. "They are all older," the mother answers. The intruder then remarks, "I bet you regretted the decision to have another one; I bet for her whole life you thought about that decision. I bet she wasn't planned."

People were not listening to the voices of parents and children. Teachers, principals, and other educators seldom ask parents and children (1) how they feel, (2) what they are thinking, (3) what their short- and long-term goals are, and (4) how these goals can be achieved. Administrators rarely make them partners in their educational experience.

The stories that follow in both chapters are all real, but the identifying details and names have been changed to protect privacy and ensure anonymity. The essential elements of the stories are told as accurately as possible and in the people's own words. The sad truth is that the stories are genuine. These parents and children have had to endure pain, embarrassment, and isolation—from their disability—in a world that emphasizes perfection and sameness. They were "square pegs" who didn't fit into societal "round holes"—and sometimes that is not acceptable to many people. While identifying details and names have been changed, the voices are theirs. The distinctive phrasing and descriptive language are used because of the power and uniqueness each person contributes.

Common themes emerged while interviewing parents of children with disabilities and students with disabilities. The major themes are:

- Psychological Feelings
- Education Programs
- Conflict
- Transition to Adulthood

PSYCHOLOGICAL FEELINGS

Emotional and Physical Safety

The special education system teaches students with disabilities that they are different and will be safe with others who are *like them*. If the education system now expects, encourages, and legislates by law that students with disabilities should be educated in classrooms with nondisabled peers, then these students need to be assured of a safe environment. Children find it physiologically impossible to learn in an atmosphere where they do not feel secure—physically and emotionally.

Teachers normally try to protect a child from physical harm. What often gets overlooked is protecting a child from *emotional* dangers—being bullied, teased, shunned, and made to feel different and inferior. A good teacher will be aware of what goes on in the classroom and will try to create an inclusive climate in which to nurture and educate the students.

Feelings of Isolation

Many students and parents were made to feel different and isolated because they had a disability or had a child with a disability. People are afraid of what they don't know and they shun those who are different. Educators, in the broadest sense of the term, should advocate for the vulnerable students, teaching people not to tolerate difference but to accept diversity. After all, disability—like race, gender, and ethnicity—is just another diversity.

Self-Confidence

Many programs and activities to boost students' self-confidence are part of school district curricula. However, the way students with disabilities are treated by other students and school personnel has lowered their self-confidence.

Sadness and Grief

Blending in and coexisting with society are not easy for an individual who is different. Both students and parents expressed thoughts of sadness and grief that are a result of their treatment by school system personnel. This sadness was seen on their faces as they told their stories.

EDUCATION PROGRAMS

Diagnosis

Research and documentation show that early intervention is paramount for teaching students with disabilities. Part of this process is diagnosing children at an early age and doing so correctly. Diagnosis, delayed or done incorrectly—over and above delaying intervention—can have a domino effect on children's lives, as seen in some of the stories below.

Education Planning Meetings

The U.S. Congress's intent when it passed the Individuals with Disabilities Education Act was to bring together all stakeholders involved in the education of a child with a disability—such as teachers, parents, special education directors, psychologists, and others—to discuss and plan an appropriate Individualized Education Program (IEP). Parents and children were to be full, equal participants in these meetings. The meetings should provide a supportive environment for parents and children.

Classroom Programs

Many times parents had to come up with their own ideas for placements and programs for their children with disabilities. They found school districts very reticent to talk about parental rights and available placements. Parents did their own research since nobody told them what was available.

Accommodations and Related Services

The IDEA specifically stated that accommodations and related services on a student's IEP must be adhered to. Yet time and again situations where the IEP was neglected had a negative impact on a child's education.

Teacher Interaction

All teachers should be trained appropriately and sufficiently in their college teacher education program to educate children with disabilities. Every teacher should have dual certification—regular education and special education. With the push for inclusion, children with and without disabilities will be in every room, and it is only fair—for both teachers and students—that all teachers know how to teach all students included in their room.

CONFLICT

When hearing the voices—stories and experiences—of parents of and children with disabilities, one would never know Congress's intent of creating a just law with parental participation and the protections of judicial due process. In addition, one could wonder what country—or even planet—the U.S. Supreme Court was on when it saw *Rowley* as proof of parent involvement with children with disabilities in the IDEA process. These narratives give voice to the plight of most Americans—unequal access to legal protections because of race, education level, income, and other socioeconomic factors—here in the land of "freedom and opportunity for all."

The language of the IDEA sets up adversarial situations where parents often have to struggle to obtain services their children are entitled to. Over and over again the language used by parents and students tells of a scenario fraught with sides, teams, and fighting.

TRANSITION TO ADULTHOOD

Transitions—be it from classroom to classroom, school to school, or into adulthood—are often neglected. A discussion should start when the child is in middle school, shaping and changing the plan as the child develops through age twenty-one. So many different layers are involved in the process of transition, particularly into adulthood, that much time and research are needed to set everything in motion.

All parents and students reported that transition planning was not done or not done soon enough, across the board—whether it was a child with a more minor or severe disability. In some cases, had appropriate transitioning been done, students would have fared much better. It was not only a school district issue, but also the state's regulations that impeded the process.

THE STORIES

Below are stories told by Isabella and Marty—two students with disabilities— and one by Moshe and Bentina, a student with disabilities and his mother.

ISABELLA

You can call me Isabella. I will tell you some of the highlights of my life in the special education system as I remember them. I went to preschool for two years because I hadn't reached my full potential yet, and they didn't want me to go into kindergarten. Preschool was great. I had teachers that understood me and let me be a very unique person. I loved preschool.

Then I got to kindergarten. I had a lot of energy, couldn't sit still, and I had attention problems. My mom and I knew there was something wrong, that I wasn't quite like all the other kids, but we expected me to be treated the same as them. My teacher just didn't understand me. There were certain situations—like she made me do a cutting activity over and over again till I got it right. One day my mom brought in cupcakes for my birthday and I was so excited. But for three days in a row, my teacher didn't sing happy birthday to me. It was things like that. You need a teacher to be kind, loving, and understanding when you're in kindergarten. It wasn't her.

I had some difficulty with some verbal math also. But I was so determined. I just wanted to please people. Today, looking at my test scores from back then, I was an average student. I wasn't stupid. My difficulties were focusing, sitting still, confidence, independence, auditory memory skills, grammar, and directions. I didn't understand directions. But I was good at talking and I had social skills. I guess some things don't change.

I was diagnosed at the end of first grade. My mom had to fight for the evaluation. The school said I had a learning disability. Before that they said I had a lot of energy and some challenges in school. They didn't want to test me. My teacher didn't think I was ready to move forward and wanted me to go into a transitional first grade. My mom fought and got me into a second-grade perceptually impaired classroom. That's also when I started to go on Ritalin.

So school went OK. In third grade I had resource room for math and reading and language arts. Those are still my difficult areas today. Elementary school was good. No major problems. I can tell about my middle school years briefly. I had my confidence issues—it wasn't there. I had resource room and some aides in certain classrooms. I remember being given tests verbally in science because I was having trouble.

I guess I don't like to talk about middle school. Middle school was hard. You're adjusting. You don't know who you are. You just try to fit in. My mom didn't fight because she didn't want me to go through any difficulties such as teachers maybe treating me differently and things like that. And I was so scared all the time to ask questions because I didn't want people to think I was stupid or whatever. No one ever said to me, "You're not stupid, Isabella, you just learn differently, that's all."

Certain things in school killed my self-confidence. My mom really tried to involve me in a lot of sports because I was succeeding in sports. So starting when I was about seven, I was in horseback riding, softball, track, and basketball. That way I would have some kind of confidence because it wasn't coming from school. She was just so happy that I had something.

I remember mom always had to fight for everything with the IEP planning team members and my teachers. Then a new director of special education started and he teamed up with her and was on her side instead of being against her and went up against everybody else. I actually still keep in touch with him today. I think it was good for my mom to have someone on her side.

In seventh grade I had an English teacher who would say, "Go home and review chapter 2." So, as a logical thinker I reviewed the chapter. But he wanted us to take notes and answer the review questions. So he thought I wasn't doing my homework for the first two or three months. I thought I was doing what he wanted. Why didn't he say anything right away?

The new director chimed in with my mom and held a meeting. The English teacher said to my mom, "Well, she should be doing her work," and my mom said, "Are you kidding? You're not providing her accommodations. She doesn't get it. This is her IEP. You need to provide her accommodations." I finally got my accommodations in that class.

So, moving on to high school, I was in a biology class and I was in Level Two, which is average. There were five levels, with One being the highest. I was struggling because my teacher wasn't providing any of my IEP accommodations. They wanted me to wait until I failed the midterm in order to move me into a Level Three class. You know what that does to a sixteen-year-old girl's self-confidence? I already had confidence issues. It just wasn't right what they did. Morally, ethically, it wasn't right. I finally got moved. I was the smartest kid in the class, had all As, and was bored. I think if I was just given my accommodations I would have been OK in the Level Two. Of course I didn't know at the time, but they legally had to follow my IEP.

I did have one support period throughout high school. I had one class—it was like a study hall. It was considered Level Five class—five kids in a classroom with one teacher. You were able to ask questions. It was a safe environment where you didn't feel overwhelmed and I loved it. I really loved it. I did have some great teachers. I actually had my preschool teacher in my freshman year. I reconnected with her all those years later. And I had some other great teachers. If it wasn't for those certain teachers I don't think that I would have been able to get through.

I had trouble with geometry in high school, but all the other math classes were good. I excelled in math. I still had trouble with all the reading and comprehension, the processing. Directions and testing are really hard for me. Mom wrote this poem and it's written from her side of the situation or perspective. She used a metaphor of a fence. The people that you have to deal with in special education are the fence. They're blocking me from getting what I need, not helping. My mom's a teacher, and seeing her child treated the way I was treated was so hard. She would do anything to reach her students, and she didn't feel like that was the situation with me.

As a child, I could see how everyone else was treated. How am I supposed to get to that place? It's like looking over to the other side of a fence. These people are not allowing me to get there. They have to be the right people to get me through everything I need to get through. It's scary.

So, back to high school. I had problems with some teachers. One science teacher always gave me a hard time. He could never see that I was a good kid. He looked at my grades and thought that I was a bad kid—I don't do my work. But that was not the case. He couldn't look past that and get to know me as a person and see how eager and willing I was to succeed. He's the one who's supposed to be saying, "Hey, this child needs this accommodation," and I know I wasn't the only one in that class who did. There were maybe three children out of twenty who needed that aide in the classroom. And he's the one who's supposed to say they need it, so supply it or provide it for them. And he didn't do that. So in a way I felt like I was being ganged up on. He didn't watch out for me. That was actually the last science class I took. I didn't need any more to graduate. My mom was just too scared to even have me try new things because of everything that went on.

But I made it through. I waited awhile to go to college because I needed a break. I encountered some great professors in college. They were understanding and let me have my accommodations of extended time on tests, things like that. I'm almost finished now—one year left. We'll see what the future holds. Thanks for listening to my story.

MARTY

Hi. My name is Marty. I'm going to tell you the story of my life as it exists to the present. Let's take a trip down memory lane. I go to school in Anytown, USA. When I was little, I had a hard time in school. I wasn't talking enough. I just couldn't. My mom kept asking the teachers if I was all right and they said yes. But I knew I wasn't and my mom knew. Finally I got tested and I had a speech delay. I received speech [therapy] until I was in the fifth grade. I still have problems, sometimes. Mom says it's like a broken record where I get stuck on a word and can't get it out. That's a pretty good description. They classified me as speech impaired in early childhood and then just a blanket learning disability. My mom asked a number of times about dyslexia and they brushed her off. I was diagnosed with dyslexia as a teenager by someone else, not the school district.

Mom came home one day all upset—she was talking about the Individualized Education Program (IEP) planning meeting and said she felt ambushed. This was before I started kindergarten. I heard her saying, "I thought everything was fine until I went to the meeting. His teacher wasn't there but said the words by phone, 'We think he is ADHD (attention deficit/hyperactivity disorder) and we suggest he goes to a special school.' My mouth dropped open. It was the first I had heard of it. And I had just had a parent-teacher conference two months before. I was blindsided." But she got to keep me in regular kindergarten because the teacher stepped forward and said, "Let me take him in my class and we'll see how he does."

I was in small classes in kindergarten and first grade. It was great. My mom pushed for a physical therapy (PT) evaluation in first grade 'cause the school wasn't going to do it. I ended up getting PT. I was doing really well. The teachers were good, helpful. But I remember an incident that was scary. I woke up one morning and said, "I'm not going to school." I was in first grade and some kids took my lunch money. The school knew and they never told my mom, so I was afraid to say anything at first. My mom had to call and talk to them.

Then I had to go to another school. The class was chaotic, a lot of kids with behavior problems. I heard them tell my mother it would be kids with issues like mine—language problems—but it wasn't. A lot of the kids I went to kindergarten and first grade with went to a different school. But I held my own. I was doing well in class.

Then I heard my mom and the teacher talking about mainstreaming me next year. It was a little scary. I wasn't sure what they meant. Then the IEP planning team said, "Well, why don't we try this year, right now." They put me in a social studies class and the kids were doing maps and other things I had never done. So I felt stupid and scared and asked to go the bathroom all the time. Anything to get out of the class. It just didn't work.

It wasn't my mom's fault. The committee people are the professionals. They are supposed to know what to do. You trust them, at first. One of the aides in my class finally was brave enough to tell my mom not to let them mainstream me next year because I was not working on a third-grade academic level. Thank God someone stepped forward to help. My mom came up with an idea on her own. She asked the school to let me repeat second grade, but start the mainstreaming process. It worked out wonderfully. I excelled.

Now I had to move on to third grade. Nobody gave my mom any information about what was available. She would research everything—look things up, talk to people—and when she went to the IEP meeting she told them what kind of class I should have in third grade. She wanted me in an inclusion class. At one point my mom walked in to an IEP meeting with an advocate because she had been fighting for some accommodation and couldn't get it. Mom presented the information and everything went smoothly. The advocate didn't have to say two words—just being there worked.

It was a little rough with all the tests that had to be done. But my teacher was great; I had a male teacher for the first time, and I discovered a love of reading for the first time. I also got glasses for the first time—no one had ever tested my eyesight in school. They helped a lot.

But another incident happened in third grade. I came home from school crying. I couldn't help it. I told my mom that the boys were saying I liked other boys. They were saying that word to me that I don't even like saying. Mom was upset and called the school. And all the school did was complain because I was crying and acting up. They never did anything to the boys who were teasing me.

I didn't like to play sports. I wasn't into basketball or football. I'm not very good at sports. I'm kind of tall and thin. I liked to read books. I did get into swimming and track. Then I got teased about wearing those shorts and those gay bathing suits. So I kept getting teased. But I'm getting ahead of myself.

I got in trouble in fourth grade for hitting another student. He kept teasing me and I told him to stop or I would hit him. I warned him three times, and then I let him have it. I was the only one who got in trouble. The other kid didn't get in any trouble for teasing me and not stopping.

I still had an IEP in fourth grade. I had trouble with language and grammar. I had test modifications that I was supposed to get but didn't always. So I failed a lot of tests. But I got an 80-something on my report card. My mom called the teacher to ask what was going on. He told her, "If he doesn't get his test modifications, I don't count the test. We have other children in the classroom that can't read and need help and they don't all have IEPs and my assistant can't always spend time with your son." So my mom picked up the phone and called the district special services and told them what was going on. She didn't want to make waves; she just wanted what was right for me. I didn't have any problems the rest of the school year. I really hated fourth grade and I wanted to quit. But my mom told me I was too young to quit school and it would get better.

It did get better in fifth grade. My mom knew I needed to build up some self-confidence, so she got me started on swimming lessons. I ended up on the high school varsity swim team. Mom thought other kids might start to look at me and say, "Oh, OK, he's on the swim team, maybe he's not so bad." I think it was really hard on my mom. But I stayed in an inclusion class and it was good.

I was given a Connor's Scale test in sixth grade by all of the teachers. All the tests showed I had issues with social situations and I was a little bit impulsive and assertive. The teachers would say they encouraged me to sit in the front because I was smart, but I always hung out in the back by myself. But the district didn't do any real testing and let me coast along with a learning disabilities classification.

Then school became hit and miss. I tried. I had the varsity swim team in seventh grade. My coach was there to help me out. The school kept trying to take my accommodations away from me. I did well because I had them. So my mom had to go to bat again. First was when the state took away the test modifications for the English language exam—you can't be read to anymore, spelling and punctuation can't be waived—the district tried to totally take those accommodations off my IEP. My mom had to fight to keep it on for every day of school, explaining the test was only one day. The school also tried to declassify me a bunch of times. They would say, "He's getting As and Bs; he doesn't need his modifications or his classification." My mom knew better and wouldn't let them take anything away.

I was really smart in science and math, so in high school I was in honors math and science. All the teachers kept telling my mom things like, "I've never had a kid like him in my class before. I've never had a kid with an IEP. I don't know how this is going to work. Are you sure you want him in this class?" And, "I've never had a kid like him before. I don't know how I'm going to be able to deal with the test modifications." And, "Oh, he has test modifications? We didn't get the IEPs yet," even though it was already the end of September.

I've heard my mom talking about the IEP planning committee. She feels like the chairperson is totally in control and they don't share information with her. They use unfamiliar language and we never know the results of the tests they give me until she goes into the meeting. Mom knows it's not just her. She works in a school and says how her students' parents don't get their IEPs or progress reports in Spanish. And how sad it is that these parents don't even realize what's going on, what they're entitled to. The parents get totally dumped on because they have no resources. They have no advocates and they can't even speak at planning meetings because they don't speak English.

Mom was really angry once because she was notified about my IEP meeting but couldn't make it at that time because she had to work. It needed to be rescheduled. She told the school a phone meeting wouldn't even be any good because she had to work. They held the meeting anyway. Boy, was she really angry!

Two times the school district sent her the wrong IEP. It was another kid's. And the initials weren't even the same as mine. Not even close. She wanted to know where my IEP went—who got my IEP? The school tried to downplay the whole thing. She was pretty upset then, too.

I'll make a long story short. When I was sixteen, I had a breakdown. I was going into a downward spiral and I didn't know how to stop. I got in trouble for something, lying, I think, and my mom grounded me—told me I couldn't go to a party I wanted to go to. I told her I should kill myself and I told her exactly how I would do it. My mom called the help line. I had more issues in school the next day and the school called mental health and they took me to the hospital emergency room. I saw a therapist but I knew what to say and he told my mom I was OK.

I was in tenth grade and was spiraling downhill pretty fast at that point. A few months later we were back at the hospital because I was threatening suicide. I had to see a psychiatrist at this point. She told my mom I was seeing things and hearing voices. I got put on medication then. But another incident happened that upset me a lot and I left a suicide note in my home and went out into the woods. I didn't really want to kill myself—I was asking for help and I didn't know how.

The police found me and took me to the hospital. Nobody called my mom even though I was a minor. She found me. She never gave up on me. I ended up in a hospital and they put me on another medication. Mom was upset because I was released from the hospital and there was no plan in place. I was still in tenth grade. The guidance counselor knew what was going on, but no transition plan was made because they thought it was too late in the year to put me in IDT [intensive day treatment], where they thought I belonged.

So I went back to school. I had another incident and got sent back to the same place and they upped my medication. I was there for a week. It didn't help me—it made me worse. I was completely coming apart. I went into the cafeteria to sit with my group of friends. They told me, "We can't be friends with you anymore. Our parents won't allow us because you tried to kill yourself." I got really hurt, and angry and upset.

I had another incident with a girl I liked—she turned me down. I ended up back in the hospital for two months. They tested me and said I had anxiety, depression, and was schizoaffective. They also found out I was dyslexic. No kidding, Sherlock! It took them long enough to figure something out.

I was in and out of treatment places and school placements. My medication kept getting changed. The people would tell my mom, "We're only releasing him because we don't feel he's going to hurt himself. Do I think he's going to be okay out there? No. But if we go for a RTF [residential treatment facility] now, they're going to deny it. Follow all the steps you have to follow, it's your only hope to get him in a RTF. We can't keep him here."

My mom was upset because she had to find her own support groups. She went through the Yellow Pages and found places and people to help her. Why couldn't anybody tell her about them? She had to carve her own way, do her own research. The school district told her nothing.

Anyway, I promised you a long story short. I am in a residential placement now, in eleventh grade. I like it here, sometimes. It can be hard—but I think they are helping me. It makes me sad sometimes. I miss my old friends. I told my mom once, "I can't hang with the normal kids. I can't hang with the kids with problems. Where do I fit in this world? Why shouldn't I want to kill myself?" It really upset her. She would try to explain to me that it's hard on other people too, because they don't know what to do. But really, there's not much you can say to make it better.

I know it was hard on her too, being my mom. She'd run into other parents in the store, and they'd ask how I was doing. But they never just picked up the phone and called her. They probably didn't really want to know. They should have just asked her if she wanted coffee. But nobody ever called. Nothing. I guess they really didn't know what to do. They never even called to ask if they could do anything *for her*. I think it hurt her that they gave up on both of us.

There are still issues with my placement. I excel in math. But I had to retake geometry. That's the highest math they offer here. My mom is going to work on (read: fight) for more math. And we have issues about my staying here another year. She wants me to. I'm not sure. I know my mom has my best interests at heart. She's scared. There is no place for me to go when I leave here unless I go home. Nobody ever bothered to talk about transition with her. It was supposed to be done, but wasn't.

I know there is this community-based placement, but because I'm eighteen now, I would have to go in with adults. And I could end up in a house with forty-nine-, fifty-year-olds. It wouldn't be really cool. There's no, and this is what stinks, there is no transition placement that's appropriate. I need a place for eighteen- to twenty-two- or twenty-five-year-olds. So that's another issue my mom has to work on. I would say "fight for," but the places don't even exist. That is one major fight that has to be forged. But there is so much involved with that—it's all political.

So, that is the story of my life up until this point. I am in my residential placement fighting the good fight to stay well and get better. I hope you learned something from listening to my story.

MOSHE AND BENTINA

My name is Moshe and this is my life as a person with a disability. I'm Bentina and this is the story of my son, Moshe—a child with a learning disability.

Moshe: I can remember kindergarten was good. I wasn't able to do the alphabet but it was good. The teacher treated us OK. I got taken out of class to get help with the alphabet 'cause I couldn't keep up. So I got help with reading. Then, in first grade I was almost full special education. You always went at the slowest pace, so in first grade you were still doing kindergarten work. It was ridiculous. It was a big class, too. In second grade we started with three grades in one class and this one teacher fought to get her own room. And it was like a little circle table and that worked out pretty good. It was a small group but she didn't let it drag. Third, fourth, and fifth grade dragged because you always went the slowest.

Bentina: When Moshe was in preschool, the teacher came to me and said that he wasn't catching on as fast as the other kids. Moshe also had a speech problem. So I took him to the pediatrician and he told me to wait a year because he was a boy. So I let it go because he was only three. When Moshe was four, the pediatrician told me the school had an early intervention program that I should take him to. I knew nothing about it. So the school evaluated Moshe and placed him in a special education program—preschool for the exceptional child. That was half days, five days a week—he was there for a year.

While he was there, he had speech and, I think, occupational therapy. He had trouble doing the work. I would do the workbook page with him, and maybe he would grasp it—but when I would go back to the page, he wouldn't remember it. Or he wouldn't get it. And he kept saying it was hard for him and I couldn't understand why because it seemed it should be simple. His evaluation came back with an auditory processing delay and his speech problem. You almost couldn't understand him for a while. I thought he was having trouble learning to read because he couldn't speak, instead of realizing that there was also a problem where he just didn't remember the letters.

In kindergarten he would go to the resource room to get help. I would work with him at home—even cook spaghetti and have him write letters with it before he ate it. I would write out his name in spaghetti, that's how he learned his name.

The school did the Wilson program. But Orton-Gillingham sells a kit for home that I bought and we did that at home. He had a wonderful support system K through second grade—the resource room teacher. She was very hands-on. When Moshe started school he was very visual and hands-on. I remember the teacher telling me that that's not the way the classrooms are set up—for visual hands-on students. And I thought—why not? We want to reach all our students.

One second-grade teacher said to me, "He got a 90 on the placement test." She was shocked. I told her he's not stupid, he has trouble reading. Just because he's got a disability doesn't mean he can't do it—you just have to give him time so he can do it. She actually turned out to be a good teacher.

In the end of third grade, after three years of fighting with the school telling them my child was dyslexic—with the school saying no—the head of the IEP planning team came to me and said, "Did you know your son has dyslexia? Do you understand how severe his dyslexia is?" I said, "No, 'cause I've been an idiot for the last three years. Of course I know."

Something I remember that bothered me—he used to eat all alone by himself in the lunchroom. In K through second grade he ate lunch in the resource room with the other kids. So by the time he got to third grade everyone had their groups at lunch. He didn't have a group. I don't know why they allowed that to go on. My son would say he was fine with it. But how could you let a kid eat all alone like that?

Moshe: Well, middle school totally sucked. It was horrible. You would go into a classroom with like three grades of class because that's how it was. I had some good teachers and one really awful teacher. She would close the door and tell us we weren't like the other kids. We didn't function like them—so shut up and deal with it. She was a bad person and a bad teacher. That was my resource room teacher.

I went to a few IEP planning meetings in middle school. They talked to you like you're some kind of idiot, like you're not even there, and I would always get upset. Also, if you were in special education in middle school they wanted you in special education for everything and they weren't shy about telling you that. They weren't shy about telling you that everyone should be on medication in the class for attention deficit disorder—which they can apparently diagnose themselves.

Someone from the IEP planning team started pulling me out during lunch to work with me. I was in their office. I remember they actually kept a list of everyone who was in special education and next to it if the kid had any siblings on a watch list. It was almost evil what went around that office. It was just wrong. That list with kids and their siblings and some of the phone calls they made, it was like, whoa. The way they would talk about students, like they weren't people, like they were problems. They were on the phone while I was in the office and they would be like, merciless, toward little kids. They thought I would be oblivious—which I am not!

The teachers didn't want us playing with the other kids in the playground. They wanted our group to stay in our group—didn't want us going around and mixing with people. I thought it was madness. Can you imagine that? They didn't want you talking to any kids who weren't in special education. One teacher told me the biggest achievement I could get in life would be working at a grocery store and that if I passed middle school I would be lucky. After that I kind of got a little mean for the rest of the year and I would talk to her like she was an idiot, like a baby or whatever. And she would say, "Why are you treating me like one of you?" The same teacher kept telling us that we kept her up at night with nightmares about us and she couldn't wait until we were out of her class.

I also remember the teacher putting my homework on the board as an example of how not to do stuff. They actually did that a lot, now that I think of it. There was a real mix of kids in our class and it was hard to learn. I said something about it once and I got, "Stop complaining." Well, I can't learn. It was almost easier to go into a mainstream class and struggle through it than to go into a special education class. What surprised me was everyone in the class got the same grade. We all got Cs. If you looked at our binders everybody had a 70 on their paper. I don't think she really graded anything.

It was always the same in middle school—we would come to class, get harassed for not doing our homework, go over what we did, and the teacher would give us a new sheet for homework, and then the bell would ring. We never learned. Every class I had with the resource room teacher—who is the evil teacher—was a waste of my life. I don't look at it as a learning experience. I look at it as a big waste of my life.

In middle school, though, I started using Orton-Gillingham [a special reading program]. It taught me how to read. It wasn't done in school—I did it on my own. My mom found the program and the place to take me. I had a mom who fought for things. I guess most people didn't. Because she found it all and she put me through it. I resented it at first. But, oh, now I can read—thank you. If the school had done Orton-Gillingham from the very beginning it would have been a lot less frustrating and I would have learned to read a lot sooner.

Bentina: Middle school. Wow. Moshe had an awful teacher who told them they were in there because they were stupid and they'd never amount to more than a stock clerk in a grocery store. He had that same teacher for three years— fifth, sixth, and seventh—and in those years I could see Moshe go from wanting to learn to saying, "Whatever." They had behavioral kids in the same room with him and he couldn't learn. The teacher would tell them, "You're useless, you're not going to amount to anything, and you're bad—that's why you're not in the mainstream classes." She used to just belittle them because they were in the re- source room.

Then I heard that the teacher was moving up to eighth grade. So I went to the superintendent—I knew they were doing the schedules. I told him not to put her with the eighth-grade students. Do it now, I know you can still do it. I was told they don't accommodate parent's requests for teachers. I had to threaten him. I told him, "That's fine. I'll have my lawyer contact your lawyer. I may not be rich, but my parents have money. I'll tie this up." It worked. I'm sure he also knew how bad the teacher was.

I would go at it with a friend on the school board. She would complain about the special education programs—the money being spent. But her kids were into sports and it's funny to me so see how the money goes to sports and nobody complains. But where's the reading specialist for the little kids who are going to be in the older grades and are killing your test scores because they can't read? I was told they're a lot of money and half of the found money went to sports. So bring in a teacher part-time. It doesn't make sense to me.

IEP planning meetings when Moshe was in middle school were memorable. The psychologist on the team laughed at me during a meeting. She said I should put my son on Ritalin and I told her I didn't want him on Ritalin. She laughed and said he was on Concerta, what did I think that was? I told her, "You know, I don't have all the answers, I'm trying to keep it all together." That's the first time I ever left a meeting in tears. When I left the meeting in tears, Moshe's teacher from elementary school came after me—she had been sitting in on the committee—and said, "Don't listen to them. He's going to make it. He's going to be fine." She helped me keep it together.

The IEP planning team was fighting with me over his accommodations. They were all riding me. I said to them, "You gotta remember he's a person. I'm a per- son. We argue at night. I'm arguing with my husband, my other child is getting the short end of the stick. What, do you think this is all easy? It doesn't have to be like this." Then they calmed down.

Moshe: High school is very real and it's fun. I go to the IEP planning meetings and I like going. It's actually necessary to go to them. It explains what you're in for next year and what you have available.

I have had some amazing teachers in high school. It's not only the way they teach, it's the fact that they care. They don't do whatever they do just to get a paycheck; they actually care. They'll see you after school, they'll write notes for you—they really go out of their way for you. And one person who really stands out in my mind as I went through everything all these years is my mom. She helped me, steered me along the right path—if she didn't care I wouldn't be anywhere. I would be so out of it, I wouldn't know what I was doing.

I have friends whose parents never really cared what happened to them in school and they are so behind me. I think their parents know but they don't want to know. They don't want to think their kid has an issue—don't want to be a parent of a learning disabled child. I almost think it's a lack of tolerance or just accepting that what you can do is the best. I used to be angry about my disability. I think I was angry about it all the time and then I found out that people who are dyslexic are statistically smarter than people who aren't—then I got happy about it.

I started looking into it, and I think learning from it—nobody could have explained it to me, I had to figure it out myself. I accepted it because you cannot not accept something that you have. When I was in middle school I had crappy counselors who would try to explain it but they didn't know how to phrase things to little kids. The counselors would say, "You don't work the way other people work. You're slow." When I heard "slow" I thought they meant "mentally retarded." They should have said, "It takes you longer." So it was actually better not to hear anything from them.

Bentina: High school is better. But I still have arguments with the teachers sometimes. Moshe was having trouble in this one class and I said to the teacher, "Let him write a report." They were clueless. I said, "It's in his IEP that he can write a report instead of taking a test. It can be different forms of evaluation." They said, "Well, we don't do that." I told them it's in his IEP; you have to do it. Their solution was to move him into a different level of the class—where he does great—but still.

I learned to read the IEP very carefully before signing it. There's always something wrong with it. I would tell them, you have to put this, this, and this, on it. The committee would always try to leave accommodations off. They don't tell you anything and they don't want you to organize with other parents. Parents aren't encouraged to meet. Ignorance is bliss as far as the district is concerned. The parents need to organize on their own.

My concern was always making sure Moshe was going to be able to make it in life. So that's why I always rode him from the beginning, because I knew he was going to have a hard time. I never expected the school to do it all. I took him to tutors and after-school programs. But I expected them to give him what he was entitled to. And they don't want to tell you what you're entitled to. At least that's what I've seen with my IEP planning team.

Moshe: My outside life is good. I have a younger sister. She was always the A kid, the one who didn't have to do any studying and came home with 100s and got mad if she got a 90. I can work for hours and the most I can pull is an 80 on tests. I'm happy with it now. But I was always frustrated with her and would wonder why I wasn't like her. And we would get into it. She'd say, "You are in the stupid classes," and I'd just say, "You are whatever you are." We had a strained relationship from it because of school. Because when you're in those special classes, they really have you feel like there's something wrong with you and then everyone else looks at it that way.

I don't get involved in any sports or activities. When I was a kid they always wanted you away from everyone so I didn't have any friends. They didn't want you to have any friends—so they succeeded and I didn't. I used to have the really big things of colored paper and tape. I would be in my room and I would make three-dimensional houses. I had, like, an architect-designed thing. I had a big room and my entire floor was covered with houses and I would make furniture and cars. That was my world. I was so bored with my own world that I would go home and there was my world. I could control it, build it. I could mold it—I could do whatever I wanted. I could make the people in it do whatever I wanted, so I always liked that. It was an escape, you know, like I don't have to be here in the real world. I guess if I could read, I would have read.

I don't know what I'm going to do when I leave high school. I always give a different answer 'cause I'm always changing my mind. People will tell me I don't really care, but I do. I care so much that I really put so much thought into it—I go on overload and then I crash. I want to go to a more local college, I know that.

And I don't want a job where I have to go sit in an office or a room all day long. If I had a cubicle, I would shoot myself. It's not just the whole ADD stuff, I can control that—it's just I have to talk to people. I need social interaction. I had none in middle school to the point where now in high school I don't shut up. Nobody from the school ever sat down with me and said, "So what would you like to do? Let's talk about what you like and how it translates into the real world." But my guidance counselor thinks I'm a complete idiot. I know because whenever I pick classes, he says, "It's going to be too hard for you." It's an art class—come on—put "OK" in the system and let it go. I don't work with him.

I work with my case manager. She's amazing. If I have issues or need to know something, I go to her. I had her all through high school. She treats everyone the same. I have a lot of teachers who have dumbed down the way they talk to me, like talk slower or louder. I'm not hard of hearing—I'm hard of learning, come on. She doesn't do that with me or anybody.

So I have ADHD, severe dyslexia, and dysgraphia. I think that's it. My handwriting is the worst. I can't even read my handwriting. I write these notes to myself because I have—that's it, I have short-term memory loss—which is why I forgot it before. This is funny. So I use Post-it notes and I put them up all over the house and in my notebooks to remind me of things I need to do. Don't you love Post-it notes? But when I try to read them I can't read my writing.

Bentina: In the beginning, it's not like my family was embarrassed about the disability, but it was like, "No one has to know." So I followed along with that for a while, and just stayed away from everyone. But then I said, "People are going to think there is really something wrong with him instead of just learning who he is." Learning disabilities—nobody knows about it—it's not like a physical disability. So other people think he's off or something, they don't know about the disability. You can't see it.

So he has problems socially; he holds himself back. And in school a lot of the kids wouldn't play with him because he was in resource room. A lot of the parents wouldn't even talk about birthday parties in front of him, or in front of me, because they didn't invite him. He's my son. You want to be my friend but you don't want to include my kid? No, I don't need you.

I would encourage him to go out and play with the kids, but he hated sports and wouldn't go. He holds himself back from boys who are very sports oriented. So I didn't want to make him do something he didn't want to do. He can draw and he has a great sense of humor. He's a good kid. If we get him out of high school I think he'll be OK in college.

CONCLUSION

In subtle and not-so-subtle ways, evidence indicates that students have needs for a place where they are comfortable learning—a place where they don't feel threatened, either physically or emotionally. Students are trying to find their way in the world   trying to fit in, succeed academically, have friendships, and gain self-confidence. Some have to turn to outside activities to boost their self-confidence because they are unable to get it from the school academic setting.

Professional school personnel stepped forward and helped students to the best of their ability—a teacher, a special education director, a coach, or an aide—for a small part of a child's education. Other professionals—whether through ignorance or intolerance—did not try to help. In some cases they even tried to hinder a learning situation. When the students were placed with teachers who were able to *think outside the box* and teach with an open mind, great things happened. However, many times teachers had preconceived notions—students were inadequate, not as intelligent as others, or in some instances irrelevant—all because of their disability. Other students teased and tormented them.

School districts failed to diagnose students early in their education and so they didn't receive the needed programs, related services, and accommodations to help them be successful. This put them on a downward spiral that negatively impacted their educational and social life. However, parents did try to access evaluations and services to the best of their abilities. The school districts let them down.

These students experienced hurt and sadness at the hands of others because they were different. One student described the feeling of being blocked by a *fence*, a fence that needed to be climbed to reach the other side where everyone else is. The fence is a metaphor for principals, teachers, and administrators—the very ones who should be building a bridge for the student to walk across. Sadness and hurt come through not only for the child with the disability but also for the parent. It is truly a family affair.

QUESTIONS FOR DISCUSSION

1. What are all the themes and subthemes in each story?
2. Select one story from this chapter. Which of the child's needs were not met? Create a narrative in which all the child's needs are met.
3. Choose one story from this chapter. Which of the parent's needs were not met? Create a narrative in which all the parent's needs are met.
4. What are the foundational causes of the issues encountered in these stories? Write an anecdotal listing of at least five.

11

Voices from the Field

Parents Speak Out

Carol Strax

Chapter 11 continues with stories—this time those told by the parents of children with disabilities. Remember, the stories are all real, but the identifying details and names have been changed to protect privacy and ensure anonymity. The essential elements of the stories are told as accurately as possible and in the people's own words. The themes running through the stories are:

- Psychological Feelings
  - Emotional and Physical Safety
  - Feelings of Isolation
  - Self-Confidence
  - Sadness and Grief
- Education Programs
  - Diagnosis
  - Education Planning Meetings
  - Classroom Programs
  - Accommodations and Related Services
  - Teacher Interaction
- Conflict
- Transition to Adulthood

At the end of the chapter will be a discussion of both chapters 10 and 11. Below are the stories of Daphne, Charley, and Molly, as told by their parents.

DAPHNE'S MOM

This case study is about my daughter, Daphne. Daphne was not officially diagnosed until she was almost five. Even before the final diagnosis was attained,
the IEP [Individualized Education Program] planning committee approved her
being sent to a full-day special education nursery school program. She received
occupational, speech, and recreational therapy in that program. The committee
chair was wonderful, so supportive of me and my child. She was such an advocate for her. But, I think they knew my husband and I were both educators and
we're educated. We know which buttons to push and we wouldn't stop until we
got what our child deserved.

The school system tested her, and the expressive and receptive language scores
were dismally low, due in part to her inability to be tested—she was not a very
cooperative test taker. They said she had pervasive developmental disorder. They
had their team of experts evaluate her, including a psychologist. This particular
psychologist was not very good. He was not the brightest light in the chandelier.
During testing he asked Daphne what her father did for a living. And then he
was surprised when she couldn't answer. She was only three. Even if she could
have answered, would she have told the psychologist, a person she didn't know?
Because of this, the psychologist decided Daphne must have autism. However,
the school district did not articulate that diagnosis for quite a while. They were
very hesitant to put it down on paper.

Daphne was also tested privately. An exhaustive survey was filled out by
me, on her behalf, on her behavior and abilities, and according to this particular
instrument she was a classic infantile autism profile. She was severely autistic.
Daphne went for a private evaluation by a speech pathologist, a psychologist, and
a pediatric neurologist. I think that was all the "ologists." The speech pathologist gave her a diagnosis of oral motor apraxia. I innocently asked if that was all
that was wrong—would she be OK when she got older, would she attain more
speech. The speech pathologist told me, "I really don't think so. I think there's
something beyond speech going on here. But I'm not an expert in that; I just focus
on speech." It was a frustratingly long process to get Daphne diagnosed.

The school district was very willing to give her the benefits, the maximum benefits. I think, quite frankly, a lot of that had to do with the fact that my husband
was very involved with a school system and an active union leader. He was very
aggressive with the school laws. They knew what I did for a living, so they felt
they couldn't push us around.

However, the school district did not buy into or articulate a diagnosis of autism
for quite a while. They were very hesitant to put it down on paper. They kept saying that she had pervasive developmental disorder or disability. I remember having to insist at the IEP planning meeting that her classification be changed from
pervasive developmental disability to autism. And they said, "You don't want
this down in writing." I told them we want her to have the right classification that

will get her all the benefits she's entitled to. I didn't want to hide from the truth. But it was like cancer used to be. People would whisper the word. So they made her classification autism.

When I first heard the term, I had heard the word *autism* my whole life. I thought I knew what it meant but I really didn't know what it could mean and no one really explained it. I didn't know what a crushing diagnosis it was.

I remember taking her to a pediatric neurologist who I thought was a jerk. He wanted to make a diagnosis on the spot. He had Daphne on the floor trying to put puzzle pieces together. She couldn't do it so her father joined her—and he couldn't do it either. The neurologist was sitting there reading a report and he said to me, "I see, ma'am, that you meet the criteria of a refrigerator mother—over-educated and lacking in emotion." I couldn't believe that came out of his mouth.

Daphne went to a special school after she aged out of pre-K. She was in pre-K for three years, then went to the special school until she was ten. This was all paid for by the school district. They placed her. She did very well in the special school, but I finally saw, more than anyone else, that Daphne needed more intensive support. So I asked the teachers in her current placement to evaluate her. They were careful with what they said because they didn't want to make waves with the school district. But they said that she would benefit from twenty-four-hour care, supervision, and twenty-four-hour structure.

I went to the school district—the chair of the IEP planning committee was such a wonderful advocate for Daphne—and told her what I wanted to do. I researched places and with the social worker from her current placement, I would check out different places. We found a great place that was perfect for Daphne, but it was three hours away. The school district agreed to place her there.

My whole family was opposed to it. I was the odd person out. In fact, they said some pretty heated things and it was awful. And I was just gulping. Saying, "Please, God, let me be doing the right thing." I thought I was, but you never know. I remember packing her clothes and then it hit me. I don't cry a lot, but I started sobbing. I called my friend who also had a child with autism and she told me, "Listen to me. Don't worry. I was just thinking of you and I'm jealous of you because you have the courage to do what I know I should be doing for my son. Everything will be all right. It is the best thing for Daphne." It gave me the courage to keep on. Daphne thrived at the new school.

When she would come home for vacations—because even though she was in a residential placement the school would close on holidays—I had to fight to get respite care. The system tried to say that I wasn't entitled to respite care anymore because she was placed residentially. I explained that the school closed for holidays. They refused. I kept calling people and finally I had to appeal and attend a meeting. I explained she was a bolter. I had locks in my house and around my property but Daphne was Houdini. They just kept saying, "I'm sorry we can't help you, she's in residential placement." So I threatened them. "If my daughter is found under the wheels of a truck on the highway, I promise you I will call my legislators and then I will call *Dateline* and then we'll see what you do for the next parent. This is absurd." All of a sudden, I got respite care whenever Daphne was home on vacation. But I had to fight so hard for it.

She attended the school until she aged out at twenty-one. That's when the fun really started. Trying to find an appropriate next placement for an individual whose needs are so great and so multidimensional was almost impossible. I kept looking for years after she was placed in her current placement. I researched placements all over and I could only find one that dealt with autism. It was full and had a waiting list—and gave preference to children who had gone through the school associated with the group home.

There was no real transition planning done by the school district. I had heard so much about that phrase, *planning for transition.* I filled out some paperwork to get on a group home list, but Daphne must have been like seventeen, maybe even eighteen, before that happened. There should also be education for parents to deal with legal guardianship after the child is eighteen. It is a horribly complex, lengthy process. I think it's another way the school district could help parents. They're technically in the school system until they're twenty-one, so it should be built in to help parents.

Aside from transition planning, we really fared pretty well throughout her school years. I realize that we had it better than other parents who had to deal with the school district and the IEP planning committee. I was a parent advocate for a brief while for the committee. And I do remember a mom from an obviously lower socioeconomic background who didn't know English that well. And the mother was lost. And I thought perhaps the school district could have pointed her to some support groups, some resources, got her in touch with people. They seemed to ignore her. I think she was treated that way because she didn't know any better and they weren't afraid she'd sue. She was treated so differently from the way they'd been treating me. Every parent and child should be afforded the same respect as everyone else.

So, Daphne's name was placed on a waiting list for a group home and one did ultimately come about locally. It was a brand-new group home that would have six female residents. None of the other residents had autism. There were some rough patches for awhile. Daphne would lose control and they would panic, call an ambulance, and the ambulance would be preceded by a policeman who would handcuff her. And then handcuff her to a gurney and take her to the emergency room where the nurses wouldn't know what the heck to do with this "screaming Mimi."

I thought I would lose my mind. I wanted to say to them, "This is not the first time in her life that she banged her head against the wall, nor will it be the last, folks. You've got to learn how to deal with it and how to stop her from doing it as much as possible. And if you can't stop her—put a pillow between her head and the wall." She was hospitalized twice on psychiatric floors and, I thought, both times unnecessarily. But she survived the hospitalizations. We did too. It seems to have gotten a lot better, thank God.

When she was at her last school placement, there was a community work plan in place and Daphne would go out on supervised work to a hotel and help with housekeeping chores. She loved it and it was good for her to have the responsibility. Unbeknownst to me, when she was placed in her group home, they do not have occupational training. So she was not able to continue with a community job. I think that is a loss for Daphne, but she is in her group home placement for better or worse and I think she is content there.

CHARLEY'S DAD

I'll tell you a story about dealing with the special education system and the IEP planning committee! My son Charley went through school until the ninth grade before he was diagnosed with a disability. And at that point they wouldn't give him an IEP; they would only give him a 504 plan. I had no idea what an IEP was. I was told he had to have a 504. You know, parents go into these planning meetings and they think, Well, they're the educators, why shouldn't I be agreeing with them. They know what's best. Boy, did I learn!

So, the school didn't know he had a reading disability until ninth grade. I was the one who discovered it—not them—and I pushed for testing. He also had behavior issues. Charley has to hear everything. He has a photographic memory for things he hears—but he has no comprehension from reading—it was all auditory. If he didn't read it out loud he couldn't process it.

Charley wanted to take honors classes. He went through college preparation classes and had passed all his college prep exams to that point, so why deny him. There were no kids with disabilities in this honors class. The school kept telling me not to worry about it, he could use his safety net—he didn't have to struggle for a college preparation diploma. But he wanted a college preparation diploma and I wanted him to have it. And the school would say, "But why stress him? He's going to a community college; he doesn't need a college preparation diploma."

I had to fight constantly to keep him in the right classes. I was nonexistent at these IEP planning meetings. I was a nonparticipant; I just sat there. They didn't address me other than when I started arguing. They talked over my head. They would send me a letter saying this was his meeting time and these were the people that would be there and I could bring someone if I wanted to. I always brought Charley's football coach. That was all they ever said or explained about my rights as a parent.

Charley gets high honor roll the first quarter of the year and I walked in on parent–teacher night and go up to the English teacher's desk and ask how he's doing. She replies she doesn't know, she has to look it up. If you have a student who has repeated almost every class because he can't read and he gets As and above 93 on every single grade, wouldn't you be excited about that? She couldn't even remember. That's when I said, "I'm done here. He just got the best report I've gotten on him. You're an idiot. Good-bye."

One teacher told me that he didn't want my son in his class because he was nothing but a problem. Charley had been in the class for two days. How could he possibly have been a problem already? The teacher told me, "I just heard things about him, I don't want him." OK. Fine. Now I trot myself into the principal's office and tell her we have a problem. We dealt with it—he got another class.

Another teacher told me he didn't have to contact me about Charley and he wouldn't talk to me. It was so very, very frustrating. I hired a lawyer. His advice to me was put everything on paper and go to the superintendent. Everything was always a fight. It was never easy. Nothing ever came easy for him and nothing ever came easy for me as his father. So we came to an agreement. I would talk to the teacher every Friday and see how the week went. The first Friday I called he was conveniently absent.

So I called on Monday and he wouldn't answer—said he was too busy to talk. So on Tuesday Charley goes into class and asks how he did on the test from last week—he had really studied hard for it. The teacher said to him in front of the whole class, "I didn't have time to grade it yet. Had your father not kept calling me and bugging me I might have had time to grade them." Charley almost hit him. He was so embarrassed and angry that he walked out of the class.

An aide from the class called me at home and said, "You need to do something. This guy is really torturing your son." I didn't even know the woman. That's when I walked into the school, right past the secretary, and into the principal's office and said, "Get him out of that class now. I don't care what you have to do, he is going to pass that class." They were ready to call the police on me because the principal was on the phone and I said, "Hang it up!" I didn't care, I saw red. My child was in the hall in tears. The principal knew I was right. Charley got another class. To be honest, I was a real bastard when it came to my son. I was awful. But they put me in that position.

Then I got on the school board. At one of the school board meetings I made a disparaging comment about the classes and one of the other board members— someone who had been on the board for twenty years—started yelling at me, "You couldn't be more wrong. My children have had fantastic educations in this school system." I responded, "Yes, and let me ask you—how long have you been on the board? Twenty years? What I find amazing is that now my son has the best teachers and I'm on the school board. Isn't that ironic? I find it extremely odd that my son had some of the worst teachers in the school, teachers who you have tried to terminate and now he's got all the great ones—since I've been on the board."

The IEP planning committee was afraid of me because I was on the school board. So they trod very lightly knowing that I wasn't someone to play with. Part of the problem is that parents are very intimidated by people in the education system and they feel they're talked down to. I felt the committee was very adversarial, and that's a problem. If a parent feels like you're attacking them or their parenting skills, they're not going to be accepting of the idea of working with the school. Why does it have to be who you know, what connections you have? The average parent doesn't know what's OK and what's not. It's not a fair situation. But my son was the first student with a 504 plan to graduate with a college preparation diploma.

Charley's doing well now. He has a good job that he likes and he lives in a town that he likes. I think things would have been very different and he would have chosen another career path if school had gone differently. Had he been diagnosed earlier on, had the teachers been more understanding, had he gotten the accommodations he needed—it would have been a much different story. It was really sad that he wasn't diagnosed until he was in ninth grade.

MOLLY'S PARENTS

My daughter Molly was diagnosed with autism when she turned three. A pediatric neurologist confirmed what my wife and I thought. And then the question was what to do. We knew virtually nothing about autism. The neurologist recommended a very aggressive course of medical treatment using a wide range of drugs that we did not embrace at that time. We attempted to place her in a local preschool and it was not working. They were not equipped to deal with a child with autism. But we didn't know what to do. We knew nothing about the law; we knew nothing about special education.

The case manager from the school district, who was on the eve of her retirement, suggested very strongly that Molly attend a school, South West, in the next town. We were very ignorant in terms of education for Molly so we placed her in this school. The district didn't give us a choice—they made the decision. We weren't told about a number of new starting-up schools for kids with autism, private schools. Our district didn't have any programs so she had to be placed out of district. But they didn't give us a choice.

At that time Molly had a number of behavioral issues. She would bite, throw things, and hit. And she did show some improvement. Molly had no expressive language of any kind. It would take a number of years before she began to utter some simple words and phrases—about four years. Her first words were "da, da."

When we attended the meeting about her educational plan, the committee told us where she would be placed and never discussed alternative placements, our legal rights, or the right to appeal. After the meeting was over, the committee gave us a pamphlet and that was it. Molly did show some limited improvement. I also arranged for a tutor to work with her at home.

So year by year we were discouraged and frustrated. As she grew older, her behaviors worsened. Finally we brought her to a pediatric psychiatrist who treated her with a range of drugs, and it did help. The drug regimen calmed her down. But in time he left the practice and went elsewhere and he was no longer on our health plan.

In the meantime, Molly was still attending South West. We would go for yearly IEP meetings and they were nothing more than grand blow offs. The committee members would tell us all of the things she had accomplished, but they did not at any point suggest that maybe other steps ought to be taken to address some of her problems.

We went through a whole slew of neurologists and x-rays and brain scans and tests—just to make sure there wasn't anything organic going on. But they found nothing. Then I switched jobs and started working in a special education classroom. Wow, did my eyes open up! I would come home and say, "Do they do this with Molly, do they do this. . . . " The teacher I was working with would tell me, "Did the school district tell you . . . you should have this or you should do this." So I started to learn. She gave me the information that we needed to help Molly. So at the meetings we knew what to ask for and knew to bring somebody along with us. We just thought the school was honest and would have been giving her what she needed.

Molly did receive speech therapy, physical therapy, and occupational therapy a few times a week. We thought she needed more. But she did not have beyond that, additional behavioral support that she needed desperately. At-home tutoring would have helped her. A lot of this we had to do out of pocket. And all the school did was complain. Some of the teachers were not adept at dealing with kids with special needs with behaviors. All we did was get complaints from the school—verbally, in letters—making us seem like we were doing something wrong.

The class was self-contained but Molly was always thrown in with boys. I'm not bad-mouthing the teachers, but these teachers were not prepared or didn't have the expertise to deal with kids with behaviors. The school refused to give her a one-on-one aide and there were not enough staff in the classroom. The school was not equipped to deal with behavioral problems. Molly was having a number of issues related to sensory deprivation and her behavior steadily deteriorated and worsened.

By the time Molly was five she was beginning to grow larger in size and her behaviors became more aggressive. We had her treated by the pediatric psychologist at a local hospital. However, unknown to us, he was not well adept at treating children with autism. He put her on any number of drug regimens, all of which intensified the aggression. Molly would go to school and we would get these letters or notes—sent to us either through the mail or attached to the notebook that Molly would bring home every day—outlining the aggressive episodes. And again, we felt as if somehow we were being blamed for what Molly was doing. All they did was complain—they never offered any solutions or suggestions. In retrospect, the school was not equipped to deal with Molly's problems. The school was just winging it. They had no program. Everything was going to be done in the future.

We were going crazy trying to deal with South West, the school district, the pediatrician, and the pediatric psychiatrist. We didn't have a network or support group to turn to. The other parents were very private. There was a group for a short time at South West, monthly meetings. I would go and they got to be very depressing. The same people would talk over and over, the same stories. There was really nothing you could take from these meetings that was of any use.

To hear other people complain was a waste of my time. I think that's what turns off a lot of parents. Having a special needs child takes so much additional work and saps all of the energy you have. You don't have much more time to spend interacting with other people. So you find yourself, for a number of reasons, steadily retreating into your own world. You can't go to a lot of other functions, social or family functions, because it's difficult. Trying to find somebody to watch your child, or if you take your child then you have all sorts of other problems. I think this is one of the major problems afflicting parents of children with disabilities. They're forced to retreat into their own solitary worlds and this is what we do. We live our lives through the backyard, through the house, and we have pretty much severed our ties to most people.

At the IEP meetings for Molly, the committee members tend to have an air of superiority and that they know far more than you. They are not interested in listening to anything you have to say. They have polite smiles etched across their faces. But beyond that there's nothing. There is no real sincerity and you get the big blow off. We spent years asking for additional support for Molly. We would plead with the committee to provide a one-on-one aide for Molly to rein in some of her behaviors before they became explosive. I would tell them, "It's not as if we aren't doing anything. Do you know how many doctors we've been to? We're very proactive. We're not just saying, Here's my kid and deal with it."

The school district people wanted to come to our house to see what kind of environment Molly had. We felt like they wanted to see if we were doing something wrong or very strange. They made us feel like we were the problem. We told them to come, we had nothing to hide. Also, at that time they knew I was working in a school, and they didn't like it because I would come to the meetings with all these ideas and suggestions for Molly's program. I knew what the children in my class were getting, so how come my daughter is getting worse? At least let her have the same things, be fair.

But South West became increasingly more hostile in proportion to the increase in Molly's inappropriate behaviors. The school assumed no responsibility in this. As Molly was on her downward trajectory in terms of behaviors, we became the focal point of their frustration. It was we, as the parents, who were responsible, not their behavioral plans—an eclectic mix of nonsensical approaches, none of which worked. They were all geared up for Molly to fail; we could see this. And IEP meetings became increasingly more hostile. They became battlegrounds, so to speak.

We hired an advocate to go with us to an IEP meeting. She was very nice, but didn't really know what she was doing and had no power. The advocate made some very useful recommendations and urged South West to provide a one-on-one aide for Molly. The school district refused, and again the meeting was another big blow off. It was clear that they weren't going to do very much of anything except blame us. The advocate said, "It's a budgetary problem. They don't have the money for whatever reason. You could hire a lawyer, but if the district can prove they don't have the money, I don't know what a lawyer would be able to do. But I don't know the politics or law about that." No one explained to us how to navigate the legal system. This is when the problems became more frightening.

Molly was now ten and the school district opened a new school. They were going to have everything at the school—a gymnasium, a sensory room, and a playground—all these wonderful things that never materialized. It was an old building that was being renovated. Molly began to go there for school and that's when everything worsened. She still had no one-on-one aide, and her behaviors were becoming more aggressive as well as self-injurious. She was eating nonedibles; she was putting things in her mouth, causing damage to her teeth; she was breaking things; breaking glass; punching; hitting; spitting; kicking. She was a mess.

The doctor prescribed medication that made the behaviors more accentuated. She didn't know what she was doing. We could never reach the doctor on the phone. I kept calling and calling and calling. The school kept harassing us, saying we weren't doing our job with Molly and stuff like that. I said to them, "What do you want? What do you *want*? We've been asking, begging for years that she needs treatment. We're not hiding anything; we were always honest about the medication she was on. Her behavior isn't as bad at home as in school." But because I would give them suggestions, the school acted like I had no business speaking out, I wasn't a teacher, who was I to tell them what to do.

The school tried to write the script. They didn't believe us. The school said, "We cannot believe she's not doing these behaviors at home. She has to be." They were adamant in saying we were liars. So they wanted to visit our home. The school sent an inexperienced young behaviorist to visit. I told her to stay some distance from Molly: "She doesn't know you. Don't invade her personal space." She wanted to give Molly a pencil to write with. I told her, "Don't do that, you might get hurt." She blew me off and gave Molly a felt-tipped pen and Molly promptly tried to stab her with it and hit her right below the eye socket. The behaviorist began crying. After that it was the end. She wrote up that Molly was too aggressive to deal with in the home.

The situation became clear to us. The school was putting together documentation that was becoming frightening in its unstated implications. The school was transporting her in a minivan, and Molly would get out of the seat belt and punch the drivers and the aide and they would cry. We told the school to use a bus. They refused. They used a taxi with an aide. The taxi was beat-up looking, seedy, dirty, dark, and smelly. I would be scared if I had to ride in it. The aide got a black eye, her lip was bleeding, was all disheveled. She couldn't speak English. The school was saying, you're going to have to institutionalize her; they were making arrangements to send her to an institution.

Molly's behavior was disintegrating. She was ten. Her doctor finally said if she has a serious episode to bring her to the hospital. She had a bad episode and we brought her to the pediatric emergency room at the hospital. We called her doctor and he didn't come. We were there for four days and it was a hellish experience. I slept there with her. No one knew much about this disability, and they would move us from one room to another in the pediatric emergency room. They just kept shooting her up with Depakote because she was going through withdrawal from all her medication. It was so scary. They were trying to find a hospital that could treat her and they couldn't find a placement for her, for autistic kids.

Then a nurse became confrontational with me, threatened me. There was an observer in the room—someone to watch what would happen between Molly and us and Molly and the hospital staff. Like a psychiatric watch. The observer was aghast because the nurse was telling me to tell Molly to be quiet and stop playing with the bed and I would tell the nurse I can't. So the nurse started with me. In the meantime, the staff told us there was a bed available at a psychiatric hospital. I explained I wanted something more appropriate. The hospital got the state involved. And everyone was getting nasty with us—the nurses, the doctors, and the person from the state—and on the fourth night they brought in an ambulance to transport Molly to the psychiatric hospital.

The hospital brought in police officers to surround me because they thought I was going to freak out. They put Molly on a gurney, strapped her down, and took her over. We were in an impossible situation. Her doctor had thrown up his hands and said, "I don't know what to do." We had no help, no one was willing to do anything. Later on, I wrote letters to the state about the hospital and our treatment. The head of the hospital was forced to resign, coincidentally, because of corruption, the nurse was fired, and the doctor left that hospital and went somewhere else.

Let me tell you about the psychiatric hospital. Molly was in the basement, in the dungeon with no windows and other children with psychiatric disorders. The doors were locked. By the way, the other girls and the aides were nice to her. We requested an aide because the boys and girls were mixed. They sleep on these concrete slabs and they gave her a pillow and blanket. It was worse than you treat animals. Animals in the zoo have it better. Molly was there for about three weeks and we took her home.

It was clear that the next step would be permanent institutionalization. Now the school district wants to provide a one-on-one aide. But the damage was already done. Molly goes back to school and the week was pretty good. Then the behaviors gradually begin to surface again. So they put her behind file cabinets to segregate her from the other students in the class. Every time I would go over there to drop her off at school, they would come out and tell me of other problems. I was having daily meetings with the principal, the behaviorist, and who knows who else, and they were all complaining about different things she had done. This was an ongoing daily affair.

In the interim, we did find the doctor who had treated her initially that we liked. He worked with children with autism. He was growing concerned about her behavior and was trying to work with the school district to develop an appropriate behavioral plan and to coordinate the treatment and the education, with no success. The school district wanted nothing to do with him. They had their own behavioral plan and didn't want any suggestions from us or the doctor. We also had somebody from an outside agency going over to observe what was going on. He was distressed that the classroom Molly was in was inappropriate for her.

We had meetings at the school that went nowhere. They became very fractious. The meeting was attended by us of course, our guy from the outside, a man from another local agency, we had a friend attend, the principal, the teacher, the school nurse, and everybody else involved. The principal was annoyed that the people she thought would be her allies were supportive of us. But, nothing changed over there, nothing. The school was adamant, rigid, uncompromising, unyielding.

Several times I would drive her to school and she would attack me. Kick me in the head while I was driving; punch me; grab my hair. I came close to having any number of serious accidents. One day she attacked me at the school. School personnel came out and took her to class. I picked her up in the afternoon and she seemed better. Then two blocks from school Molly really went after me. I pulled over to the side of the road and took her out of the car. I was wrestling with her on the sidewalk and people across the street came over to help me; they were very nice. Our doctor was able to get Molly hospitalized out of state at a wonderful facility. She was there for three weeks and they changed and regulated her medication.

When Molly came home she went to the school for a few more weeks. I was driving her. We started the process of looking for another school. We had to do all the research. We went to many different schools, and either they didn't want to accept Molly because of the behavior problems or they only accepted the children from a younger age, so they could mold them into their way of teaching. We were upset. The doctors had done wonders with her medication, she was on track, and we didn't want her back at that school. What were we going to do? The school year ended and we were desperate to find another school for Molly.

We were visiting every place we could find and we were down to one last place, Ivy School. It was the last straw, our last hope. I went inside and instantly developed a fondness for the director of the school, and I was impressed with everyone else. The only problem was Molly would have to tolerate a half-hour drive. The district agreed to transport her in a bus with an aide to Ivy School. It only took two hospitalizations; any number of meetings; confrontations; the expense of time, energy, and money before she was placed in this school that most specifically met her needs. And this could have been done much earlier in time.

This new school worked wonders with Molly. She was twelve years old at this point. It has been a very wonderful experience. We no longer have all the major problems. The sad part is if we had hit on Ivy School, or the district had told us about it in the beginning, Molly's life and ours would have been very different. If Molly had gone to Ivy when she was younger, we would have been spared, as would Molly, the pain, the horror of a number of hospitalizations, and the constant fighting with school administrators. We could have been spared all this. This was a living hell, a living hell.

This school works with our doctor and would have from the beginning. They work as a team with everyone for the benefit of the child, even outside people. Ivy has a very integrated team approach that works. And they provide the kind of services that the children need. They customize the education plan to the child. We brought Molly over to the school and sat down with a whole team of people and put together an IEP for her. They put together a plan that was flexible enough to make accommodations when necessary. When the school wrote or called us they would say, "These are the behaviors we are seeing and this is what we are trying." They didn't blame us and they had suggestions to try.

We started talking about a transition plan last year. Molly is fifteen. Ivy would like to make the transition to primarily teaching her life skills and de-emphasize academics. But we insisted that they still give her a healthy diet of academics, and they are. They have been very accommodating.

I think our district should have been more forthcoming in the very beginning about our rights—legal issues and accommodations—and kept us better informed. Honestly, we assumed that they were telling us the truth, that they were doing what was best for our child. But nobody has ever talked about transition for when she has to leave this school.

Plus, the school districts don't have a clue about transition because the people in the school business don't know about adult services, and the people who know about adult services don't get invited into the schools. The same thing is true when we had these emotional crises. There are no places to treat children with autism. Hospitals can't treat them, doctors can't treat them. We wrote letters to assemblymen, senators, other people in government positions to try and get them to do something and we got the big blow off. In the end we simply became exhausted.

It has been difficult. We cut ourselves off from family and friends. Some friends were put off by Molly. They didn't know how to handle her. They didn't want her to play with their kids. And getting a babysitter is hard, so our social life is down the tubes. This year we managed to go out for dinner three times. We've never gone away by ourselves, not even overnight. Our honeymoon was the last time we went away. Neither of our families could handle watching her. And to go somewhere with Molly is very, very difficult. This has had a significant impact on our families. You find yourself cut off from other people, from co-workers. I don't get invited to things that are going on with people at work. If I bring Molly to work the people in maintenance are great with her. The people in the office are not; they have a hard time dealing with her.

And what happens if something happens to us? We were on our way to pick Molly up from day camp last year and a car ran into us. We were hurt, but minor injuries. It makes you think, what would happen to Molly if something happened to us? That's a shock. Who is going to watch her after we are gone? We live with this every day. What will her fate be? This is frightening, when you realize this. You carry this weight around with you.

CONCLUSION

The themes and subthemes are clearly expressed in many different ways throughout all these stories—regardless of the disability and whether students or parents are informing us. Both parents and children were isolated because of a disability. People didn't know how to deal with the situation, so the parents and children were shunned. Some were treated as if they had a contagious disease.

Attending education planning meetings for the child has mixed results. Sometimes the process goes smoothly and team members are very supportive to parents' needs. In some cases, if a parent shows up with an advocate or lawyer, events move smoothly. But in many cases, parents reported that the opposite happened. They were not made to feel welcome, not spoken to as an equal, and their requests were ignored or dismissed. They reported having the IEP planning team members speak over their heads, using jargon and language they couldn't understand, and their rights were not explained to them. Parents reported being ambushed during their child's IEP planning meeting.

Interestingly, parents also reported that if they were connected politically, had financial means, or were well educated, they were often treated in a different manner from other parents. Parents believed that those who had no political clout, were from low socioeconomic backgrounds, were uneducated, or did not speak English frequently did not have their child's needs met.

Parents had to fight to get their child an appropriate placement. If they didn't have to fight for it, they had to find it. Nobody suggested program options for their child. Parents were left to their own devices to locate placements, thus making a difficult situation more time consuming and arduous.

Teachers and administrators, in many cases, had preconceived notions. School districts would put families on *watch lists* if one child had a disability. Parents were made to feel guilty, as if they were not doing enough or the right thing for the care of their child.

The issue of transition is a theme that resonates very clearly throughout the stories—from the easier to accomplish transition of what educational program the child will go to after high school graduation, to the much more complex and harder to attain transition of group-home placement. Governments on the local, state, and federal levels have cut funding, and group homes are among the tragedies. They are expensive to run and in short supply. Where will all the children with more severe disabilities go when they age out of school? When the parents are no longer around to take care of them, where do the children go? This is a serious concern of all the parents involved.

What is amazing is the ability of these parents and children to persevere, not yielding to the despair they must have felt many times. It takes great courage to go on in the face of adversity and to continue to look for the opening in the fence and ultimately, the bridge that will take them through to the other side.

The process of navigating the special education system does not have to be one of sadness, torment, grief, and conflict. The process should be an equal partnership where children, parents, teachers, and administrators interact together to provide the best education possible for each child. If parents don't trust in their school district personnel to be transparent—to tell them their rights, diagnose early and correctly, remember their child is a person and not a disability, and have their child's best interest at heart—then they are not going to be willing to enter into a dialogue and work as a team toward the end goal, the child. Children, not a commodity to be bargained over to find the cheapest fit for an education plan, are the end of the means, not the means to an end.

QUESTIONS FOR DISCUSSION

1. What are the key themes and subthemes in each story?
2. What information do parents need to understand and participate in their child's education? Develop a script to educate parents about special education using lay language parents can understand: no jargon, acronyms, or legal terms.
3. Pick one story from this chapter. Which of the parent's needs are not being met? Create a narrative in which all the parent's needs are met.
4. Select one story from this chapter. Which of the child's needs are not being met? Create a narrative in which all the child's needs are met.
5. Why do you think the voices of children and parents, describing their feelings and emotions, are left out of textbooks about special education?
6. What are the foundational causes of the issues encountered in these stories? Write an anecdotal listing of at least five.

12

❖ ❖

Voices from the Field

Education Professionals

Carol Strax

A border separates school administrators from parents of and children with disabilities—but is it a fence? Is the fence wire mesh with barbed wire across the top of it? Is it made with wood, where some slats have been moved aside, some broken through with holes? In this chapter we will explore *the other side of the fence*. Thoughts and feelings about the special education system—in the present and in the future—are examined through the eyes of various stakeholders in the special education system. These stakeholders include school superintendents, principals, private school principals, advocates, lawyers, adult educators, and professors.

Superintendents and principals are paid to run a school district or school—make it operate well—for all their students, on a budget. They are under pressure to meet all the demands being placed on them by the federal and state government, taxpayers, and parents. Children are placed in their care for approximately 185 days a year. They are charged with the daunting task of *educating all* with a budget that, in this current fiscal crisis, is dwindling. Pressure to lower the number of children with disabilities grows. And when this system goes awry, advocates and lawyers get called in by parents. How do our school superintendents, special education administrators, and principals believe all the components of the system—the good, the bad, and the ugly—are functioning?

Perhaps it's time to do something to change the system—to remove the fence. Find a new future for special education. What follows are the narratives of professional stakeholders involved in the education of children with disabilities:

- School administrators
- Advocates for children with disabilities
- Adult educators

SCHOOL ADMINISTRATORS

Administrators have to work not only with children receiving special education services, but also with an entire school population. They strive to meet the needs of all people in a school district—people who may have competing interests. Their perspective is one that oversees the entire school or district. Do they see the system as a fine-tuned instrument, or are there areas that need tuning up? Administrators' viewpoints concerning special education follow.

Private School Principal

A principal of a private school for children with disabilities, who previously worked as a public school principal and superintendent, speaks out. This is someone who brings a unique perspective to political issues in special education, having transitioned from being responsible for the education of all children in a school district to leader of a school for children with disabilities. The principal's narrative follows.

When parents come in here, they're so beat up and so downtrodden you want to give them some glimmer of hope. So we have a college board and we list all the colleges our graduates attend. Not that we're about colleges, but it helps the parents. A number of our graduates eventually go to Ivy League schools and other good colleges.

We started a tradition of having an alumnus speak at graduation. This one young lady said the best thing. She said she had real difficulty in school—people told her she would never go to college, the regular horrible routine—before she came here. Then she said, "I can't tell you how good it feels to be an adjunct at Harvard." That is the kind of message you want the kids to hear, that anything is possible. Our students leave here with certain skill sets and one of them is advocacy, so they know how to ask for extra help if they need it.

It's a disgrace—the special education system in public schools. In order to get into special education you have to fail in the mainstream, you put them in special education, you don't remediate them, they continue to still suffer terribly, and your solution is to put them back into the mainstream with the same program that failed them initially and that's progress. And you haven't done a thing to educate the teachers, who I think are trying their best. They're just uninformed.

When special education first came out, it was used as a way to segregate our schools. If you went into a special education classroom it was predominantly minority. And the city is predominantly African American and that message was picked up by the community, and advocates for the community said, Don't let those people tell you there's anything wrong with your child, they're just trying to put them down, hold them back, and I think it was true. Unfortunately, I think there's still a mind-set that to get special education services is in some way insulting on some level. We also have the gross misinformation in people who are educators about what disabilities are, especially learning disabilities, and how to remediate them.

The stuff that our kids write about their experience is just remarkable in a very discouraging way—what people said about them, how they were treated, what message they were given—so the system is messed up.

And this is my confessional here: I was part of the problem when I was in the public sector as a principal and superintendent. I thought inclusion was the way to go. I know this is not politically correct; however, I've yet to see a convincing piece of research on inclusion. What you get is a bromide that it's good for the kids to be in a classroom with other kids as role models and models for appropriate language, and that's better than being isolated. And, see, that's a reaction to when we put kids in a basement and didn't let anybody see them. And so it's born of, I think, a nice notion, but it misses the point.

Homogeneous versus heterogeneous is another, I think, misguided sense of making kids feel good about themselves when they're not. I don't believe in heterogeneous grouping. I know that is also not politically correct. If we're going to help kids you teach to a skill set that kids possess so they can move to the next skill set. You put in heterogeneous grouping for kids in language arts class, you're doing everybody a disservice. Teachers teach to the middle, the top get bored, and the bottom doesn't get it. The problem with it is it's politically based. I think the thought is, mistakenly, that it's somehow egalitarian. It's not. It's a disservice to those kids.

Someone told me, and I'm paraphrasing here: if you put a goat in front of the classroom about 60 percent of the kids would learn to read with a goat instructing, but 40 percent of the kids are going to have some degree of difficulty, some degree, and depending on who you talk to, 10–20 percent of those kids are going to have really significant issues learning the language. And so what do we do, we put a goat in front of the classroom and we're very proud of the 60 percent who read. I find that very sad.

Some parents never even tell their kids they have a learning disability. They treat it like an embarrassment, something to be ashamed of. Schools have made them feel that way. But, if you tell kids, give it a name, it's like saying it's not a bad thing, not a thing to hide or feel ashamed about. Some kids have—I wouldn't even call it a learning disability—I would call it an instructional disability, or a curriculum disability. They were not properly instructed. I really believe that every kid would benefit from a structured sequential approach to teaching language and reading. And writing. It has to be done in a very structured way with a good, solid, structured program.

I've got the statistics to show that the way we teach works, no question about it, it works—we can do it. But we continue to do stuff that doesn't work and continue to blame the kids, blame the parents. Schools should be using programs that have been proven with research to work. We should use the same care with the instructional choices we make that we do with prescribing medicine. Unless we have some research that indicates that a drug is good with a certain illness, I shouldn't be prescribing that drug for you. "You know, it worked for Carol, try it." But you're not Carol. The first step, we should only use research-based programs, and the second step, fidelity to the program is also important. Use the program the way it was designed to be used and with the population it was designed for.

The underlying premise in the way the system is set up is that it is going to be adversarial when parents walk in and that the superintendent is only going to be interested in the monetary aspects of the special education placement. So that's why they separated the superintendent from the process. They have to be very careful not to interfere with the diagnosis and placement process because of an assumption that it was going to be adversarial right from the get-go.

Why would the assumption be that the superintendent would not be the same educational leader for the most needy kids as well as the least needy kids? I think that's troubling and it sets a bad tone. I would argue that if the superintendents were more involved then special education directors and department chairs would feel less compelled to be parsimonious and not give the kids the kind of services they really need.

The system is broken. I think the reason it's adversarial is that parents haven't been told the truth about how their child is functioning. Parents are told, "Oh, he's a late bloomer." Well, late bloomers don't bloom, they wilt! Tell parents the truth: "Your child has a significant deficit and here is what it is." We don't share information with parents and we use platitudes and generalities. When everyone is sitting down at a planning meeting for a child, parents are very nervous, wondering what is going to happen with my child, and it is overwhelming. The system is really broken.

The problem is the way we go through these meetings. The school is going to have to do an intervention. And if we don't have something in our repertoire that will work, no matter what gets decided it won't produce the desired results. The results are terrible. The committee doesn't want to recommend what they don't have to give. It suffers from being a bureaucracy. And it's interesting that the original creation of the bureaucracy was a good thing because there was a multitiered system where the elite got treated differently than the poor and the underclass, and the bureaucracy was meant to make it equal so that everybody got good service and that's what is missing. I don't know how to solve that, except it takes a complete overhaul in terms of the results that get produced. If the programs are producing positive results, it changes the parent's worries going in and makes them more likely to trust the process.

Now they have RTI—Response to Intervention. Here's the problem with RTI. You have to wait until you fail to get increased services. It's not how the medical model would work. If you were in the hospital, you're not quite sick enough, let's try water, and if doesn't work we'll try aspirin, then maybe we'll think about operating, but you've got a long way to go because you're not nearly sick enough. Who would say that? And to me, that's what RTI is. It's too complicated. I think it was well intentioned; the discrepancy model had problems in itself. I can honestly tell you that if every school taught the way we teach in K–3, every kid would benefit from it and you would have significantly less caseloads and people could do a better job. Just do it right—direct instruction, smaller class sizes, group homogeneously for reading and math, get a program that is research based, teach teachers how to teach—and it would be revolutionary. Maybe the system that doesn't work now would actually work.

The thing about all of this, as a society, we're throwing away tremendous potential and just being careless. It's almost like a Gatsbyesque piece here—Daisy and Tom weren't bad people, they were just careless people—and that's what we're doing with kids. And we can't be careless with kids. So I'm infuriated. And it's lack of knowledge. I don't think these are bad people. I don't think they're evil people; it's lack of knowledge.

Public School Principals

This account is a combination of several public school principals. Their thoughts regarding special education, told in their own words, are below.

Special education percentages are at a very high rate. I would look at a variety of factors—not just pedagogy—health factors, and parent factors. One of the biggest problems we are having in this country right now over this national debate, over educational reform, is we're focused solely on structure. I understand that the work of the classroom has a powerful impact, the principal has a powerful impact on the work of the classroom teachers, but we neglect those variables that I just mentioned. They play into what happens in the classrooms especially around literacy.

Also, it's very hard to declassify a student. Once the monster has been created it's very hard to reel back from it. And some schools have special education programs, so in order to keep the programs running you need a certain number of special education students. No one wants to lose their job, so you make sure that you have the needed number of students to keep it running.

I think Response to Intervention (RTI) is really used to more accurately classify students because there has been an overclassification of kids with specific learning disabilities and we are using it for prevention. We are focusing on providing interventions for students prior to classification, progress monitoring, and working with the general education classroom teachers. I think RTI is a positive. It shifts the focus from special education to general education. It's a general education initiative.

RTI has changed people's philosophy and belief about when a child is struggling and how important it is to monitor the progress of that child before we rush into classification. Also, when we do classify a child, we're not just looking at an IQ test, we're asking teachers to come to the table with data to show that they have tried XYZ interventions in the classroom, at the classroom level. People are also starting to realize that sometimes the RTI services we can provide for students are better than the special education services. Once a child is classified, it's ongoing forever.

I think we are going in the right direction, but sometimes you have a situation where all of a sudden classifications spike in a particular grade and a lot has to do with the teacher. We just didn't have the right teacher. And that's all it takes sometimes, a year with a not-great teacher. Not that she is a bad teacher, just not in the right place. She didn't have the experience for where she was placed.

With RTI I believe we get the kids quicker and earlier and the accountability is placed more on the classroom teacher to say no one else is going to come in and fix this problem. It's not the reading specialist who is going to come and fix this child's deficit, or the math specialist. I think historically that's been the mind-set of classroom teachers, especially with special education students who were included in their class. RTI is not the barbed-wire fence to keep kids where they don't belong. I have children in my school that are classified as autistic and I could tell that these children are not autistic as far as I'm concerned. They might have some characteristics of children with autism, but that's all.

We want our process to become more analytical. Not just take a look at student test scores. We're having teachers say, "You know what, he's been failing these tests, he's not engaged, let's classify him." We want teachers to really be reflective and say, "OK, what are the strategies, what are the skills, how does the student learn?" And that's part of our RTI, to have a leadership team with representatives from every area. So our teachers have studied what RTI is about. And again, it is not the barbed wire. It is just ensuring that we really get to know students. We're asking teachers to track children's independent reading level. Whether it's research based or not, I think that term gets thrown around so loosely, I think it's a good way of measuring kids' progress and they can assess them using a benchmark system.

We had a class of children that had been together in a self-contained classroom for four years, kindergarten through third grade. And everybody knows who the kids are. It became dysfunctional and we had to start splitting up the kids and dealing with a lot of different behaviors. We created a full-time co-teaching model because the special education children will be going into a larger class for the first time in their lives. When the class lists came out, every parent in the district and every child knows the names of these children because they were in a self-contained class for four years. I think nine, ten years old is a good time to integrate them into an inclusion class. If you have a good teacher who can differentiate instruction and you have good staff, you can be very successful.

Another point is that it's not just one cause that leads to an effect. These students were together in second [grade] and were very successful. They had a very experienced teacher and teaching assistant. Then they go into third grade with a teacher who was not very experienced in teaching self-contained classes.

Suddenly the dynamics change. There is not an adult who is skillful in engaging the students, and the learning difficulties are exacerbated. It made it a difficult situation to manage all year by that principal. So there's so many politics, but there's also the personal dynamics and then the skill of the teacher dynamics that factor into it.

The key is to put the strongest teachers into co-teach positions. I have taken the best general education teachers the school has to offer and placed them in the inclusion classrooms. This will change the perception of the class and the general education parents not wanting their kids in it. There was one parent who was concerned about her child leaving a self-contained room and going into an inclusion class because the reading level was so low. We worked with her and she's OK with it now.

Of course, on occasion, we can't make a parent happy. If we are unable to come to agreement then it moves on to litigation. We have a few cases like that. But for the most part, our system runs smoothly and parents are happy with placements and programs. The Special Education Parent Teacher Association (SEPTA) was very strong in our district. But their activity has diminished in the last few years. I'm hoping it has something to do with the fact that they see we're addressing their needs, we're not dismissive of them, and it all has to do with our relationship.

Superintendents

This narrative is a combination of public school superintendents and assistant superintendents. Their thoughts on the major issues in special education follow.

I think the major issue right now is funding. The thinking is that too many students are placed out of district, so the push is to bring as many back into the districts as possible. Districts need to be careful with the percentage of students that are being classified. I think that's why the whole issue of Response to Intervention was instituted. RTI is used to see if not as many students would be classified because it all adds up to the dollars, so to speak. I think that is the major political issue, but nobody will ever come out and say they are against special education. It's like being against motherhood and apple pie. We are all very sensitive to students, and that is our role as educators.

There is a lot of debate over RTI. You would have to look at it by schools and their implementation models. There is no statewide role telling you how to do it. The politics behind RTI looks from the perspective of how much are you overseeing and regulating local schools and where does that come into play in politics. Depending on who the governor is and what their philosophy is behind it, how much are you telling the districts you must do this kind of a program and in this manner and in this time frame. So where and how the state department comes into play, I think, plays a major role in how these areas are developed. If they aren't overseeing RTI and saying you must do it this way, then you have to look at each district separately.

So some districts have a specific RTI model and others don't. One district may use the Orton-Gillingham program with pullouts three times a week to help a student with a reading difficulty. Another district may say the teacher will give you extra support in the classroom with no pullouts. It depends on what the school has to offer.

The federal special education department is telling us to look at minority over-classification. So the state has rolled out analysis of that, and the idea is to see if minority kids are being overclassified. And RTI is an intervention created to help lower that number.

Then you have No Child Left Behind (NCLB). The one good thing that came out of NCLB was the emphasis on accountability with regard to special education. For too long I saw the perception by the special education teachers as, "Well, they can't do it, they're special education." And while some of them maybe can't, many could. It asked more of them and you ask more, you get more. And I think the accountability was good in that respect. Now to force some of them to take these tests where they would sit there and start to cry, that's cruel.

I think we have come full circle with special education because we've seen the philosophy change from pulling them out and saying that provides a better forum to saying it wasn't a better forum for them. It excludes them. An inherent belief is that these children can't learn to the same levels of the average nucleus student, and it's not necessarily true. So the accountability in some respects did raise the bar, but I also think it provided the key to needs, the push to provide more services and resources. And that costs money.

The word we talked about in education for years was *balance*. The pendulum swings from one end and then it goes back to the other end. You have to have a balance. It's the same thing with special education expectations. You have high standards but you also have to have expectations that maybe some of the students aren't able to do it—so *balance*.

I think we are going to be in some hard times with funding. I believe it is going to be frozen; I don't think it is going to increase. The special education lobby is so strong that they will put pressure on to see it doesn't decrease. But it may have to. IDEA funding is an entitlement grant, and with any entitlement grant, where do you put the parameters around that grant? It is an established law what the criteria is to get classified. So they could change the criteria and make fewer children eligible for learning disabilities, for example, which is the largest category of classified children. That would play into the funding issue. I think people are starting to analyze the cost-effectiveness of some of these programs.

The new Race to the Top grants, this is the second round, is all based on early preschool reading. Remediate early and classify fewer children. Again, it is a cost-saving measure along with being good practice.

Some changes that I think will be coming because of austerity measures involve grants. Different grants—Title I, IV, all different categories of entitled funds are going to be put together with special education, and the government will disburse the money locally in block grants. Then it becomes the local person's problem how to divvy it up, not the federal government.

The IDEA reauthorization, which is supposed to be done this year, is pending until the changes are done on No Child Left Behind, particularly in terms of testing requirements. It will be interesting to see who undertakes the task of the IDEA reauthorization statewide. The superintendents' lobby group is complaining about the funding—all the funding going to special education. They are going to be looking at the number of regulations being put on the schools. I can't imagine changing much in terms of the regulations. Full funding for educating a special education child was supposed to be 40 percent of what it cost. Twelve percent was actually the most reimbursement received. The Obama administration was talking about full funding but is ignoring that issue right now since the economy tanked.

But I do believe we are going to see changes in special education programs—the money is not going to be there. Perhaps it will be RTI classifying less children, the requirement for being classified as LD will be more stringent, and you will have fewer numbers of special education children needing to be serviced. We will have to wait and see.

Special Education Directors

This narrative is a combination of special education directors. Their account follows.

To be successful in special education, you have to know the law, but you have to be very careful about knowing when to make use of your knowledge of the law. I found that when people get the sense that you're running your meetings based on requirements of the law, you usually lose your meeting early on in the process.

I believe that parents need to understand the process, their role in the process, the importance of being informed and knowledgeable participants. I have dealt with cases where parents didn't want to give us consent to evaluate and cases where I felt parents were asking us to do something for a student that I felt was going to be harmful for the kid. I just said to the parent, "You have the tool available and probably for you and for us, it's better if we let an impartial hearing officer give us a decision on this." We, as a district, would push if we felt a child needed to be evaluated.

The IEP [Individualized Education Program] team should approach the meeting as a decision-making process—not have their minds made up ahead of time—and parents should be involved in the process. If parents believe that is what will go on, you are building consensus. I know there are others where this is not the case. The meetings are autocratic and parents don't really have meaningful input. If you let the system work the way it was supposed to, we may not have to deal with all of these impartial hearings. I know that it is my job, to listen, to help build consensus, to help the team move forward.

One problem is that I haven't found a parent yet who finds *reasonable education progress* an acceptable level of support for their child. Yet the law states special education requires only *reasonable educational benefit*; we don't have to *maximize potential*. That can lead to adversarial situations with parents. And sometimes parents get beat up as they go through the special education process because they want what's best for their child. And the law provides what's reasonable, not what's best.

I would like to see a commitment to the fundamental principles of the law. That's collaborative team-based decision making about kids with disabilities and all the members are informed and active participants in the meeting. Decisions are made at the meeting, not before the meeting. Superintendents don't get to dictate the outcome, even when their budget might depend on an outcome.

Beyond that, I think the intent of the law was to ensure access. I think the moves recently have been designed more to ensure that kids make progress, meaning, moving beyond access to accountability. I think special education is more about personal connections between teachers and kids. I am waiting for the pendulum to swing back away from accountability, frankly. But I am clearly in the minority in that area.

I feel like the good work that's done in special education is done when the teacher sits down with a kid and connects and motivates and works to ensure skill development and then measures progress. So if what we are doing is preparing kids for tests and spending valuable instructional time working on accountability, then I think we missed the boat.

ADVOCATES FOR CHILDREN WITH DISABILITIES

Advocates step in and help when parents are struggling with school districts. Entering into a dialogue with schools can be overwhelming for parents of students with disabilities. It is confusing and time consuming. An advocate can bridge the gap to help parents get the services their child is entitled to.

Attorney

This is a recounting of the thoughts from an advocacy lawyer who works with many parents of children with disabilities.

Special education is a very classist system. So I find myself representing many relatively affluent families who have been able to afford to send their children to an appropriate school and are seeking reimbursement from the state. But systemically the consequence of funding their children, given the limited resources and paucity of resources for special education, is actually regressive. So I consider my own work, in a sense, contributing to the problem.

Special education is a very multifaceted issue. The delays inherent in the legal system are also totally unacceptable, but commonplace. They render the system, frankly, laughable. It is a very, very broken system. I think the judges recognize this. The ultimate issue is very simply this: If you have a relatively modest family, in terms of family income, and that child is being disserved in his or her placement, that family, in essence, in this system, has no choice. They can't self-place, unilaterally place, because they can't afford to. So they are stuck with whatever *the best* the public school has to offer. And the public school system knows the families who have limited resources; it's no great secret.

So that immediately advantages the public school system because it knows those families who have no real alternative. Where are they going to go? The school can pacify some small proportion or ratio of families who have means, and the irony is, they end up spending money on the families who have the means to begin with.

Clearly, what has to occur is that districts have to be honest about their ability to educate a particular child. A survey was sent out to all the schools in a very broad area asking, "Do you have any students that fit this profile that you are unable to educate?" One district responded that they had one child. Every other district denied that they had any child whose needs they weren't meeting. It was a bold lie, an absolute lie. One of those districts had a child of that specific profile in a private school. So the system really needs to start with a recognition that there are youngsters whose needs are not being met.

I get several of these youngsters in here every week, and I have for the past twenty-five years, who are being miseducated, grossly miseducated by the public schools. And the public schools, at these times of increasing budgetary shortfalls, do not have the resources to meet those needs. Obviously the solution is you either have to have the public schools better equipped to meet the need or you have to have private schools. Now the advantage of private regionalized schools is that every public school is not trying to meet the need of every kid. You would have a group of schools collaborating with one private school, which is intended to meet those kinds of particularized needs, whatever those may be—dyslexia, Asperger's, or psychological issues.

We have a dearth of programs in this region, in this state. It leads to pressure to send children out of state. And states have now passed regulations saying, "All children will be back in state in one year." But there is no place for them to come. Parents are at a tremendous disadvantage. Parents are at an even greater disadvantage in certain areas because there isn't an appropriate school for their child. So even if the parent has resources, "OK, I'm going to send my child to X school," where is X school? It doesn't exist. And parents are desperate. They will look at any school that appears to be a specialized school to find a place appropriate.

All of this dramatizes the broader issue, which is misplaced priorities, and they are not going to change around special education. Many of us were hoping that this presidency would lead to some of that, but it doesn't appear to really be true. In terms of the future, we're either going to have more addressed to all the issues—such as housing and jobs, along with special education—or not at all. I don't think the government is going to pick out special education and address it more. I think you need a broader consciousness-raising, and this, among other issues, will get attention. Without it, special education will be ignored, marginalized.

People need to be organized. Those that are involved are intensely involved. It's about their child. But those involved are often focused on themselves, which makes organizing everyone very difficult, because they focus on their own needs. This approach is too myopic and not likely to have success. Your particular child is not likely to be advantaged in a regressive system. You need to have a system that is much better for *everybody* or your own child won't get help. And any organizing needs victories so people think what they do has some impact. You have to inspire them. And let school districts know that this group is watching over them.

So for the future of IDEA, the classism has to be remedied. There has to be a very particular statutory direction that impartial hearing officers have the right and responsibility to order a placement with reimbursement or with funding, so it's not simply a reimbursement statute. The other issue is adherence to timeline, which is both a state and federal issue. Timelines right now are being avoided, worked around, and evaded, and it's just impossible. Your average case can last from three to four years. Those are two key issues.

Parent Advocates

This narrative is a combination of parent advocates who work to improve the special education system by speaking about parental rights, putting different parents in touch with one another and disseminating information related to resources for children with disabilities through a website. Their account follows in their own words.

I go to meetings in a lot of different districts as an advocate for parents of children with disabilities. So I can really see what's going on and how evil people are. I hear all these horrible cases. It breaks my heart. If you don't have a strong advocate with you or know what you're doing the school district freaking screws you. We try to teach parents, don't ever go alone to a meeting about your child, tape-record everything. And they won't understand. They say, "What do you mean? These are professionals, I trust them." We try to empower the parents because school districts will beat you down.

Parents can't stand up because they've had such horrible experiences in school. They tell me they're afraid of being blackballed. They start off thinking, "But the school people are the professionals and they're the educated people, I trust them." The district will say to the parents, "Give us another year, we need more time." So they trust the school.

Also, the district will say, "You're the only one who can't get along with us." They isolate the parents. The school puts it all on them. "The other people I can work with. If you would just stop being so unreasonable it would work." I'm also a parent of a child with a disability. My district told me, "Quit your job and stay home with your child 'cause there's nothing we can do for him." I told them, "This is 2004. Women work. I think there is a law that says you have to educate him."

We try to get parents organized and motivated, but it's a pretty apathetic group. It's hard to get people motivated because all they see is their own child. Right now their child is getting what he needs, so they back away. But there is a bigger need out there, and most parents can't see beyond themselves. I know it's emotionally draining; it dominates your life. But it needs to be done. Parents have so much more power than they realize if they would group together. Districts know we are watching them so that helps a little. And sometimes we send letters from a lawyer and that will work.

Right now my group works on the independent education evaluation policy that each district has. If you disagree with the in-house evaluation, the school district one, you can seek an independent one at district expense. That's your right by law. But for a neuropsych they will reimburse you $1,200. Well, you can't find a neuropsych for $1,200. It's more like $7,000. You would think a district would want that evaluation to see what is going on with the child, but no. We are telling all the parents to get an outside evaluation done because if you have to go to hearing you will need one. Otherwise, you have no power. The rulings have been so unfavorable without an outside evaluation.

The best way for parents to get informed of their rights should be by the district. But districts don't do it or don't do it adequately. Most people don't understand what they get given about the law. It needs to be explained in language parents can understand. And schools don't do that. So you have groups like ours that try to do that role.

We are also working on getting a school put on the state-approved list, because the school district can't legally place a child there without litigation. It has been a long and tedious process and we are not getting anywhere yet.

Districts don't have programs for a lot of the children. So they get placed out of district or out of state. But now there's a law that says all kids have to be brought back into state. I know it's expensive to educate a child. I don't think regular education parents know the cost of special education. I think there would be more outrage if they knew. But if districts stopped spending so much money on impartial hearings they could afford to educate. Districts will just put a kid into an existing program, instead of trying to fit a program around the kid. Unless parents know what to fight for, they don't stand a chance.

I think changes need to be made to the IDEA. Not get rid of it because then we'd have nothing. Maybe not changes to the IDEA, but enforcing it. The districts think they can function without following the law unless somebody stands up and says, "You are violating the law." Also, the IDEA is ambiguous. For example, it states that reports are supposed to be given to parents in a reasonable time period before the meeting. Well, what's reasonable? I think a week ahead is reasonable, but the districts might think ten minutes is reasonable, while you're sitting in the waiting room before the meeting. The weak link in enforcing it is the parents' not standing up and saying, "I have rights by law, you have to do this."

So that's why we started this group. And I got a lawyer to do free consults one night a week. He listens to the parents and then he'll send a letter out the next day to the school district. Simple things the district will change, just because of that letter. But you shouldn't have to send the letter out. I know it's hard for lawyers to deal with us. It's very emotionally taxing and I know we get a little out of control sometimes. It's because of what the districts do to us, to the vulnerable population.

When parents go to a meeting about their child's IEP, districts use language and jargon that the parents don't understand. I think it's to remove their [the parents'] power. The committee is talking off a tape—it's all set up ahead of time what everyone is going to say. And we encourage parents to record the meeting, so the school gets very hostile. They'll say, "Well, are you really going to be that contentious that you need to record? Can't we all just get along and work this out? You don't need to record unless you think you're going to a hearing." They try to pressure the parents.

It also depends on the personality of the person chairing the meeting. I went to one last week where the chair was very hostile and degrading to the parent. She told the parent what a horrible parent she was because she wouldn't agree to the placement. It also depends on the parent's wealth or knowledge level. One parent was getting pushed around so I went with her to the meeting. I knew they had the services she wanted. I went and she got them; they couldn't hide.

The services cost money and they [the district] don't want to spend it if they can get away with it. If you're educated, and can show up with a lawyer, know the law, bring an advocate who knows the law, you have a better chance of getting the service your child needs. As a parent, you are supposed to be a full participant in the meetings. But the committee tries to tell what they're going to do, fait accompli, and these people may never have even seen the child.

Like my child was only in the district for ten days before I got him placed elsewhere. I said to them, "You don't even know who he is. I could give you a picture and you wouldn't know him. I could give you information about him." But they still say, "We know better than you." It makes you distrustful. Your information is not important to them, because they know more. They have more education than the parents; they have the training, so the parent is superfluous.

All these meetings can have a parent representative attend. This is someone that the school district brings in. I'll never forget at one meeting I was talking about how I was placing my child in a boarding school that was the appropriate placement for him. The parent representative started saying, "You are a horrible mother. You're going to send your child away? You just adopted him. Why did you bother adopting him?" She went on and on. I was so upset. She didn't know who I was, who my child was. She knew nothing. The district told her what to say, to make me feel inadequate and guilty about finding a placement out of state that was appropriate for my child.

Ever since then I decline a parent representative at the meetings. I tell other parents to decline. A parent of a disabled child acting as a district representative at these meetings will sell another parent down the river. They will be on board with the school's agenda, as long as they're getting what they want for their child.

It's hard to get people in the community to support your efforts, the organization. I don't think a lot of the parents of the general education kids are that sympathetic because I don't think they really understand what it is to have a disabled child, especially severely disabled, so they don't get involved. They don't realize the struggles you go through. We try to encourage other people to join our group, like politicians, to bring about more awareness and strengthen our position with the school districts. But it's hard.

I think you should publish a book "This Is What You Need to Do": parent rights, the laws, and how to survive the special education process, how to maintain your sanity. Tell parents how to access resources and what is available. A lot of resources exist out there and if parents could access it you might not have to be on the school district all the time, making them crazy. Then maybe everyone would be happy.

ADULT EDUCATORS

Entering the special education arena requires people to learn a new language. This language encompasses the legal—laws and rights—and terminology—what those acronyms stand for and mean. Adult educators are people who attempt to inform parents of this. They do not work for the school district and they do not work for the parent. They are neutral. They educate about rights, terminology, and where resources exist.

Parent Educator

I see my job as educating families to give them the resources that they need to participate in their child's education planning. I don't go in and advocate for parents. I believe that we—parents, school districts, and educators—should be partners in the education process. And I think any good partner should know what their role is intended to be. You need to know the rules and how to play with the other team members. Otherwise you're only out for your own agenda and no one is going to want to play with you.

I'm very pro Response to Intervention (RTI). Unfortunately, it's not done according to the process in most places. It's a very big system change. There are many districts who know it's required as of July 2012 and haven't even started talking about it. I worry about that. I believe that the next generation of advocacy for students with disabilities is inclusion and is getting them included and building capacity for our general educators to support students. Not just students with disabilities, but students with vulnerabilities whatever their socioeconomic background, students of color, or students that are at a lower level. RTI is a lot of promise to help build the capacity and support those kids. But it needs to be done right. My district does it right, but a lot don't.

I'm going to be writing a new curriculum for families for accessible instruction materials. I really believe that it holds such a capacity that I think we need to educate parents. Parents are how you build capacity. Parents' asking questions and demanding their rights is how we build capacity. We push each other. So I offered to write a curriculum for families so they understand what their rights are and how they start navigating the special education system.

It won't just be about parent rights. I try and give parents the tools they need so they can participate most effectively. I'm not from a perspective of advocacy, but much more from a perspective of collaboration. Because I went through all those stages with my children. I feel that I've accomplished the most when I sit down at the table realizing that I'm actually a member of that committee. And when I understand what I'm entitled to and can have the conversation and trust in my ability, I accomplish the most. So many times I sat at that table, I didn't know my rights well enough, and so it was very intimidating and made me feel distrustful. I really try to educate families so they feel empowered enough to sit at the table and participate in the conversation effectively so they can be a part of a team to develop good outcomes for their kids.

I believe we have to shift our advocacy before we come under a spotlight. With the current fiscal crisis, budgets are being reduced and cut, so a lot of regular programs are going to disappear—like sports, language, music, and art. Well, eventually that advocacy for special programs and placements is going to come back and bite us because it is going to fuel the anger of regular education parents. I think we need to be proactive about supporting our general educators so they can support our special education kids and build a really, truly inclusive society.

What I'm hoping will come out of this financial crisis is that we'll be forced to include students with disabilities in our community. It's very expensive to house an adult with a disability in a separate setting. It's much less expensive to have them part of the community. Schools should work on independence so that these kids could work in some capacity. There is not going to be an adult system to take care of my daughter. She needs to work at something. That's why there's so much depression in the developmental disability community. Human beings were meant to be productive to feel fulfilled. So schools and society need to shift the focus away from entitlement and focus on nurturing independence and productivity.

IDEA got us invited to the table. Now for the next round we need to figure out how we're going to be included in the meal. I see a backlash coming. At community budget hearings special education families are singled out as using up so much of the school budget moneys. I think it's going to be a significant backlash. The focus is still on, "What's my individual due process right? What's appropriate for my kid?" rather than, "How do we protect services? How do we come together, stakeholders, and protect to the greatest extent that we can, protect services for all our kids? Not just for the kid who can hire the lawyer, but for all our students." And I think that's going to take a different approach, a collaborative approach.

Parent Education Coordinator

My main goal is to disseminate as much information as possible to as many people as possible. So I go out there and do presentations. But I have to be invited someplace to do it. I rely on our relationships with school districts to promote information. I'll say to them, "Offer this for your parents. I'll help you explain it to them." We'll deal with other agencies to make connections and network. I will try to get to Special Education Parent Teacher Associations and more neutral places like libraries.

We have a lot of different people speaking about different topics, and a good amount of the time we get a poor turnout. I don't know if the information is not reaching the right people, people are apathetic, or it's just too overwhelming.

Transition is a topic that's very important to me. I go into school districts and talk about services—what's involved in securing services and all the different options. I try to get the schools thinking about creative ways that they could develop programming, thinking outside the box and understanding what transition is. It ends up being "panic moment." Either parents are not worrying about it, thinking some other system is just going to automatically take over, or they are relying so heavily—because they trust the school—that the school district will tell them what the deal is, and that there must not be that much to know.

When you see parents of kids who are getting ready to age out, they are really getting very worried, and rightfully so. Transition is pretty much focused on at the high school level, and we've been trying to push it back to start at the middle school level and earlier because parents and children need time to accept and think about it. But it's still really not happening. I have parents of kids who are graduating and they say, "I never heard of any of this. No one has told me anything." And that is so scary.

So where is the weak link? Where is it breaking down? You would think that school districts would be happy that we are here to relieve them of some of the burden. I think school districts are leery of us coming in and speaking. Advocates do great work, but it can end up being an adversarial situation for schools. We are neutral. We are not advocates. We give information—tell parents what they need to know. It is a little bit tricky because of that.

We are not an advocacy agency. We help parents work collaboratively with the school districts. Parents will ask me where they can find an advocate. I'll respond, "Why do you think you need an advocate?" And really, the primary reason is because they don't understand what the law is. They don't understand what the school is legally supposed to do or not supposed to do, and that causes fear and so they rely on somebody else. But I will remind them, "You are relying on someone else, that their information is correct and that they're going to speak for you in the way that you want them to. Especially because you don't really get to know them unless you've been working with them for a while."

I tell parents, "We are here to help you find your own voice, to learn what it is you are confused about and what you don't know. That way you can go and represent yourself appropriately, be involved in your child's education, and get the best services planned for the future, accordingly." That's how we differ from advocacy groups.

Schools need to put somebody in the position of transition counselor. Somebody who is very familiar with the entire process and what's available outside of school. Ideally, it would be somebody who is part community, part adult services, and who knows what's going on outside of school, because that's what it's about, bridging the gap. So someone who understands the education but also understands the world on the outside and the services in the other systems.

CONCLUSION

Interestingly, a number of issues are common to all stakeholders interviewed. RTI is consistently brought up by all parties interviewed, with varying degrees of favoritism. There seems to be agreement that RTI is a cost-saving measure insofar as the goal is to classify fewer children. Stakeholders seem to also agree that if RTI is done right, it is a good intervention. One interesting comment was that RTI is a regular education initiative, so it doesn't have the special education stigma attached to it. Stakeholders believe that districts implement the RTI process differently and in some places it is not done correctly with full understanding by those involved. Many parents see RTI as a process designed to keep their child from being classified, thereby withholding needed services.

Another commonality is education. Stakeholders believe that a parent educated in the law and their rights is an asset. Parents strongly believe they need to know their rights. Disagreement comes through when discussion centers on disseminating this knowledge: who should do it, where it should be done, and when it should be done. An area that also generates the same disagreement is transition planning. Everyone agrees it needs to be done and done sooner, but that is the limit of agreement.

A great divide stands between administrators—superintendents, principals, and special education directors—and the other stakeholders—parents, children, advocates, and adult educators. Administrators believe that the special education process in their districts runs smoothly, for the most part. The other stakeholders believe the special education system needs a lot of work.

Parents, advocates, and attorneys believe that IEP planning meetings are not appropriately done. Even special education directors acknowledge that some districts do not run meetings in a suitable manner. Parents attending these meetings believe them to be adversarial, and are very distrustful of the process and committee members, effectively closing the door on collaboration between all stakeholders.

Special education is a complex process. Little things along the way can snowball into major problems and have very powerful negative effects on children's education and lives. Students, for the most part, enter school with the notion that they will be accepted and treated fairly, and they have trust. Special education has the ability to kill those feelings. It can be insidious, slowly over time eroding a child's self-confidence bit by bit—slowly making him or her feel more and more isolated.

This negative scenario is certainly not the case for all children with disabilities. Some escape this treatment. However, for too many this is the case. The expression "fair is not equal" in special education means that sometimes children with disabilities need more support than others to be full participants in the classroom. These students should never receive fewer services than they need.

Education is not a factory even though special education is a large complex system with no magic answers. Only with caring and compassion for all children, true collaboration, and trust can the bridge be built over the fences that separate children, schools, and their communities.

QUESTIONS FOR DISCUSSION

1. Explain the Response to Intervention process. At what point in the implementation process do you see potential for its breaking down?
2. Why do you think the viewpoints expressed by the administrators differ from the viewpoints of the children, parents, and advocates?
3. What information do parents need to know about due process in special education? Create a presentation—using lay language, no education jargon, and no acronyms—designed to inform parents of children with disabilities about their due process rights.

13

Schooling Tommy in the Future

The Ideal

Marshall Strax

INTRODUCTION

Children with disabilities, their parents, teachers, administrators, advocates, attorneys, and adult educators all have a key role to play in the micropolitics of special education. The children—in the middle—are pivotal in the growing special education saga. However, the children should not be in the middle but at the end—of every decision-making process concerning their own education. This chapter shows how we can move the children from the messy middle to the desirable end.

Special education is a microcosm of the macrocosm of life in a capitalistic United States. Competition creates winners and losers in every arena of American life, as success is measured by one's accumulation of resources—financial, political, and social status. The resources of the United States are vast—among the largest in the world. How these resources are spent becomes a matter of politics, as the distribution of resources is arranged to the liking of those who profit most from it—those who wield the power to maintain intact arrangements that benefit them. "History shows no examples of the powerful voluntarily relinquishing their power to the powerless" (Smith and Max-Neef 2011, 13).

People compete for the vast resources available in every area of American life. Sometimes the resources are put into infrastructure and services that serve the common good by developing the human capital of all citizens; other times they are invested in conquest and private corporate entities that benefit the rich and powerful as a conscious choice. For example, resources can build schools, do research, and implement new models for educating all children, or they can provide increased wealth for the rich and powerful through corporate subsidies and a full spectrum of tax abatements.

Key players—children with disabilities, parents, teachers, administrators, advocates, attorneys, and adult educators—in the micropolitics of special education are critical in understanding how special education works. Several barriers to progress seen through their eyes are given voice in this book, along with suggestions to overcome these obstacles and create a new future for special education.

BARRIERS TO PROGRESS

Throughout the case studies presented in this book (chapters 2, 6, 8, 10, 11, and 12), adversarial relationships between families of children with disabilities and school and state agency personnel emerge as a major source of disruption to the education of these children. On the one hand, children want to be like all other children—to go to school and play with their siblings and friends. Parents desire to maximize the potential of their *cared-for* (Noddings 1984) children—seeking to protect them from physical and emotional harm and to develop all their educational potential.

On the other hand, school administrators and other education personnel are responsible for educating all children in a school and managing the financial resources under their purview (see chapter 5 for details). People's valuations of what is important—their thoughts, beliefs, and ideas, both rational and irrational, concerning socioeconomic status, abilities, and distribution of resources—constitute what they believe are important. "Whether through our upbringing, schooling, reading, or whatever, we all have relatively fixed valuations concerning the world about us, and whether we like it or not, we carry them with us into our work and social science" (Smith and Max-Neef 2011, 57).

For example, parents realized that the ground rules of significant discourse are an expression of power (Bowers 1987). After meeting with school personnel, parents report (in chapters 10 and 11) feeling inadequate and unable to contribute to a meeting conducted in a language they do not understand—one of education jargon, legalese, statistics, and acronyms. Administrators were sometimes not aware of the need to—or were unwilling to—educate parents about a full range of programmatic options for their children and their due process rights. Parents rarely believed they were equal participants in meetings with school personnel.

Some parents and children are aware of unequal treatment of other parents and children by school personnel. Parents who served on school districts' Individualized Education Program (IEP) planning teams described how other parents—without financial resources, political relationships within the school districts, knowledge of programmatic options and due process rights, or the support of expert testimony—were coerced into accepting substandard IEPs for their children. Other parents described the full range of programs their children received *after* they became members of their local board of education.

Participants in the New England Inclusion Education Leadership Summit (IOD.UNH 2009) agreed that leadership is the biggest barrier to change in the way children with disabilities are educated. Each new generation of school leaders is socialized into the leadership profession by the existing generation of school leaders and professors of school leadership. Attitudes toward children with disabilities and their parents are passed down. Unduly technical, classical, top-down, and neoscientific concepts of bureaucracy still prevail. Relying on concepts such as objectivity, superficial rationality, task analysis, accountability, the division of people into categories, and the sanctity of expert knowledge, school leaders essentially colonize the children and parents.

The Individuals with Disabilities Education Act (IDEA) (2004) requires school districts to provide a free appropriate education in the least restrictive environment (see chapter 4 for details). This landmark legislation that originally passed in 1975, with regulations adopted in 1977, ended the era of exclusion of students with disabilities that had existed since the beginning of public schooling in the United States. However, the act did not end segregation; it provided only for a student's education in the *least restrictive* environment—with a child's nondisabled peers to the greatest extent possible.

Educators interpreted the mandate for least restrictive environment as the concepts of mainstreaming and inclusion (see chapter 7 for details). However, these terms, not defined by law or regulation, are open to individual interpretation. Over the last thirty-four years, vast improvements have occurred in the educational opportunities for children with disabilities. However, the current Special Education approach, couched in a medical model—of categories of disabilities needing to be cured—leaves many children segregated for part or all of their school day. In addition, the language of discrimination still exists. Consideration of *inclusion* implies contemplation of *exclusion*!

Parents as well as some administrators express concern over the human, programmatic, and financial costs of late and improper diagnoses of children with disabilities. For example, children not diagnosed with both reading and language disabilities until age seven or later experienced frustration with the academic curriculum, a long-term and expensive remediation process, and other obstacles to learning.

Parents and administrators point out how early and correct diagnoses and early intervening remedial education—such as the well-researched Orton-Gillingham approach to language—would have enabled the children to be successful in school with their peers. In some cases, the inability to read or properly communicate led to children's developing behavioral issues that were difficult and costly to remediate.

Children with disabilities and their parents all report very poor transition planning from public school to adulthood. In fact, many parents report virtually no transition planning at all—just a brief statement of a postsecondary goal added to an IEP with no meaningful parent input. Most children were not invited to be full active participants in this process. Administrators describe very little knowledge about transition. Adult educators point out that after offering their services to train school district personnel free of charge, very few districts accept their offer. Parent participation in free transition workshops is poor.

> We have the opportunity now to analyze with true honesty the map that shows where we have navigated, with all its hazards and successes; all its tragedies and glories and then we may be wise to unearth the alternative map of the route we did not navigate and see whether we can find in it orientations that can rescue us from our existential confusion. (Smith and Max-Neef 2011, 20)

A MODEL FOR CREATING THE FUTURE

Different valuations and perspectives lead to different uses of language to describe one's world. Max-Neef (2010) suggests that when one is speaking and interacting with other people who have lived their lives in a different social, cultural, and contextual environment, one's own language is totally inadequate. An opportunity to invent a new language is created—communication that is coherent with the environment and the experiences of the other.

A new model to educate children with disabilities in the twenty-first century should begin with a reconciliation of the many ideas, perspectives, and differences in thinking of the stakeholders in educating children with disabilities. As shown in figure 13.1, reconciliation is achieved—at both the intragroup and intergroup levels—through a cyclical process of (1) dialogue, (2) consensus, and (3) implementation.

This process begins with dialogue. Freire (1968/1970) believed that people who are oppressed and exploited through systemic structures beyond their control

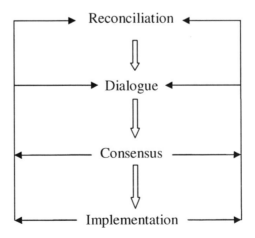

Figure 13.1. A Model for Creating the Future

need to meet and critically explore and understand their situation, investigate possibilities for liberation, and create a plan to achieve it.

First, parents and older children can get together and conduct a bottom-up discourse on the local level with the goal of understanding and solving common issues encountered in the special education system. A plan for the future education of children with disabilities can be developed. Once the players reach consensus, this discourse would continue between like players across ever-larger geographic areas. Other major stakeholder groups, such as school administrators, are already organized and involved in intragroup dialogue.

Second, groups of parents and older children on the local level need to enter into a conversation with other stakeholder groups with the goal of developing a plan for the future education of the children. However, before different groups of key players are brought together, sensitivity training should take place. Each group of stakeholders in the education of children with disabilities will benefit from knowledge about the belief system and language of other groups.

Knowledge, with proper sensitivity training, will enable participants to develop an understanding for the source of the other's belief system. Comprehending the differences of the other stakeholder's belief systems should lead to an appreciation of why the terrain of special education is divided. Stakeholder groups would benefit from interactive presentations by panels of other key players.

For example, school administrators could learn the belief system of parents who seek to protect the physical and emotional well-being of their child. Panels of parents could share their ideas, beliefs, goals, and emotions with an audience of administrators. Parents could gain an appreciation for the pressures and obligations that drive administrative behavior.

Adult educators capable of facilitating critical dialogue can provide both groups with successful strategies for collaborative discourse and negotiation. Key players in need of adult education include parents, school administrators and other school personnel, the community, and social policymakers at every level. In addition, adult educators who are not employees of school districts can educate parents about the full spectrum of programmatic options for their children and their due process rights. This will prepare parents to be equal participants in dialogue with other stakeholder groups.

Intergroup collaborative discourse can commence on the local level. When consensus is reached among all stakeholders on future courses of action, experimental or pilot programs would be implemented. Through a cycle of feedback, exchange of new ideas, and reimplementation, pilot programs would be refined. Successful plans from various localities could be compared and through a continued process of dialogue, consensus, and implementation the best ones could be exported to larger geographic areas. This process would enable bottom-up creative solutions to educating children with disabilities within any social policy created by federal and state politicians and educators.

A NEW FUTURE FOR SPECIAL EDUCATION

The model for creating the future through cyclical dialogue, consensus, and implementation is useful for moving special education forward. This model brings key players together at many political levels to work collaboratively to remove barriers to the educational success of children with disabilities. Following are suggestions for use of the model.

Peace in Our Time

All children with disabilities—and their parents, teachers, administrators, advocates, attorneys, and adult educators featured in this book—decried the adversarial relationships between stakeholders in the special education process. Many spoke of relationships being divided by metaphoric obstacles such as fences, barbed wire, and mountains. They agreed on the sources of these barriers, including different life experiences, perspectives on education, levels of involvement with the children, lack of transparency, distrust, educational language usage, inadequate program implementation, and the power differentials between stakeholders.

The model, which provides sensitivity training, successful techniques for discourse and negotiation, and trial and error through a cycle of dialogue, consensus, and implementation, would create an atmosphere where all participants could develop a new language and process of discourse that is acceptable to all.

Diversity or Disability

Disability Studies and disability rights advocates believe in a social model of disability. The full spectrum of children's abilities (Fleischer and Zames 2011) should be analyzed for strengths. Early intervention and diagnoses of strengths and weaknesses give educators direction to develop all the potential in the children. There is human capital in every person. Developing children's potential brings real security to one's community, state, and country.

Advocates of the Special Education approach—a medical model—to the education of children with disabilities believe in classifying a child as a person with one of thirteen categories of disabilities. Advocates of Disability Studies and supporters of the Special Education approach at any level of decision making could meet and reconcile their differences using the model of cyclical dialogue, consensus, and implementation.

Social Policy or Individual Choice

In the past, changes in social policy such as passage of the IDEA have led the way to full integration of children in American schools (see chapters 3 and 4 for details). Further changes might or might not include definitions of disability, full funding of the IDEA, and full inclusion for all children. Many people believe children with disabilities and their families have been colonized. Powerful politicians not in a relationship with them have created systemic structures—including the IDEA—that have the power to alter their destinies and lives.

Believing in parental choice, many parents are vested in the identity politics of their child's classification of disability. Others believe in segregated classes and segregated schools. They prefer social policy that reflects their beliefs. Through a bottom-up dialogue beginning at the local level, interested parties can propose social policy reform that flows from consensus.

Leading Change

As previously discussed in this chapter, innovative change should begin with consumers of special education services participating in a process of critical dialogue with the goal of developing consensus for a plan of change. Before consumer groups can meet with education leaders in a cyclic process of dialogue, consensus, and implementation to reconcile differences of ideas for change, education leaders will need to enter into their own process of significant discourse.

Current school leaders could develop an understanding of the belief systems of parents and children with disabilities through sensitivity training that would include encounters with panels of parents and children. Adult educators, not employees of school districts, could provide the leaders with the background knowledge necessary to benefit from the sensitivity training.

School leadership programs—at both the administrator and teacher levels—require change. As Jorgenson points out (IOD.UNH 2009), leadership program curricula need to focus on inclusive education. The curricula would include ideas for new models of working with children and their parents, languages of communication, and rules of discourse. An inclusive structure and learning environment at the college and university level should be mandatory. The best way to learn inclusive education is to be inclusively educated through the use of cyclical models of dialogue, consensus, and implementation.

Smooth Transitions

The need for transition planning—from school to adulthood and already mandated by the IDEA (2004)—and the lack of knowledge about transition by all key players other than adult educators provides an ideal opportunity to take advantage of the collaborative planning process in the new model. Stakeholder groups could meet on the local level and enter into a critical conversation about the transition process and the results they would like to see for their children.

For example, parents in a school district could meet and develop a list of transition goals and information and services that they need to learn about to achieve these goals. Then they could invite an adult educator knowledgeable about all aspects of transition planning, including difficult topics such as finding adult group homes, financial trusts, and navigating the college and university choice and acceptance process to assist them in meeting their goals.

Next, intergroup collaborative discourse would commence on the local level. When consensus was reached among all stakeholders on the ideal procedures for transition planning, pilot procedures would be implemented. Through a cycle of feedback, exchange of new ideas, and reimplementation, the pilot program would be refined. Successful plans from various localities could be compared and contrasted and through the cyclical process the best one could be exported to larger geographic areas. This process would enable bottom-up creative solutions to transitioning students with disabilities to adulthood.

SCHOOLING TOMMY IN THE FUTURE: THE IDEAL

In the United States we strive to have an inclusive society, one where all people— with all their complexities and diversities—are accepted equally. However, even with all the civil rights legislation in the last fifty years, including the IDEA, this ideal has not been reached. Keith Jones (IOD.UNH 2009) suggests that children with disabilities have been hidden away and segregated because of their physical manner and demeanor. Counts (1932) suggests that teachers and schools could be a driving force for social change. Social change for Tommy was (in chapter 2) and continues to be done (in chapter 9) with some level of integration and toleration. Now is the time for full inclusion and acceptance for Tommy.

Full inclusion is the education of all children together in the same classrooms where all related services and accommodations are provided in the room. This goal will be Tommy's education in the future. A very small number of children (less than 1 percent) may not be able physically to attend the same classrooms with other children because of severe violent behavior, incarceration, or clear and present danger to themselves or others.

These children could still attend the same classrooms as other children through distance learning. This technology would provide the children with the same broad academic program options as other children. Some children may be kept out of these classrooms as a result of parental choice. Tommy is certainly not one of these children.

Social policy such as a future IDEA should mandate full inclusion. Due process would then be the avenue for a parent or public entity to remove a child from placement in a full inclusion program. However, as previously pointed out, *inclusion* implies consideration of *exclusion*. The word *inclusion* will not be used anymore because Tommy and all other children will no longer be *excluded* in any way.

All the components to educate Tommy in the future exist today. Implementing an ideal education for children with disabilities will require educators, consumers, and other stakeholders to get together and use the reconciliation model at every level of controversy to develop shared implementations of already-existing model programs. Parents will need to organize with other interested key players to drive local, state, and federal social policy with the goal of developing the full human capital of all children.

First, early and correct diagnoses are critical, allowing for early intervention to remediate academic, cognitive, emotional, social, and physical characteristics that impede a child's ability to learn. Identification of disability might be done using a three-dimensional matrix. For Tommy, one axis would delineate his spectrum of disability. For example, Tommy might present with a need for remediation of fine and gross motor function, speech articulation, and self-confidence.

A second axis would delineate the spectrum of severity—from mild to severe—of each disability on axis 1. For example, Tommy might exhibit severe gross motor functioning, moderate fine motor functioning, moderate speech articulation, and mild self-confidence issues. The third axis would demarcate Tommy's competencies of academic functioning in all the subject areas taught in school, including physical education and the arts. This process would inform diagnostic and education professionals about Tommy's cognitive, academic, social, emotional, and physical skills in need of remediation and support, thus enabling the delivery of his complete program—including related services and accommodations—within the classroom. The matrix model of diagnosis and identification of disability is useful with any child.

Universal design—creating public policies, structures, and programs with equal access for all people—will facilitate change (Sapon-Shevin 2007). New social policy—unlike the current IDEA—should provide people with limited financial, political, educational, and information resources with equal access to all provisions of law. All buildings and facilities would be completely accessible to all people, requiring a revision of current architectural and building codes.

Classrooms can be designed to accommodate the physical, behavioral, and social learning needs of all children in a noncompetitive environment, where everyone participates as an equal. Curricula that meet core content standards for learning will require materials giving all students an opportunity to succeed. Delivery requires differentiated teaching methods in the classroom. Creative scheduling at the secondary level allows guidance counselors to place Tommy in appropriate classes and activities that match characteristics diagnosed on a three-dimensional matrix.

Tommy would take the full range of academic courses, fulfilling all the prerequisites for postsecondary education. Any therapies still needed at this time could be provided within academic classrooms. For example, a physical therapist could work with Tommy during physical education class, and an occupational therapist might develop therapies associated with manipulating equipment in science laboratories and using technology in any academic classroom.

Model programs exist for educating Tommy and all other children with and without disabilities (Sapon-Shevin 2007; IOD.UNH 2009). New models can be created by key stakeholders through the process utilizing dialogue, consensus, and implementation. All children are valuable assets in the education of other children. As Arnold B. Danzig states in chapter 8,

> The measure of a person's life is less about one's individual accomplishments and more about the ways one person's life affects the lives of others. In this regard, my wife would always say our daughter was not handicapped; rather, she was gifted because she changed the people around her—parents, siblings, teachers, caregivers, bureaucrats—with great ideas concerning social responsibility, chronic care, the meaning of vulnerability, the limitations of medical practice, and so on.

Many educators "throw up their hands" and say, "How can we educate children with medical fragility or severe and profound disability?" Current schools for these children are often technological tours de force. For example, a school for students with medical fragility or severe and profound disability might be a segregated school with 60 students. Through new construction, that school could expand to 180 students. The additional 120 students from a neighborhood school would end segregation, as all children could be educated together. The technological tour de force of this school would make it a desirable choice for all children.

The next step is to export the model programs to other schools within school districts and then across wider geographical areas. Many principals, teachers, teaching assistants, and support service personnel—such as psychologists, social workers, school nurses, and speech and language, occupational, and physical therapists—know how to successfully educate all children together. They are a resource for other schools and school districts. Most parents interviewed for this book prefer to have their children with disabilities in schools and classrooms with their siblings and neighborhood friends.

This effort will require the involvement of all the key players—parents, school administrators and other school personnel, the community, and social policymakers at every level. Working together to create a new and innovative future for children with disabilities, stakeholders can reconcile differences as they occur through a cyclical process of dialogue, consensus, and implementation. This will not be a quick and easy process. Commitment, creativity, and hard work will be needed to maintain momentum.

Meaningful change takes several years to implement. Colleges and universities need to develop programs that include sensitivity training, course work on new conceptualizations of disability and diagnosis, and the delivery of education services to all children. Likewise, parents and other community organizers should educate other members of their communities and convince policymakers at the local, state, and federal levels to allocate significant resources necessary for change.

CONCLUSION

Now our journey through special education in the past, present, and future is coming to an end. On this journey the micropolitics of special education was scrutinized through the eyes of children with disabilities, their parents and advocates, adult educators, and school administrators. The perspectives of these parties are critical to understanding special education in the present and planning for the future. Their stories give voice to the other chapters of the book.

This book introduces (in chapters 1 and 13) a new model of special education with the goal of transforming special education, as we know it, into a system grounded in caring, compassion, and the common good. Beyond the administrative aspects of special education and the Individuals with Disabilities Education Act (IDEA), micropolitical issues place kids in the middle, affecting how children with disabilities are educated. We hope this book encourages everyone to be moved to action and to refuse to accept mediocre solutions to the problems that exist in educating children with disabilities. Together, we can succeed!

In a final letter to the Canadian people, opposition leader Jack Layton (2011) wrote, "My friends, love is better than anger. Hope is better than fear. Optimism is better than despair. So let us be loving, hopeful, and optimistic. And we'll change the world."

Technology is changing the world. Kaku (2011) gives us a glimpse into the future of the intersection of technology and biology that could open doors to educating Tommy in the future that can only be predicted and dreamed about in the present. The next thirty years should bring significant change to the field of rehabilitation of not only physical disabilities but of the whole range of the disability spectrum. Unlocking the secrets hidden in the human genome system can open the door to the possibility of understanding intellectual, cognitive, and psychiatric disabilities, and by extension, techniques to rehabilitate the underlying causes of these and other disabilities in vitro or post vitro.

Smith and Max-Neef (2011) point out that "Igor Sikorsky, a famous aeronautical engineer of the early 20th century . . . hung in his office lobby a sign that read: 'the bumblebee, according to the calculations of our engineers, cannot fly at all, but the bumblebee doesn't know this and flies'" (180).

BONNIE

. . . Bonnie rolled down the path to the arts building and stopped in front of the door. The clouds had passed and the warmth of the sun on her face and body were a welcome relief from the cool breeze that continued to blow. The door opened and she drove to the theater and onto the stage. There he was. Tall and handsome, Mikhail met her on the stage.

Swan Lake *began. At first they slowly danced to the music, she using a wheelchair and he his handsome, muscular, sensuous body. As he danced with her the pace quickened and around and around they went. All of a sudden he reached down and lifted her out of the wheelchair she was using. A man and a woman in a ballet dancers embrace. He swung her around and around—locked in that embrace—with her hair flowing in the air. Her face radiated peace and relaxation. Around and around they went across the stage, flying like a bird. And she was* free*!*

QUESTIONS FOR DISCUSSION

1. How do you think the vast resources of the United States should be used to improve special education? Why?
2. Do you believe in full inclusion for children with disabilities? Why or why not?
3. What is your understanding of the matrix for diagnosing and characterizing children with disabilities? Do you think the matrix is superior to the current system of identifying children with one of thirteen categories?
4. Think about a conflict of ideas that you have been involved with. How would you have reconciled differences using the cyclical model of dialogue, consensus, and implementation?
5. How would you educate Tommy in the future? Describe the details of his education program.

REFERENCES

Bowers, C. A. (1987). *Elements of a post-liberal theory of education.* New York: Teachers College Press.

Counts, G. S. (1932). *Dare the school build a new social order?* New York: John Day Co.

Fleischer, D. Z., and F. Zames. (2011). *The disability rights movement: From charity to confrontation.* Philadelphia: Temple University Press.

Freire, P. (1970). *Pedagogy of the oppressed.* Trans. M. B. Ramos. New York: Herder and Herder. (Orig. pub. 1968.)

Institute on Disability. University of New Hampshire, producer. 2009. *Including Samuel.* DVD. www.iod.unh.edu.

Individuals with Disabilities Education Improvement Act, P.L. 108-446, 118 Stat. 2647 (2004), now codified, as amended, at 20 U.S.C. § 1400–91 (2006).

Layton, J. (2011). Canadian opposition leader Jack Layton dies. Audio transcript. August 23. Retrieved from www.democracynow.org.

Max-Neef, M. (2010). Chilean economist Manfred Max-Neef on barefoot economics, poverty and why the U.S. is becoming an "underdeveloping nation." Audio transcript. November 26. Retrieved from www.democracynow.org.

Noddings, N. (1984). *Caring: A feminine approach to ethics and moral education.* Berkeley: University of California Press.

Sapon-Shevin, M. (2007). *Widening the circle: The power of inclusive classrooms.* Boston: Beacon Press.

Smith, P. B., and M. Max-Neef. (2011). *Economics unmasked: From power and greed to compassion and the common good.* Devon, UK: Green Books.

Index

About the Editors and Contributors

Carol Strax, EdD, is an associate professor of education at Dominican College in Orangeburg, New York. She is the former president of the New England Educational Research Organization and has held many leadership positions in the Eastern Educational Research Association since 1999. A qualitative researcher, her interests include inclusive education, the use of service dogs with people with disabilities, and children's literature.

Marshall Strax, EdD, an advocate for people with disabilities, is a professor of education at the College of Saint Elizabeth in Morristown, New Jersey. He is a former president of the New England Educational Research Organization and Eastern Educational Research Association. His interests include the intersection of disability studies and special education, the politics of special education, and higher education and disability.

Bruce S. Cooper, PhD, is professor of education leadership and policy at the Fordham University Graduate School of Education in New York City, and the former president of the Politics of Education Association. His interests focus on school politics, finance, and unionization, which are discussed in his handbook, *On Education Politics and Policy*.

David J. Connor, EdD, is an associate professor in the School of Education at Hunter College, City University of New York. He is the author of three books and numerous articles in a variety of academic journals. His interests include disability studies in education, learning disabilities, inclusive education, and social justice.

Arnold B. Danzig, PhD, is professor in the College of Public Programs at Arizona State University. He has authored numerous articles and books on school leadership, family involvement in schools, and school-to-work transitions. He is coeditor of the 2012 volume of the *Review of Research in Education, Citizenship, Democracy and the Public Good*, which will be published by the American Educational Research Association.

Anna Dunn, MD, has extensive experience in running subacute rehabilitation services and performs consultations in trauma and cancer rehabilitation. Dr. Dunn was one of two physicians who devised a third-year medical school course in pain and rehab care. She presented the course at the Accreditation Council for Graduate Medical Education (ACGME) Annual Assembly.

Lisa Luciano, DO, currently holds the position of practicing physiatrist in the Rehabilitation Medicine Department at St. Peter's Medical Center, Robert Wood Johnson University Hospital and the Shore Rehabilitation Institute. Dr. Luciano authored several chapters in the *2004 Physical Medicine and Rehabilitation Board Review Book*. She also authored the Rheumatology Self-Assessment and Resident Review Course from 1998 to 2003.

Allan G. Osborne Jr., EdD, a retired principal, has authored numerous articles, monographs, and textbooks on education law. He writes the "Students with Disabilities" chapter of the *Yearbook of Education Law* and is on the Editorial Advisory Committee of *West's Education Law Reporter*. A past president of the Education Law Association, he was the recipient of the McGhehey Award in 2008 in recognition of his contributions to education law.

Catherine Hall Rikhye, EdD, created and served as director of the Office of Inclusive Education in the New York City Department of Education. She was associate professor of special education at Hunter College of the City University of New York and Dominican College. Currently, she is a lecturer in the Department of Curriculum and Teaching at Teachers College.

Charles J. Russo, JD, EdD, is the Joseph Panzer Chair in Education in the School of Education and Allied Professions and adjunct professor in the School of Law at the University of Dayton. Having authored or coauthored more than eight hundred publications, Dr. Russo speaks extensively on issues in education law in the United States and twenty-five other nations on the six inhabited continents.

Thomas E. Strax, MD, is professor and chair of the Department of Physical Medicine and Rehabilitation at UMDNJ-Robert Wood Johnson Medical School and vice president for medical rehabilitation and medical director of the JFK Johnson Rehabilitation Institute. He is the recipient of many prestigious awards including the 1995 NYU Medical School Alumni Award and the 2005 Frank K. Krusen Award.

CPSIA information can be obtained at www.ICGtesting.com
Printed in the USA
BVOW020450280212

283939BV00002B/1/P